IDIOT'S GUIDES.

AS EASY AS IT GETS!

Self-Hypnosis

by Synthia Andrews, ND

ALPHA

A member of Penguin Group (USA) Inc.

This book is dedicated to Sherry Rogers, who demonstrates with every breath the power of holding an intention.

ALPHA BOOKS

Published by Penguin Group (USA) Inc.

Penguin Group (USA) Inc., 375 Hudson Street, New York, New York 10014, USA • Penguin Group (Canada), 90 Eglinton Avenue East, Suite 700, Toronto, Ontario M4P 2Y3, Canada (a division of Pearson Penguin Canada Inc.) • Penguin Books Ltd., 80 Strand, London WC2R 0RL, England • Penguin Ireland, 25 St. Stephen's Green, Dublin 2, Ireland (a division of Penguin Books Ltd.) • Penguin Group (Australia), 250 Camberwell Road, Camberwell, Victoria 3124, Australia (a division of Pearson Australia Group Pty. Ltd.) • Penguin Books India Pvt. Ltd., 11 Community Centre, Panchsheel Park, New Delhi—110 017, India • Penguin Group (NZ), 67 Apollo Drive, Rosedale, North Shore, Auckland 1311, New Zealand (a division of Pearson New Zealand Ltd.) • Penguin Books (South Africa) (Pty.) Ltd., 24 Sturdee Avenue, Rosebank, Johannesburg 2196, South Africa • Penguin Books Ltd., Registered Offices: 80 Strand, London WC2R 0RL, England

International Standard Book Number: 978-1-61564-630-2
Library of Congress Catalog Card Number: 2014938373

16 15 14   8 7 6 5 4 3 2 1

Interpretation of the printing code: The rightmost number of the first series of numbers is the year of the book's printing; the rightmost number of the second series of numbers is the number of the book's printing. For example, a printing code of 14-1 shows that the first printing occurred in 2014.

Printed in the United States of America

Note: This publication contains the opinions and ideas of its author. It is intended to provide helpful and informative material on the subject matter covered. It is sold with the understanding that the author and publisher are not engaged in rendering professional services in the book. If the reader requires personal assistance or advice, a competent professional should be consulted. The author and publisher specifically disclaim any responsibility for any liability, loss, or risk, personal or otherwise, which is incurred as a consequence, directly or indirectly, of the use and application of any of the contents of this book.

Most Alpha books are available at special quantity discounts for bulk purchases for sales promotions, premiums, fundraising, or educational use. Special books, or book excerpts, can also be created to fit specific needs. For details, write: Special Markets, Alpha Books, 375 Hudson Street, New York, NY 10014.

Publisher: *Mike Sanders*
Executive Managing Editor: *Billy Fields*
Senior Acquisitions Editor: *Tom Stevens*
Development Editor: *Kayla Dugger*
Senior Production Editor: *Janette Lynn*

Cover Designer: *Laura Merriman*
Book Designer: *William Thomas*
Indexer: *Brad Herriman*
Layout: *Ayanna Lacey*
Proofreader: *Virginia Vasquez Vought*

Contents

Introduction

Did you finally break free of a bad habit, only to end up a few months later back in the same rut? Do you want to release the underlying cause of self-sabotage but find yourself confused by conflicting emotions, thoughts, and beliefs? Do you beat yourself up about not being able to make the changes you desire?

Habits and self-limiting choices are often created by subconscious patterns learned in childhood—patterns borrowed from parents, family members, and society. While the first step in change is making the decision *to* change, success demands that we also engage the subconscious mind and learn to harness and direct its power. Fortunately, self-hypnosis is an excellent tool to bridge the gap between the conscious and subconscious; it offers incalculable support in your quest for the best life possible.

This book provides steps and strategies to use self-hypnosis, walking you through the process with easy-to-grasp concepts and simple do-it-yourself skill development. The techniques can be used to break bad habits, build confidence, attain goals, support optimal health, and understand hidden motives. Picking up this book is a declaration that you are ready to be the driver in your life, setting your own course and determining your destination.

Congratulations! You are embarking on a life-affirming journey as the conscious designer of your life!

How This Book Is Organized

This book is divided into five easy-to-use segments. Each segment approaches a different aspect of the self-hypnosis practice.

Part 1, The Magic of the Mind, explains what self-hypnosis is and why it works and reviews common myths and misconceptions. It also explains the three keys to successful self-hypnosis, offering skill development for each key. Basically, this part helps you understand yourself and your inner toolkit.

Part 2, Designing Your Own Self-Hypnosis Program, leads you step by step through the method of self-hypnosis. It explains how to make goals and action plans that work, induce a hypnotic state, and write suggestions that empower your subconscious mind with the information it needs to create change. This part also includes a troubleshooting guide to address problems as they arise.

Part 3, Taking Charge!, provides strategies for overcoming limiting behaviors, addictions, fears, phobias, and emotional trauma.

Part 4, Vibrant Health Through Self-Hypnosis, gives you advice and sample scripts to help you overcome stress and support optimal health.

Part 5, Unleashing Your Highest Potential, takes self-hypnosis to the heightened level of reaching your fullest potential through confidence building, exploring past lives, developing higher intuition, and deepening spiritual connection.

Extras

Throughout the book are useful tidbits that provide specific tips, inspiration, and interesting information. Watch for the following sidebars:

HYPNOTIC CONNECTION

These sidebars reveal interesting facts and provide connections to books, articles, and research about hypnotic techniques.

MESMERIZING MORSEL

These inspiring quotes engage your heart and mind in positive change.

SUBCONSCIOUS SCAFFOLDING

The tips in these sidebars help in building a solid framework for successful self-hypnosis.

DEFINITION

Here you find definitions of common words, jargon, technical terms, and key concepts.

WISE COUNSEL

"Safe and effective" is the motto for self-hypnosis. These sidebars offer ways to avoid common pitfalls, keeping you from harm's way.

But Wait! There's More!

Have you logged on to idiotsguides.com lately? If you haven't, go there now! As a bonus to the book, we've included links to hypnosis audio for full-body relaxation, easy hypnosis induction, boosting confidence, achieving your ideal weight, glimpses into past-life possibilities, and coming out of a trance you'll want to check out, all online. Point your browser to idiotsguides.com/self-hypnosis, and enjoy!

Acknowledgments

A heartfelt thank you to my clients and patients who, through 30+ years, have taught me the power of the relaxed mind to explore and release limitations.

Many thanks to the great teachers I've had in the power of trance work and imagery: Iona Marsaa Teeguarden, Deborah Valentine Smith, Jasmine Ellen Wolf, and Margaret Vassington.

A huge thank you to my spiritual editor, Johanna Sayre; my agent for this project, Marilyn Allen; and the editors and staff at Alpha Books, who offer great support along with creative freedom.

Trademarks

All terms mentioned in this book that are known to be or are suspected of being trademarks or service marks have been appropriately capitalized. Alpha Books and Penguin Group (USA) Inc. cannot attest to the accuracy of this information. Use of a term in this book should not be regarded as affecting the validity of any trademark or service mark.

The Magic of the Mind

Inside of you is a powerful force filled with awesome possibility. It is waiting in your subconscious mind, ready to awaken. This potent force is your intent—your ability to choose a direction and make it happen. You might be one of the millions of people who don't use this remarkable power to its fullest. If so, self-hypnosis may be the tool you've been looking for. With the techniques in this part and throughout the book, you can unlock the magic inside your mind and empower your intention to create the life you were born to live. The steps are easy; the results are remarkable!

Self-Hypnosis: Your Path to Victory

Every person I've ever talked with, including myself, has at least one thing in common: we all have something in our life we want to change. Isn't that the reason you picked up this book? Maybe you want to change a harmful health habit like smoking or overeating. Perhaps you're trying to overcome a fear, such as public speaking or confrontation, or want to create more prosperity, success, and ease. Whatever you're trying to change, the answers you seek, the resources you need, and the solutions you must engage are to be found within.

Self-hypnosis is a method to access your subconscious mind, the place where the source of your problems and their solutions reside. The self-hypnosis process offers an opportunity to talk to your inner self and hear the small voice that may have been missing in your conversations about what you want and where you want to go. No matter how big or small the change you're trying to make, self-hypnosis is a tool that can assist you in unlocking the door to success.

In this chapter, I talk about how your subconscious mind works and what self-hypnosis can do to get it working for (rather than against) you.

The Power of the Subconscious Mind

Have you ever wondered why some people are able to make positive changes while you struggle? Author and positivity psychologist Shawn Achor suggests that success lies in a person's ability to choose a worldview or reality in which change is possible, obstacles can be overcome, and happiness and achievement are obtainable. In other words, your reality must include the possibility of positive change. Right now, ask yourself: do you really believe you can make the changes you're after? Do you believe you can make your goals a reality? If not, that may be why you haven't yet made the changes you seek. Fortunately, *you can choose to shift your reality!*

The challenge in shifting to a positive worldview can be as simple as not recognizing your limiting attitudes and beliefs. Quite often, the origin of your limiting behavior lies in the *subconscious* mind, the part of the mind that is below the level of conscious awareness and therefore difficult to interact with.

The subconscious mind is important in self-hypnosis for two reasons: it holds all your unexamined beliefs and learned behaviors that drive your life (called your *subconscious programming*) and it holds your authentic self, which is the source of your creativity, intuition, and inspiration. It's the source of your inner wisdom and provides access to your unused potential and strength of character. Communicating with your subconscious programming allows you to change your life script, while communicating with your authentic self allows you to uncover and express your path and purpose and develop the innate skills you were born with.

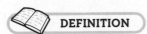 **DEFINITION**

> The **subconscious** is that part of your mind that is not consciously known or felt but has tremendous impact over the quality of your life. **Subconscious programming** is the unexamined attitudes and beliefs that drive your behaviors.

Subconscious vs. Conscious Mind

The conscious mind is the part of your mental process you're aware of, while the subconscious is responsible for all the mental functions that happen below your level of awareness. The conscious mind, often called the *outer mind,* is objective, handling your daily awareness, observations, logic, and rational thinking. Here is decided what you'll wear, what to put in a presentation, and what will make you happy. The underlying assumptions the conscious mind uses to analyze information, make decisions, and solve problems are supplied by the subconscious, which makes the subconscious supremely important in determining your success.

The subconscious mind manages body functions, such as heart rate, breathing, posture, and so forth. Additionally, it holds the programs that create your foundational beliefs about the world and how it works. Often referred to as your *inner mind*, it maintains your ideas of who you are and where you fit in. In determining what you believe and expect, your subconscious mind creates your habits and directs where you're willing to invest your energy and effort. Often, the programing in your subconscious mind is inherited from parents and social conditioning and does not reflect your true self.

It might sound like the conscious and subconscious minds work against each other, but actually they don't. When the subconscious presents a belief, even if it makes no logical sense, the conscious mind finds ways to rationalize and support it. For example, you may have been trained to believe that only people who struggle and work hard get rewarded in life. Following this dictate, you work very hard, stay crazy hours at work, skip vacations, and never take sick days. Yet for some reason you never really get ahead. Instead of examining your belief for flaws, your conscious mind will present 100 reasons why your hard work doesn't produce the results your subconscious belief expects: the boss doesn't like you, you're being taken advantage of, and so on. While these things may be true, they also may not. Or at least they may not be the reason you aren't getting ahead. It's possible your subconscious script might be what's holding you back.

SUBCONSCIOUS SCAFFOLDING

The outer mind is often used to designate your critical capacity, especially your self-criticism and judgment, while the inner mind is often used to designate your authentic core self. The term *subconscious mind* is used to designate unconscious programming and conditioning.

Self-Talk and Limiting Subconscious Programming

The subconscious is programmed with the messages you pick up from your environment, beginning with your parents and family. Your subconscious mind is molded and firmed through social interactions, the culture you grow up in, and the experiences you have. You reinforce those programs with the internal commentary of continuous, repetitive self-talk. These repetitive thoughts and the types of words you use become the mechanism through which your programming is maintained.

Here are some examples of negative repetitive thoughts that uphold a limiting mental program:

- Winning is for other people.
- I'll never be good enough.
- I'm such an idiot.
- Why am I so stupid?

- I can't believe I'm such a loser.

- I'm a failure.

- The world is getting so much worse.

- You can't trust anyone.

- There's just no point.

- Why try? I never win anyway.

- I'm too fat to find a partner.

- Nobody will ever love me.

- It's all my fault.

- I can't do anything about it.

- I can't, I won't, I'm not, I'll never ….

Every time you let thoughts like these take control of your conscious mind, you reaffirm the underlying subconscious beliefs that create them. Worse, even though these statements are obviously unfounded, your conscious mind finds ways to rationalize them and make them believable. *I can never win because it's rigged for the people at the top. I can't trust anyone because everyone is out for themselves. Nobody will ever love me because I have too many personality flaws.* Even though people break into fame and fortune, heroic acts of altruism are performed daily, and flawed people find love, these rationalizations sound perfectly true to the conditioned mind. Luckily, it's as easy to use repetitive self-talk that builds you up as takes you down. All that is required is to make a conscious choice and pay attention.

The Genie in the Magic Lamp

Your subconscious mind is like a genie living inside the magic lamp of your mind. It hears your thoughts, listens to your words, and pays attention to your repetitive self-talk and then does its best to create a world that is consistent with what you describe. In short, every success, every failure, every trauma, every resolution, and every repetitive thought is woven into the matrix that is your subconscious mind. Born out of this matrix are the conditions of your life.

The subconscious is not discerning. Regardless of whether your words support who you are or tear you down, the subconscious believes what you say and think. So every time you describe yourself in limiting terms, your subconscious does its best to enact the story, no matter whether it's helpful or hindering.

MESMERIZING MORSEL

"Whether you think you can or you think you can't, you're right."

—Henry Ford, American industrialist and founder of the Ford Motor Company

In many ways, you're caught in a catch-22; your repetitive self-talk reinforces the subconscious beliefs that are reflected in your repetitive self-talk! So which came first, the chicken or the egg? Where do you begin to make changes?

Fortunately, you don't have to choose. You can make a shift by working with all aspects simultaneously. You just have to make it a conscious choice *and you can!* Alongside your limiting view of reality is an infinite view with unlimited resources. The assets you need are an inherent part of you, submerged and often ignored, yet nonetheless ready and able to activate as soon as you decide to expand your view of reality to include them. Are you ready to engage a new worldview where your dreams really can become reality?

Self-Hypnosis Explained

The technique of self-hypnosis is simple. It consists of three basic steps: inducing altered awareness through deep relaxation, introducing a suggestion or hypnotic script for the goals you want, and returning to normal awareness. Simple, right? Actually, it is! Once you learn how to interact with the subconscious, you'll be off and running toward establishing your goals and proving the effectiveness of self-hypnosis.

It's apparent by now that your ability to make positive change is significantly tied to how well you're able to contact your subconscious mind, yet the subconscious mind is wily. It doesn't reside in a specific anatomical location and it's difficult to nail down. Consequently, many shy from harnessing the tremendous power it contains. That's where self-hypnosis comes in. Moving beyond the need to define the subconscious, it provides an effective method for direct connection to it. Using self-hypnosis helps you identify and align with your true self to direct your goals and create your success.

Hypnosis is really nothing more than a state of focused concentration that is purposefully induced. It creates receptivity to suggestion. Because this state is different than your ordinary awareness, it's called an *altered state* or *trance*. It's characterized by deep relaxation with a focused, alert, and clear mind.

In this state, your outer mind—the conscious, critical mind—relaxes, making it possible to interact with your inner subconscious mind. Predetermined suggestions given to the subconscious at this time can replace limiting beliefs. Because the critical mind reinforces your doubts about your ability to change, side-stepping it allows the subconscious to receive with ease the suggestions you want to embrace.

Like hypnosis, self-hypnosis induces an altered state and supplies suggestions, but instead of someone else inducing the trance and making suggestions, you do it yourself. It's not difficult. You unwittingly induce hypnotic states many times every day. Have you ever driven with no memory of the trip? This is called *road hypnosis*. Have you wandered around the house looking for your lost keys, only to eventually find them on the table that you're sure you searched several times? The refrain "I've lost my keys" became so real to your subconscious that you actually looked directly at them yet didn't see them.

The great thing about self-hypnosis is that you're in control of the process, the agenda, and the timetable. You can use the process just about anytime and anywhere. The altered state in hypnosis makes it possible to rewrite old programming held in the subconscious mind and change it to support a new reality.

Deactivating Limiting Programs

The goal of self-hypnosis is to deactivate the limiting programs that undermine your goals and desires and replace them with positive suggestions that continue to work after the session ends. Some suggestions given during hypnosis are meant to activate when triggered by specific cues. This is called a *posthypnotic suggestion*. When you give these suggestions to yourself, they are called *auto-suggestions*—for example, giving yourself the posthypnotic suggestion to relax whenever you hear words that usually trigger your stress response. Posthypnotic suggestions are used to maintain the goals of the session.

 **DEFINITION**

Posthypnotic suggestions are suggestions made to you when hypnotized and specify actions to be performed in response to specific cues after you awaken. **Auto-suggestions** are posthypnotic suggestions you give to yourself.

Modifying underlying programs is important. Otherwise, as you try to institute change, internal parts fight with each other and enact conflicting life strategies. This creates resistance and confusion, which manifests as chaos in your life circumstances. In fact, the degree of chaos in your life is an excellent indicator of how many conflicting programs you have running.

Deactivating subconscious programing doesn't happen magically; it occurs through the old adage "know thyself." It requires self-observation and self-reflection, two attributes often overlooked. As already discussed, observing the self begins with paying attention to your self-talk and, equally important, how the words you use make you feel. Conflicting feelings, chaos in your circumstances, states of confusion, and resistance are all indicators of multiple programs that are not in harmony. Chapters 4 and 5 provide excellent guidance in how to engage and communicate with all aspects of the self so they work in harmony for the best outcome for you.

Self-hypnosis gives you direct access to the subconscious, making it easier to know what the programs are that need to be addressed. With dedication fueled by the compelling future you're creating, discipline is a breeze.

The Three Keys to Unlocking Self-Hypnosis

Using self-hypnosis is easy. There are no special tools, expensive equipment, or involved training. Although some methods of self-hypnosis suggest using some type of device to focus on, such as a swinging pendulum or a candle flame, most self-hypnosis uses guided imagery. All you need are specific words, which are discussed in the chapters ahead. Then, by reading a script you wrote or listening to an audio download, you lead yourself step-by-step into a hypnotic trance, provide yourself useful suggestions, and come back out. This book will help you develop the skill you need to powerfully change your life. (Downloads that sync with this book can be found at idiotsguides.com/selfhypnosis.)

The three keys, which are discussed in more detail in upcoming chapters, open the gates to successful self-hypnosis. They work in every situation, and using them infinitely increases your ability to attain your goals:

- Key 1: Instant relaxation

- Key 2: Engagement of mind, body, and emotion

- Key 3: Communication with the subconscious mind

These three keys are natural and easy, making hypnosis comfortable and safe. Remember, you've been using self-hypnosis most of your life, you just haven't been aware of doing so. Have you ever been so involved in a daydream that the outside world disappears? Or so focused on solving a problem that nothing else exists? These are altered states in which you're receptive to new ideas and able to receive new suggestions more easily. Anytime you're relaxed and deeply engaged, you're in an altered state—a state different from your everyday level of awareness—and an element of self-hypnosis is present.

 SUBCONSCIOUS SCAFFOLDING

While terms like *trance* might seem scary and elicit zombie-type images, self-hypnosis is safe. There are no recorded instances of people being hurt in any way. Chapter 2 reveals all the common misconceptions of hypnosis.

Owning Your Potential

Self-hypnosis helps you help yourself. The more you use it, the easier and more effective it becomes. It's a technique you can employ quickly and practice almost anywhere: in the elevator on the way to a meeting, in the driveway as you rehearse your proposal to your spouse-to-be, or even in a restaurant before you start eating your meal. The bottom line is that self-hypnosis provides you with conscious control of the direction of your life. As you increase your skill and commitment to use it, you increase your quality of life until one day you notice that nothing is the same; you've achieved a new vantage point and overcome problems you never thought you would.

More importantly, self-hypnosis puts you in touch with your authentic self, that part of you that is aligned to your path and purpose. By deepening your knowledge of self, you can discern the direction of true fulfilment. Self-hypnosis can expand understanding of your weaknesses and strengths and provide a means for self-improvement. The stillness it brings imparts inner peace.

Self-hypnosis may be the most important tool you've ever used to help shift your life in new and better directions. All that is required is choice, a desire for something new, 15 minutes a day, the ability to daydream, and the belief that change is possible.

Have fun! The rest of your life is waiting!

The Least You Need to Know

- Choosing a reality in which change is possible is essential to a positive outcome.
- The subconscious mind is where change begins; it is the home of the beliefs and attitudes that direct your behavior.
- Self-hypnosis is a safe, natural, and effective method to access the subconscious mind.
- The three keys to successful self-hypnosis can be used anywhere, anytime to ensure ultimate victory.
- Self-hypnosis give you control over your life, as well as the ability to effectively create positive change.

The Many Facets of Self-Hypnosis

You may be eager to start the process of attaining your goals through self-hypnosis, but are still beset by doubt. After all, you might have watched old movies where hypnosis is depicted taking over a person's free will or been told that audio programs with guided imagery have hidden messages. Are you wondering if these things are true? Can self-hypnosis cause harm?

This chapter provides a summary of some of the most respected uses of self-hypnosis, with examples of the resulting changes in people's lives. I also address misconceptions about hypnosis and where they arise. Most importantly, you learn when self-hypnosis is better served with the guidance of a professional hypnotherapist.

In This Chapter

- Learning the many uses of self-hypnosis
- Putting to rest myths and misconceptions about hypnosis and self-hypnosis
- Understanding and avoiding potential issues when using self-hypnosis

Benefits and Uses of Self-Hypnosis

Self-hypnosis helps you take responsibility for your life. Once you become aware of your own limiting programming and decide to change your view of reality, you stop behaving like a victim and cease blaming other people for the difficulties in your life. As long as you believe other people are keeping you in limitation, *you are giving them the power to do so!* You hand over your self-determination and agree that you're a limited, powerless human being.

Yes, you might think, sometimes other people have control over your circumstances; often you're limited by conditions beyond your control. And frequently that is true. For example, the opportunities for a person born in the Depression era of the 1930s were different than for those born in the boom of postwar 1950s. However, the key to happiness and success lies in the manner you respond to differences as much as the fact of them. Wherever you are, and whatever is around you, you still have choices that can make things better.

 MESMERIZING MORSEL

"Man can live about forty days without food, about three days without water, about eight minutes without air, but only for one second without hope."

–Hal Lindsey, author

The effectiveness of self-hypnosis can be seen in the wide variety of people who use it and the benefits they receive. Self-hypnosis is used by CEOs of major corporations to maximize effectiveness in meetings, by athletes to optimize performance, by students to learn quicker and perform better on exams, by cancer patients to diminish side effects of treatment, by patients before surgery to minimize complications, and so forth.

Uses of self-hypnosis fall into three main categories: promoting physical health, getting to underlying issues, and supporting self-improvement efforts.

Promoting Physical Health

Hypnosis has a long history of involvement in medicine. It's best known as a stress reduction technique, so stress relief is an excellent arena to employ self-hypnosis. While you need some stress in your life to challenge your development and promote the use of inner resources, a life with unmanaged stress can create serious health-related problems. (Part 4 focuses on this category of self-hypnosis.)

Pain management is another arena where both hypnosis and self-hypnosis are used extensively. They have even replaced anesthesia in emergency surgical operations, as reported in many stories of war zone disasters requiring surgery with only hypnosis available for pain. In fact, doctors in the American Civil War were trained in hypnosis for use in field surgery.

HYPNOTIC CONNECTION

A 1995 report in the *Journal of Pain and Symptom Management* related that hypnotic analgesia was shown to significantly reduce pain during surgery.

While you might not plan to rely solely on self-hypnosis as anesthesia during a surgery, you might want to consider using it prior to a procedure to support your body and immune system during the operation. Many women use self-hypnosis to naturally manage the pain of childbirth. Some people find it helpful to lessen the pain of migraines, ease the discomfort of burns and injuries, and manage chronic pain syndromes. Self-hypnosis can help you increase your control over pain and thereby increase the quality of your life.

No matter the medical procedure, self-hypnosis can be used alongside it to your benefit. It's typically considered *mind-body medicine*. By working with the power of the mind to improve the healing of the body, you can improve your body's response to medical treatments and procedures, increase the effectiveness of drugs and therapy, and support the immune system in fighting disease. For example, cancer patients use hypnosis to increase the effectiveness of chemotherapy to destroy cancer cells while also decreasing the discomfort of side effects. I also have a claustrophobic patient who induced the relaxation of self-hypnosis and talked himself through an hour-long MRI procedure, something he never thought he could endure. And you might be excited to learn that hypnosis has an excellent reputation for curing warts!

You can create a self-hypnosis program to positively impact any part of your health picture, ranging from overcoming bad health habits to creating ideal healing environments. You may not be able to change the fact that you have a certain illness, but self-hypnosis can give you a powerful tool for supporting your body in the best way possible.

DEFINITION

Mind-body medicine is a holistic approach that takes into consideration the impact of the mind and emotions on physiological processes.

Hypnotherapy: Getting to Underlying Issues

Hypnotherapy is hypnosis used in psychotherapy by trained psychologists, psychotherapists, and psychiatrists. It's probably the best known therapeutic use of hypnosis. One way hypnotherapy is used is to dislodge deeply buried memories of trauma that impact current well-being and happiness. The therapist employs hypnotic regression, giving suggestions that lead a subject back in time to re-experience the past event and process the varied emotions. Benefits are found in using this form of hypnosis to decrease posttraumatic stress disorder (PTSD), relieve anxiety, and improve mood disorders.

Uncovering memories of trauma is best not undertaken alone. In conjunction with supervised psychotherapy, self-hypnosis can be a powerful tool to manage the aftereffects, as many people recovering memories of past trauma find that difficult memories can rise at odd times. Having a tool to calm the body and mind until professional therapeutic help is available has been lifesaving for some. (If this is your area of interest, Chapter 11 provides a script for it.)

Addiction recovery is another arena where the use of hypnosis and self-hypnosis produce excellent results. For example, in the *American Journal of Clinical Hypnosis*, numerous studies over the last 20 years show the dramatic benefit of using hypnosis in the treatment of addictions to nicotine, alcohol, cocaine, and even heroin. You can achieve less discomfort from withdrawal symptoms, experience fewer cravings, and create a better prognosis for long-term success.

 HYPNOTIC CONNECTION

A July 2001 article in the *International Journal of Clinical Experimental Hypnosis* reported a 90.6 percent success rate for the cessation of smoking using hypnosis, according to the University of Washington School of Medicine.

Hypnosis and self-hypnosis are also used to alleviate long-standing phobias, such as a fear of spiders, heights, and flying. Regardless of the issue, most phobias have deep-seated origins, and using self-hypnosis in combination with standard therapy is a very effective approach.

Supporting Self-Improvement Efforts

Chances are you picked up this book looking for ways to maximize your potential or to improve some situation in your life. It was a good choice; self-hypnosis has tremendous power to connect with and enhance your natural abilities. Interacting with your subconscious mind, you can reduce resistance to living a happy and successful life while at the same time uncovering hidden abilities.

Hypnosis can help you expand current skills. Imagine getting better test grades because you improved your test-taking ability and enhanced your memory. You can also use hypnosis to learn more easily and progress faster in your training than you might imagine possible. Hypnosis is useful in reversing unwanted behaviors, resolving relationship fears, overcoming inhibitions, and removing limiting beliefs.

The biggest area of self-help hypnosis is thinking for success. Many positive-thinking gurus link affirmations with the power of deep relaxation to create the mindset of success. Whether public speaking is your nemesis or fear of taking a risk paralyzes you, hypnosis is a dynamic tool for change.

Myths and Misconceptions

Even though the use of hypnosis and self-hypnosis is well established, you might be hesitant due to the many misconceptions surrounding the subject. Urban legends abound of subjects feeling fear while in a hypnotic trance or being forced to do things against their will. It's important for you to know that you're always in full control during both hypnosis and self-hypnosis and can come out of a trance whenever you want.

Many mistaken beliefs about hypnosis can trace their origins to the impact of movies in which the technique is mischaracterized to promote a terrifying plotline. In these movies, subjects are hypnotized and programmed to unknowingly perform terrible acts, forced to forget they have children or even their own identity. Although these are obvious fallacies derived for entertainment, they can stick in the back of your mind and create discomfort for you. Stage hypnotism, which seems to support the idea that hypnotists can make people to do things against their will, is also a culprit. Other misconceptions are fostered to get you to believe that hypnosis is a cure-all that can eliminate the need to make change.

Let's take a look at the misconceptions and shed light on both fearmongering and exaggerated expectations.

Hypnosis Makes You Lose Control

The idea that in a hypnotic trance you could lose conscious control is a prevalent fallacy. You might derive great benefit but miss the opportunity because of the fear that you'll lose control of your willpower and do something embarrassing, immoral, or even illegal. The truth is that you cannot, under hypnosis, be compelled to do something contradictory to your values.

Participants in stage shows who do silly things under posthypnotic suggestion are picked because their body language tells the hypnotist they are eager to comply for the enjoyment of being part of the show. Stage hypnotists avoid asking anyone whose body language suggests they will not enjoy being the center of attention.

> **SUBCONSCIOUS SCAFFOLDING**
>
> The use of hypnosis in many movies and television programs tend to portray it as a means for seduction, criminal profit, or the attainment of supernatural powers. You can disprove this for yourself by looking at some of the many studies published by the National Institutes of Health (NIH) on hypnosis.

The truth is, when a suggestion is made that goes against a person's beliefs, the individual automatically comes out of hypnosis.

You Can Lose Consciousness

You might be afraid you'll lose consciousness while hypnotized and not be aware of what is happening, and perhaps be taken advantage of. Or maybe you're concerned that during self-hypnosis, the trance will leave you incapacitated in the event of an emergency, such as a fire. You might worry that if you're too relaxed you won't respond to the necessity for immediate action. Movies capitalize on this by showing a person struggling to break from a trance to respond to a threat and being unable to. You might wonder if, at the end of the session, you'll fail to return to normal awareness.

Being afraid of not being able to react to a threat is a reasonable and important concern. You might be relieved to know that a hypnotic trance does not induce a loss of consciousness. No matter how deep the trance, you're always aware of what is happening around you. In fact, the relaxation of a hypnotic state is characterized by an alert and aware mind in which you have heightened cognizance.

The pleasant state of relaxation is not a coma; your brain does not cease to function. Should an emergency arise during your session, you can be sure you'll be aware and automatically come out of the trance. You can always be roused. You'll respond to the phone ringing, someone at the door, the fire alarm, and so on. Especially in self-hypnosis, you're in charge and in control of the entire experience. There has never been a recorded case of anyone not emerging from hypnosis. So relax, this is fun!

You Can't Be Hypnotized

If you're curious to know whether or not you would make a good hypnotic subject, take the test in Chapter 3 and put your mind at rest. While not everyone can enter a deep hypnotic trance, everyone can learn to use relaxation to increase awareness and promote well-being. Half the fears you might have about whether you can or can't be hypnotized arise from preconceived ideas you have about what hypnosis is. Chapter 3 establishes a more realistic view of the trance state and helps dispel this fear.

All that's required to hypnotize yourself is that you're open, willing, curious, and desirous of change. You may not understand the gentle yet profound altered state of consciousness that is a hypnotic trance and instead imagine that it entails a loss of consciousness. When you experience the alert, heightened awareness of a trance, you might not believe you were hypnotized at all. Over time, and with practice, you'll learn that the deep relaxation of self-hypnosis is a trance state.

It's true that if you do not want to be hypnotized, you can't be. However, if you desire to hypnotize yourself, you can.

Hypnosis Is Mind Control

In a sense, hypnosis is mind control—it's putting you in control of your mental programming! During hypnosis, you're always in full control. You don't surrender your will to the hypnotist or, in the case of self-hypnosis, to the recorded guided instruction. As previously emphasized, you're not brain-dead. In the heightened mental state of hypnosis, you're cognizant of every suggestion that is made. You may choose to accept or reject any one of them.

Because with self-hypnosis you develop or choose your suggestions (see Chapter 7), the only reason you would reject your script is if it isn't in alignment with your values and core beliefs. Fortunately, by the time you write your script, you'll have learned the three keys to self-hypnosis and have tools that ensure that you listen and respond to your inner wisdom, resources, and values.

Hypnosis Makes Change Effortless

Hypnosis is not a trick you play on yourself or a magic force that you employ. This is one of the most damaging myths about self-hypnosis, because believing it sets you up for failure. The truth is that through accessing your subconscious mind and listening to your core values, hypnosis makes change easier. However, it cannot magically change your life; you must participate in the process.

Self-hypnosis is a powerful tool to support your goals. It helps you identify what you truly want and brings your plans into alignment with your deeper soul needs. It highlights your resources and helps remove obstacles in your attitudes and programmed beliefs that get in your way. It harmonizes inner conflict and allows your highest potential to emerge.

Self-hypnosis offers an extraordinary opportunity. However, change requires conscious choice, dedication, and commitment for self-hypnosis to succeed.

Hypnosis Is a Spiritual Practice

Nope, hypnosis is not associated with any religion, belief system, or philosophy. It's simply a method for you to obtain deep relaxation and then use that state to make useful suggestions to your subconscious mind. You can be a member of any group and still be able to effectively use self-hypnosis. It has nothing to do with the occult, the New Age movement, or even psycho-therapy. It's a distinct modality that can be used in many arenas.

Hypnosis can be applied to any practice to obtain better results. You've already seen that it can be used in psychotherapy to uncover and work with hidden trauma and in medicine to promote healing. In addition, many people use it to deepen meditation and augment spiritual practices. However, there is nothing exclusively spiritual about self-hypnosis.

Self-hypnosis is an innate skill that we all have and use in a variety of situations.

Hypnosis Might Remove Memories

Once again, movies and stage hypnotists are the source of this concern. You've been led to believe that after hypnosis you won't remember what went on during the session or worse, troublesome memories can be removed and therefore perhaps your good memories can be lost as well.

Because your memories help form who you are, losing them means losing your links to self and to the continuity of your reality. While you may want to change your reality, losing your memories is not how you want to do it!

 HYPNOTIC CONNECTION

In 2004, Columbia Pictures released the movie, *The Forgotten,* in which two parents who lost children in a plane crash are part of a research program to erase memory. Although the plot included aliens and government monitoring programs, it was terrifying for the doubt it introduced—that memories of people we love can be erased through mind control.

The truth is that hypnosis can help your mind retrieve memories, as is used in hypnotherapy, not the reverse. While you can be fully aware in a hypnotic session, posthypnotic suggestions can be made that on waking you'll forget what happened. This is done to help ease trauma. However, it's rare that you would fully forget. In self-hypnosis, you may fall asleep and have the sense of for-getting. However, most people fully remember everything that was said to them during hypnosis.

A Trance Is Scary and Uncomfortable

Hypnosis is deep relaxation. It does not feel like being drugged. Relaxation is neither scary nor uncomfortable. Rather than feeling drugged, you feel more alive and awake. Chapter 3 explores the feelings and experience of being in a trance, so it's enough at this point to say that in a trance, you are awake, aware, comfortable, and safe.

If for any reason you become scared or uncomfortable during a session, you will immediately wake up.

Are There Dangers to Using Self-Hypnosis?

You're probably feeling ready to jump in and write a self-hypnotic script to increase your chances of getting the raise you're after or writing the next Great American Novel. While self-hypnosis can help you do both, there are times when this technique is best used with caution.

Hypnosis causes heightened awareness of the body and emotions, so if you suffer certain conditions, you could find it overstimulating. While self-hypnosis could ultimately be a great tool, if you're this type of person, you need to explore hypnotism with the professional guidance of a hypnotherapist to ensure both safety and effectiveness.

 WISE COUNSEL

Here is a summary of some situations when self-hypnosis may be a phenomenal tool, but professional hypnotherapy supervision is advised:

- You've suffered severe abuse and/or trauma.
- You have sensory processing disorder, autism, or severe ADHD.
- You suffer *extreme* anxiety with panic attacks, have bipolar disorder, or have severe PTSD.
- You have thoughts of hurting yourself or others.

For example, if you've suffered severe physical abuse, torture, or mental or psychological trauma, you would benefit from the guidance of a professional hypnotherapist before using self-hypnosis. Powerful emotions and memories can return you to earlier mental states where you may not be able to maintain your own safety. Handling these issues is difficult enough—causing things to surface without proper support can initiate retraumatization and increase rather than decrease pain.

If you have an overresponsive sensory processing disorder or have forms of autism or attention deficit hyperactivity disorder (ADHD) in which inner physical sensations are heightened, you'll want professional support to use hypnosis. In these cases, skin sensations, smells, lights, movements, sounds, and other sensory stimuli can be overwhelming. The more you relax and feel your body, the more likely overstimulation will occur. Ultimately, using self-hypnosis to live more easily in the body may be very helpful, but professional guidance is strongly recommended.

If you have periods of anxiety and occasional panic attacks, self-hypnosis is an effective tool for getting through these episodes. However, anxiety and panic are messages from your inner self that underlying issues need attention. By all means, use self-hypnosis, but don't ignore the underlying issues. Seek professional help and give yourself the support you deserve.

Bipolar disorders have a manic phase where it feels like you can do anything. During this phase, realistic control is more important than a tool that could fuel risky behavior. For example, a patient with bipolar disorder believed her manic phase was her healthy state and consistently went off medications during this phase and engaged in risky business ventures. She used self-hypnosis to help her believe in her invincibility, which eventually resulted in financial ruin. A professional hypnotherapist to help her manage and understand her illness would have been a healthier choice.

If the pain you're carrying has become so great that you have thoughts of hurting yourself or others, you need to seek professional help immediately. Talk to someone you trust and ask for support to consult a mental health professional. You can also call the National Suicide Prevention Lifeline at 1-800-273-8255 and speak with a caring person who can support you, or join an online chat at suicidepreventionlifeline.org.

The Least You Need to Know

- Hypnosis is successfully used to support medical treatment, to promote psychological health through hypnotherapy, and as a successful tool in self-help programs.
- Many of the myths and misconceptions about hypnosis come from movies or onstage shows.
- During a hypnosis session, you're aware of your surroundings, in control, and able to emerge at any time.
- You can never be made to do something against your will or counter to your values with hypnosis.
- If you've suffered severe abuse or trauma; have sensory processing disorder, autism, or severe ADHD; or suffer extreme anxiety or panic attacks; seek professional guidance in using self-hypnosis.

Key 1: Instant Relaxation

Self-hypnosis is effective because suggestions are being given during a relaxed and open state of mind. Consequently, the first obstacle to overcome in using self-hypnosis is the natural concern of not being able to enter a trance. You may be one who thinks you can't be hypnotized, and hopefully, the information here will show you that you can.

This chapter explains the many reasons why relaxation is useful and provides guidance to obtaining deeper states of relaxation. The exercises in this chapter are the foundation of the induction in Chapter 7, so time spent learning relaxation techniques now will significantly improve your self-hypnosis later.

In This Chapter

- Learning the first key to self-hypnosis
- Undergoing a relaxation exercise
- Understanding altered states and brain wave connections
- Discovering the feelings and signs of a trance

The Importance of Relaxation in Self-Hypnosis

On the shelves of every library and bookstore, you'll find many volumes on self-help methods that extoll the use of positive affirmations to overcome negative thinking. While your negative thoughts are natural and normal and may not need removing, some came be severely limiting (see Chapter 9). If you notice a negative thought and quickly counter it with a positive affirmation, it's thought this action will help deactivate negative programming. But why should you wait for a negative thought? Many methods suggest you can speak a positive affirmation to jet start the day in a constructive, confident, and optimistic direction.

MESMERIZING MORSEL

"The significant problems we have cannot be solved at the same level of thinking with which we created them."

—Albert Einstein, theoretical physicist

Positive affirmations as well as auto-suggestions used in self-hypnosis are uplifting yet often lack the ability to become potent seeds for change. You might find using affirmations to counter negative thoughts produces an internal battle between consciously desired change and your subconscious beliefs. As a result, the potential for growth-oriented affirmations is never actualized.

For positive suggestions to work, they must land in fertile soil. The thought seed of your suggestions must be able to take root in order to grow. This requires you to cultivate a receptive state of mind. Because the beliefs that guide your attitudes and actions are created and maintained in the subconscious, accessing them through the conscious mind produces conflict and limited results.

Self-hypnosis is a powerful tool because of the shift you create in your state of mind, producing a trance that allows direct conversation with your subconscious. As seen in Chapter 1, your hypnotic trance is characterized by deep relaxation with a focused, alert, and clear mind that is receptive to suggestion. A positive affirmation landing in the subconscious of a relaxed mind has the ability to create transformation.

Developing the Skill to Instantly Relax

The ability for you to relax at will is the first key to self-hypnosis. It's the essence of establishing a trance in the process called *hypnotic induction.* If you're like most people, you're having one of two reactions: You're either asking "What's so hard about relaxing?" or asking "What? How can I possibly relax when I'm so stressed?" Shockingly, you might not know how to really relax. You might equate relaxation with not working or with sleep. Relaxation is definitely not sleep and surprisingly, you can work—and work more effectively—when you're relaxed.

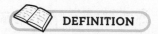

DEFINITION

Hypnotic induction is the process of consciously establishing a trance.

Relaxation is relief from tension in your body and your mind. It's the withdrawal of your attention from the external world of distracting incitements to an intricately more interesting inner world of creative thought. Your body can't completely relax as long as your mind is thinking worrisome thoughts. According to psychoanalyst Wilhelm Reich, the father of body-centered psychotherapy, every muscular tension is held in place by a tension-producing thought. So if your body is tension-filled, it's the reflection of your tension-filled mind.

The trick to relaxing at will is learning to direct your mind away from external diversions—like what so-and-so is thinking about you right now, what stock to sell in tomorrow's market, or all the unfinished business left at work—and toward awareness of your internal state. Becoming more aware of your internal environment and the stores of creative energy within you is one of the benefits of self-hypnosis.

Are You Hypnotizable?

You might find it very easy to be induced into a trance or you might be completely immune, but the vast majority of people fall in a middle range of susceptibility where, with practice, they can easily be hypnotized. Despite popular belief, being intelligent doesn't make you less able to be hypnotized. Traits that increase your ability to be hypnotized include being able to think outside of the box, being open-minded, and having an interest in how the mind works.

The main ingredient for your success in self-hypnosis is belief. You need to believe that it's actually possible for people in general to be self-hypnotized and that it's a desirable or useful state for you to be in. It doesn't seem to matter whether or not you believe you're personally able to be hypnotized; you just have to be open to the possibility.

Want to find out how hypnotizable you are? Here are some questions that will indicate your predisposition:

- Do you daydream?
- Can you follow instructions?
- Have you ever been so involved in a project that you lost track of time?
- Are you able to imagine yourself as a character in your favorite movie or book?
- Can you imagine the sound of a train or alarm clock?
- When you read or hear about a painful event, does your body cringe?
- Does your mouth water when you think of biting into a lemon?

If you answered yes to the majority of these questions, consider yourself a candidate. The greater your imagination and the ability to concentrate, the easier it will be to be reach a trance state.

> **SUBCONSCIOUS SCAFFOLDING**
>
> In the early 1960s, Dr. Herbert Spiegel created the eye roll test. He determined that there is a 73.9 percent correlation between being able to positively perform this test and being able to be hypnotized. Here's what it entails: Can you roll your eyes up while closing your eyelids? This might be easy for you, or you might not be able to do it at first, but after a few tries and some concentration, you should be able to master it. According to Dr. Spiegel, the time it takes to master the eye roll test is synonymous with the result you get when inducing hypnosis.

Relaxation Exercise

Learning how to induce a hypnotic trance will be far easier if you have some practice in relaxing. Relaxing is a skill. The more you develop it, the faster you'll be able to initiate it, until eventually you'll be able to shift into a relaxed state with a few brief instructions. To start, let's combine two commonly used exercises you might already know: the head-to-toe inventory and getting heavy.

The first time you do this exercise, you'll need about 20 free minutes. If you can actually lie down or sit in a comfortable chair, that would be best. With practice, you'll be able to instill the relaxation response at will with only a few deep breaths.

The exercise starts with your feet and moves up through your body. If you're in a safe space, get comfortable and follow the instructions as you read. Even if you can't follow the instructions, however, your body is listening and as you read, chances are excellent that you'll experience some degree of relaxation relative to what is safe for where you are. You can find a download of this exercise at idiotsguides.com/selfhypnosis.

Track 1

Begin:

Relaxation is easy and natural. Your body wants to relax; just listening will allow relaxation. You can make that more effective by using your attention. So right now, bring your attention to your feet—inhaling, tightening all the muscles in your feet as strongly as you can, curling your toes, and flexing your ankles. Squeeze all the blood from the tissue in the entirety of both of your feet. Holding your breath, exhale and allow your muscles to completely relax.

Inhaling, imagine blood rushing into all of your muscles, filling your feet with warmth and making them very full and heavy. And as you exhale, your feet become so heavy. In fact, they become so heavy they feel glued to the floor. Taking a normal breath, let yourself feel relaxed and heavy.

When you're ready, move your attention to your lower legs. Inhale and tighten all the m bones and your calves—tightening, tightening, and holding your breath. Hold your b and relax the calf muscles. On the next inhalation, see your lower legs filling with b getting warm and heavy. On the next inhalation, just feel how very heavy your legs and you

Now inhale, tightening and relaxing your thighs, front, and back. On the inhale, hold. Squeeze them and relax with the exhale. Exhaling relaxation, become so heavy. On the next inhalation, allow blood and warmth to fill your thighs, making them feel so large and so heavy. Breathing naturally, notice how relaxed your whole lower body is feeling.

Inhale into your buttocks and into your pelvic girdle, tightening all the muscles as tight as you can. Inhale and tighten, and hold. Hold and squeeze before releasing as you exhale. On your next inhalation, allow blood and warmth to rush into your pelvic girdle. Completely relaxing and opening, notice how heavy you feel through your whole lower body—and how very relaxed, sinking into the floor.

On your next inhalation, tighten up your abdomen and lower back. Tightening as tight as you can do it, squeeze all the blood out of the muscles in your lower back and abdomen. Squeeze and hold your breath, holding and then releasing on an exhalation. Allow blood and energy to flow into your abdomen and lower back. Allow your lower back muscles to fully and completely relax, to feel heavy and free.

Inhale into your chest and upper back, inhaling and tightening the muscles as tight as you possibly can. Squeeze the blood out of the muscles, tightening your whole chest segment. Hold it for as long as you can and then release into the exhale, relaxing into the floor.

As you inhale, blood and energy flow into your upper body, and your whole body sinks into the floor—so relaxed, so free. Even as you're sinking into the floor, you're floating above the floor. Taking your attention into your arms, all the way down to your hands, inhale and squeeze all of those muscles—your hands, your forearms, and your arms. Squeeze all of the tension out of those muscles, all of the blood out of those muscles. Hold your breath and then exhale relaxation, letting your arms sink into the floor. Notice all the blood and energy flowing with your breath into your arms. Exhale, sinking into the floor and becoming heavier and heavier.

With your next breath, tighten your shoulders. Inhale into your shoulders and neck and tighten the muscles as tight as you can, squeezing all the blood out of the muscles in your shoulders and neck. Hold that breath for as long as you can and then release with your exhale. Release the muscles into the floor and inhale energy, space, and freedom into the muscles now. There's relaxation in your shoulders and your neck, making you feel so free and so heavy. At the same time, it feels so light, like you're just floating.

On your next inhalation, take your attention into your face and head and squeeze your muscles as tight as you can possibly squeeze them, squinching your face up as small as you can. Hold your breath and then exhale and relax all the muscles in your face. Let the tension in your face melt right off of you.

As all of the tension in your body is melting right off of you, you sink into the floor deeper and deeper. Notice how comfortable it is to be this relaxed. Notice how open and free you feel to be this relaxed. Know you can be this relaxed anytime you want, just simply by breathing in and breathing out and intending relaxation.

SUBCONSCIOUS SCAFFOLDING

Throughout the book, using your breath to pace the exercises you do will significantly increase the body-mind connection and effectiveness.

Once you've done the full exercise a few times, you can begin to shorten it. To start, say "One" as you inhale and tighten and then exhale and relax both legs from feet to buttocks. Next, say "Two" while you inhale and tighten and then exhale and relax the entire torso. Say "Three" as you inhale and tighten and then exhale and relax both arms and both hands. Say "Four" as you inhale and tighten and then exhale and relax your neck, face, and head. Finally, say "Five" as you inhale and exhale and feel how your whole body is relaxed, heavy, and alert.

When this process becomes fast and easy, you're ready for instant relaxation. Simply say "One" while imagining that you're inhaling relaxation and exhaling tension. Next, say "Two," inhaling relaxation and exhaling tension. Say "Three," inhaling relaxation and exhaling tension. Say "Four," inhaling relaxation and exhaling tension. Say "Five," inhaling relaxation and exhaling tension. After five, say "I am deeply and completely relaxed." You will now experience deep, calm, peaceful relaxation.

If you skipped the full step-by-step exercise to jump to the counting-to-five shortcut and are now discouraged that you're not relaxed because it didn't work, how could it? As with every skill, you need to train your body and mind to become proficient. Relaxing is natural and it doesn't take long, but you do need to start at the beginning. Lie down and give yourself over to the exercise; allow your training to become an ingrained ability.

Learning how to relax at will enables you to use the state of relaxation to induce a deeper hypnotic trance. In the meantime, you can use the technique to take a power break anytime. Just counting to five and imagining relaxation will help you counter stress and increase your poise, presence, and ability to think more creatively.

Now that you know relaxation is a key element, begin using it to induce a hypnotic trance. Using the progression of the relaxation key, you should be able to induce a state of awareness between sleep and wakefulness where your attention is withdrawn from external events and concentrated on inner visions, sensations, and feelings. The result is a calm, alert, and focused state in which you're directly connected with the subconscious. In this altered state, you're in a prime position to cultivate new habits.

Entranced: Altered States for Altering Habits

The idea of using a trance to connect to the subconscious might seem scary and historically unfounded. However, the use of trance states has existed in multiple cultures for thousands of years. It was used in the Sleep Temples of ancient India, Egypt, and Greece, where people were taken to be cured of insomnia. The ancient Maya also used altered states to develop their under-standing of astronomy and mathematics. Modern use was brought to scientific study through the work of an Australian physician, Dr. Franz Mesmer, in 1770.

Although Mesmer's specific body of work was ultimately rejected by mainstream science, the therapeutic use of trance states was not. It gained widespread support in the 1880s due to the work of Scottish surgeon and scientist James Braid and in 1892, hypnosis was unanimously endorsed at the annual board meeting of the British Medical Association.

 HYPNOTIC CONNECTION

In 1956, Pope Pius XII gave approval for hypnosis to be used medically by professional health-care providers.

As Chapter 2 revealed, altered states of awareness as used in modern self-hypnosis help millions of people overcome phobias, develop skills, think more clearly, achieve better health, manage pain, and realize success. Certainly a large part of the appeal of self-hypnosis is that it gives users control of their mental, physical, and spiritual health.

What Is an Altered State?

So what is an altered state, and how does it differ from normal, ordinary awareness?

There are many different state of awareness that reflect different levels of consciousness. Every day you move in and out of different states with little mindfulness of the transition. The most obvious change of awareness is moving from sleep into wakefulness. However, even sleep and wakefulness have different levels. In sleep, you have two basic states: nonrapid eye movement (NREM) sleep in which you do not experience dreams, and rapid eye movement (REM) sleep in which you dream.

Generally, waking awareness is lumped into one state and referred to as ordinary awareness, not paying attention to the fact that you shift in and out of different states throughout the day. A normal state of wakeful awareness is the state in which you move from one task to another with fluctuating thoughts, emotions, and body sensations. Focuses come and go as your mind travels on well-worn paths of repetitive thoughts, your emotions react in predictable patterns, and your body responds to both.

Altered states can occur under several influences. When sufficiently engaged in an activity or thought process, your state of awareness can shift, and you become deeply engrossed, experienc-ing heightened concentration and focus. Time passes unnoticed as sensations and body awareness slip into the background. This represents one type of altered state.

Another type of altered state that you're well acquainted with occurs in the state between waking and sleeping called the *hypnagogic state*. In this transition, the brain is relaxed and open. Vivid images come and go accompanied by body sensations, unexpected sounds, and sudden body movements (such as jerking or eye rolling). Quite often during the hypnagogic state, you can have sudden insights into problems you've been struggling with, or you may have feelings of deep spiritual connection. The hypnagogic state is very similar to a trance state, as both exhibit something called alpha brainwaves. However, don't get confused that hypnosis is the same as being asleep; a hypnotic trance establishes an alert awareness that you don't have in sleep.

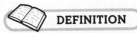 **DEFINITION**

> The **hypnagogic state** is the state between waking and sleeping characterized by alpha brainwave states and often occurring with odd sensations, visions, sounds, body movements (such as sudden jerking and eye rolling), and deep insights and perceptions.

Understanding how the brain works helps to demystify the trance state and explain why and how different states of mind are useful.

Brainwaves and Consciousness

Your varied states of consciousness are associated with different ranges of your brainwave frequency. Brainwaves are electromagnetic waves emitted from your brain and measured on an electroencephalograph (EEG). Like all electromagnetic waves, brainwaves are measured in hertz (Hz): the lower the hertz, the slower the frequency.

Your everyday awareness occurs within the beta range of 12 to 40 Hz and represents your conscious mind. In beta states, you carry on daily functions, problem solve, and make decisions. Waves in ranges directly above beta, called *gamma waves*, and those directly below beta, called *alpha waves*, are both useful states for self-hypnosis.

Alpha brainwaves (8 to 12 Hz) are associated with mental states of trance, meditation, and hypnagogia. They are characterized by deep relaxation and mental alertness. Alpha is considered the gateway into the subconscious, as it's the first state that directly links with the subconscious mind. Attaining a trance in the alpha range produces an excellent effect for you to achieve the goals of self-hypnosis.

Gamma waves (40 to 100 Hz) are relatively newly understood as a range of brain activity associated with profound states of elevated consciousness. Some experienced meditators and advanced practitioners of self-hypnosis are able to shift into this range after many years of practice. Gamma waves synchronize all the areas of the brain, harmonizing the brain's activity and binding information from different areas together into perception. If you plan on using self-hypnosis to deepen your spiritual connection, this is the range you'll ultimately seek.

The following table provides information on these and other brainwaves and their association with self-hypnosis.

Brainwave Summary

Brainwave	Frequency (in Hertz)	Natural Occurrence	When Induced
Delta	0.5-4	A deep, dreamless sleep with no mental images or awareness of the physical body (NREM stage 3).	It's a very deep trance state that can be felt as a point of stillness.
Theta	4-8	This occurs in sleep (NREM stage 2).	This is used by experienced hypnotherapists for regression work. It occurs with disconnection from the body.
Alpha	8-12	A hypnagogic state and early sleep. The muscles are active and the eyes roll slowly and may open and close (NREM stage 1).	This is the most accessible state for self-hypnosis with deep relaxation, mental alertness, and body awareness.
Beta	12-40	Waking consciousness with various degrees of body a wareness. These waves are found when problem solving, planning, and organizing.	This is the normal state of awareness.
Gamma	40-100	Super-beta. These waves help synchronize all areas of the brain so you become super focused. It is the state many scientists and artists achieve when working.	This creates a heightened state of awareness and elevated consciousness.

Although it sounds like altered states occur spontaneously, the good news is that you can learn to alter your brainwave states through intention. The relaxation method used in the beginning of this chapter is a start toward shifting into an alpha frequency range. Techniques through the rest of the book will build on this fundamental step.

> **HYPNOTIC CONNECTION**
>
> In 1958, psychologist Joe Kamaya determined that certain sounds induced altered brain states. He discovered this when watching the effects of sound on brain waves while the subject was hooked to an EEG. After listening to the sound and experiencing the mind state, the subject could reproduce the mind state simply by imagining the sound. This research became the basis of biofeedback.

Breath: Connection Between the Body and Mind

Intentionally changing brainwave states and altering consciousness begins with bringing your attention away from the outside world to focus it internally. Attending to the outside world is often considered a mental function (conscious outer mind), while attending to the internal world is often thought of as being in the body (subconscious inner mind). When you bring your intention inside, you're basically getting out of your head and into your body.

Your breath is the doorway between your mind and your body. When you focus your attention on your breath, your attention is focused in your head as you inhale and air passes through your nose and then moves deeply within your body, taking your attention with it. When all else fails, simply following the breath will institute a change in your awareness.

This is very important since the breath is used as the meter for every exercise. Instructions are given with respect to inhalations and exhalations. As your breath slows, so does your mind.

Get in the habit of noticing your breath as you go through your day. Don't try and change it or judge it, just notice it. You'll begin to see how closely related your mental states are to your depth of breath. Again, there is no need to change anything; just observe.

The Characteristics of Being in a Trance

Compared to another person, you have a certain degree of hypnotizability, as well as a varied response to being hypnotized. Trance states are so natural that the first time you're hypnotized you might not think you actually are in a trance. As you develop results or when some piece of unknown information emerges, though, you'll realize that the level of awareness you're in is a powerful state of self-discovery.

Using the relaxation key is a good step toward inducing a trance. However, you might be wondering what a trance feels like. Here are some representative experiences you might have in regard to trances.

What Does It Feel Like?

Moving into a trance is similar to falling asleep except that you don't actually go to sleep or lose consciousness. With eyes closed and lying or sitting in a comfortable resting position, you're deeply relaxed yet able to hear and sense things around you. You're hyperattentive to sounds and movements, although they might seem to come from a great distance. If you're using a recorded induction, the voice on the machine might sound as though it's inside your head or very far away.

As you relax, you might notice that, on its own, your breathing slows and deepens. Your muscles become softer and heavier with each breath. You may feel a sense of distance between you and the room. You might feel as though you're very light, even floating just above the bed or seat, or feel very heavy, sinking so deeply that you're falling through the furniture. The passage of time might become distorted so that seconds seem to take an eternity or an hour goes by that felt like 10 minutes. Most people feel a pleasant, euphoric sense of peace.

Another interesting aspect is that although you can easily move, you won't feel inclined to. Your body might feel heavy and glued to the furniture. You can test that you're able to move by giving yourself a suggestion to move and then doing it. For example, if you give the instruction to raise a finger or move a foot, you can do it with ease.

Trance states can be induced through touch, as anyone who has received a massage, Reiki, acupuncture, or other forms of bodywork knows. Touch-induced trance is one I use regularly in my private practice. Many people receive massage and bodywork specifically for the experience of peaceful upliftment that deep relaxation and altered states provide.

Not surprisingly, amazing things can happen when you intentionally relax.

 HYPNOTIC CONNECTION

In the late 1700s and early 1800s, hypnosis was called *mesmerism* after Dr. Franz Anton Mesmer, who was the first to scientifically explore hypnotism. Trance was induced using touch to interact with a person's "animal magnetism"—what we might now call *life force*. This is also the origin of the word *mesmerize*.

When in a trance, you might experience changes in perception. You could feel as though you're watching the scene around you from a distance or suddenly notice that one object in your vision becomes very large as everything else fades into the background. The sounds around you may fade away. You may have a heightened sense of knowing, focus, or mental acuity. You may access psychic information by seeing visions or receiving instructions. You may hear musical tones of extraordinary clarity. It would not be unusual for you to experience a heightened awareness of physical sensations.

Because trance states are highly suggestible, when you're in a trance, you might be easily influenced by surrounding stimuli. For example, if you hear someone say they are cold, you might shiver. For this reason, making sure you're in a protected environment before going into a deep trance is an important precaution.

It's improbable that you'll forget what happens while you're in a trance, although time and distance might be distorted. Details might be vague to you, but in self-hypnosis, the depth of trance is automatically curtailed by the need to stay focused on the objectives of the session.

Physical Signs of a Trance State

As you relax and enter the alpha brainwave state, natural physical signs occur indicating you're in trance. These are expressions you often experience in the hypnagogic state between sleep and wakefulness. They are as following:

- You may have increased eye watering; tears might stream down your face.

- The rapid eye movement of REM sleep may occur.

- Your eyes might roll upward.

- Your muscles may twitch or jerk, causing sudden jolts through your body.

Basically, these signs are good indicators that you've successfully achieved the first key in self-hypnosis: instant relaxation!

Using Your Mind Power

Learning how to create an induction script and use relaxation as a hypnotic tool occurs in Chapter 7. However, if you do nothing more with self-hypnosis than use the relaxed state taught in this chapter to observe yourself, you'll take huge steps forward in your self-understanding.

With just this one skill, you'll begin to notice connections between thoughts, feelings, muscle tensions, attitudes, and beliefs. You can begin the process of self-reflection that helps remove bitter roots that influence you to engage limiting patterns. With no more than this, you can begin to plant seeds of change.

Try it. Spend time every day simply relaxing. Notice the quality of your thoughts and how you feel. Don't make any changes, just notice. If relaxed attention alone can be so powerful, imagine what else is in store as you proceed to learn all the keys of self-hypnosis and propel yourself into dynamic action.

The Least You Need to Know

- Practicing the skill of instant relaxation will allow you to relax at will.

- The most important traits for you to be hypnotized are an active imagination, an open mind, and your belief that in general, hypnosis is possible for you.

- Using altered states provides direct access to the subconscious, allowing you to plant powerful seeds for change.

- Altered states of awareness correlate to specific brainwave emissions.

- Intentionally shifting brain states allows you to observe emotions, thoughts, body sensations, beliefs, and attitudes.

- Trance states are often accompanied by physical signs and induce a pleasant, euphoric sense of peace.

Key 2: Engagement of Mind, Body, and Emotion

Self-hypnosis is a technique of words; there are no devices. Words lead your body and mind into relaxation, provide suggestions to reprogram your behaviors, and lead you back to normal awareness. Words create the effect you want because they move beyond information and engage your imagination. Well-chosen words produce images in your mind that feel real. They make you laugh or cry and stimulate your body so that you squirm in excitement or cringe in avoidance. Through imagery, you speak directly to your subconscious in a language it understands.

The words you use in hypnotic suggestion construct a new view of reality. The ability of your subconscious to believe this reality and shift attitudes and behaviors to create it depends on how engaged your mind, body, and emotions are, as you learn about in this chapter. When the images are vivid and you feel emotionally connected—tasting, smelling, and feeling the ambience—the subconscious believes.

In This Chapter

- The role of engagement in achieving your dreams
- How to use visualization, body awareness, and emotional connection in self-hypnosis
- The alignment of your mind, body, and emotions

Developing the Skill of Full-Spectrum Engagement

The second key in successful hypnosis is full-spectrum engagement. This skill entices your mind, body, and emotions to invest in the script you provide. It encourages your subconscious to believe in a new vantage point.

Engagement used in induction ensures a deeper trance for you; engagement used in hypnotic suggestions increases subconscious receptivity to the change you seek; and engagement as you come out of trance leaves you feeling refreshed and alert.

In the preceding chapter, a series of questions helped identify if you were more likely to be hyp-notizable. One question was "Are you able to imagine yourself as a character in your favorite movie or book?" Most likely you answered yes. Imagine it now; imagine living a life different than your own. Create the character you want to be. Take on the body posture, facial expression, and movement of your ideal. What kind of clothes do you wear? Feel the clothing draped on your body and notice the texture as it slides across your skin. What kind of day is it? Are you inside or outside? Experience the temperature of the day; feel the wind on your face. Notice the smells, sounds, and tastes around you. Imagine your character in the adventure she was born to pursue. Notice the emotional intensity and your interest in finding out what happens next.

Your submersion into a story to the degree that you're so engrossed in what is happening that you become lost in the images, sensations, and emotions is what makes good entertainment. It also makes for a good hypnotic script your subconscious will believe and *want* to create.

Imagine having a life that engages you as much as a good story. What would it feel like to be as aware of your surroundings and alive to the potential of the moment as in your daydream fantasy? Imagine how much more energy would be available to you, how exciting life would be! This is full-spectrum engagement, and the more you can write it into the script you develop as your self-hypnosis program, the greater your success will be. The three tools you need to engage are all within: *visualization,* body awareness, and emotional connection.

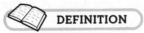 **DEFINITION**

Visualization is constructing images in your mind's eye that enact desired outcomes.

Visualization: Connecting with the Power of Your Mind

You're probably quite aware of the technique of visualization. This is the prime method for engaging self-hypnotic suggestion—the visualization in your mind of the reality you want to create. For example, if you're pursuing career advancement, the script you write to confidently attain your goal will include seeing yourself happily in the job you desire.

You might proclaim you're unable to visualize and therefore hypnosis won't work for you. In general, when you declare an inability to do something, you're ensuring that you can't. You create images in your mind's eye whether you think you do or not. It's a natural part of how your brain works.

You unconsciously create images all the time. When you speed to work late as you imagine the boss's anger, or when you anticipate the pleasure of your grandchild as you give her a present, it's impossible not to envision the angry or happy face you expect. This is a natural function that you use consciously when you daydream. Do you ever daydream by describing a scene with words? No; you see it and live it in your imagination as you did in the skill development exercise. The more you like the daydream, the more vivid it is and the more it engages you. This is what is meant by visualization.

Imagery: Primordial Language

Visualization in self-hypnosis works because imagery is the language of your subconscious. Images and symbols convey more than thought; they convey emotion. The imagery of your dreams, your visions of inspiration, and the sudden connections you make through symbols are all avenues of communication between your subconscious and your conscious mind.

Images create effect because they bypass your critical mind's desire to control and direct your actions. They speak to deep places within you, sparking your creativity and reminding you that you're more than your intellect. The words you choose to create your self-hypnosis suggestions become powerful tools when they evoke images that communicate with what is unique and authentic within you.

In this book, you will intentionally choose the images of your self-hypnotic suggestions and personalize your script to match your own experiences. Many hypnotic scripts use the soothing image of water, evoking the rhythmic sound of waves with the gentle bob of a raft to deepen the level of engagement. But what if you had a traumatic experience and nearly drowned in a water accident? That imagery would produce the opposite effect for you. With self-hypnosis, you pick the images that work best for you and, as a result, create purposeful engagement.

Does Visualization Really Work?

When you focus on a visual image, your internal energy concentrates on creating it. You might believe visualization is mere imagination and therefore doesn't have any impact on improving your capabilities or making your life better. The experiences of athletes, actors, and CEOs say otherwise. They find imagery an invaluable tool in optimizing performance.

According to brain studies, visualization and repetitive thoughts produce the same mental instructions to your body as actions. Using mental imagery improves motor control, attention, perception, planning, and memory. In other words, imagining your way through an exercise routine, scene in a play, or speech increases your ability to perform successfully.

> **HYPNOTIC CONNECTION**
>
> A 2004 publication in the journal *Neuropsychologia* reported research conducted at the Cleveland Clinic Foundation in Ohio, which found that thinking through an exercise helped maintain muscle strength, even when the exercise was not physically performed!

Basically, visualization is a constructive use of your body's responsiveness to your thoughts, allowing you to prepare for events by practicing them in your imagination. As you see yourself successfully performing an activity, your body develops the neural pathways that support it. In hypnosis, visualization provides the opportunity to feel the reality of what you believe you want. Immediately, your body and brain change as your body sensations and emotions are linked into the visual stimuli.

Body Awareness

Your body believes every word you say. Try it. Repeat "I am so tired" over and over and watch what happens. If your habit is to constantly tell yourself you're tired, you'll reach a point where you're barely able to function. Every time you say "I am so tired," you paint a picture in your mind of exhaustion—body slumping, dragging feet, long and slack arms—until that is exactly how you begin to look! Then night comes, and suddenly you feel alive and have energy to go out dancing! You must have stopped telling yourself how tired you are! Or more to the point, your mind, body, and emotions became engaged in a new direction.

Your body responds to your thoughts, releasing hormones and chemicals in order to prepare you to meet upcoming challenges. The adrenaline high you get before a sports competition, meeting, or other high-stakes event sharpens your perceptions, focuses your mind, and prepares your muscles for action. The endorphin high you get before engaging intimately with your partner prepares you for pleasure. Essentially, your thoughts are your emissary into the world, preparing you for what is ahead. In the preparation, your thoughts might also be predetermining outcomes.

The Impact of Repetitive Thoughts

Your body's ability to respond to your thoughts is a survival mechanism meant to help you prepare for and overcome life-threatening situations. The ability works against you, however, when your thoughts have no useful outlet. Continuous worry causes the release of stress hormones that turn off digestive function, leaving you unable to "stomach your thoughts" and possibly creating an ulcer. Perpetually reliving conflict keeps your body primed with the desire to fight and results in tight muscles that stay rigid and ultimately develop trigger points of tension.

HYPNOTIC CONNECTION

In a CD lecture released by *Sounds True* in 2004, neuroscientist Dr. Candace Pert revealed research supporting her theory that the body is the subconscious mind that holds memories, attitudes, beliefs, and inner wisdom in cellular memory.

Your repetitive thoughts move beyond preparation to determine the limits of your perceptions. You perceive the meaning of events in light of your thoughts and beliefs. If your belief is that the world isn't safe and your continual self-talk is "people can't be trusted," every kind offer that comes your way is viewed with suspicion until people get the vibe and don't offer anything—thus confirming your belief. Now you lose connections that may have brought you great opportunity and happiness.

The body's responsiveness to thoughts is what makes it a master tool for engagement. In self-hypnosis, you replace thoughts that limit you with ones that expand you and, as a consequence, you feel your body open to anchor new vistas.

Muscle Memory: Instructing the Subconscious

Your ability to direct your subconscious mind with a new script becomes infinitely more believable when you can feel the intensity of the new script in your body. Are you able to imagine the sound of fingernails raking across a chalkboard or the sound of screeching tires before a car crash? Do the sounds you imagine make you cringe? Can you recall the sound of crickets on a summer night and use it to make yourself relax?

Your brain's neural patterning related to your muscles retains a memory of your experiences: your trauma and injuries, emotional ups and down, learned activities, and so forth. This is called *muscle memory*. Because your muscles respond to your mind, they remember your habitual thoughts and feelings. Muscle memory is reflected in your posture and movements and is part of the information that relates to your attitudes and beliefs.

Muscle memory is an important tool in creating self-hypnosis scripts. In addition to making the script more realistic, incorporating body signals allows you to use muscle memory to retrieve the program of your script after the hypnotic session is over. For example, if you're creating a script to help reduce stressful reactions at work, you might make a suggestion that every time you bring your hands together in a specific position, you feel deep relaxation and peace. Your muscles now link your action with your feeling and help carry out the directives of your program.

Muscle memory is a form of *procedural memory*—memory that guides performance of actions. The strength of muscle memory increases through repetition of an activity. The more you perform something, the more natural it becomes until it requires little thought. This occurs below the level of your conscious awareness.

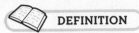 **DEFINITION**

> **Muscle memory** refers to the memories stored in the neural patterning of your brain that relate to body experiences and associated emotions. It's a form of **procedural memory,** or memory that increases through repetition of an activity until it can be performed subconsciously.

Practice makes perfect, but you only get perfect at what you practice. If you're repeating a mistake over and over, you only get better at the mistake. Muscle memory doesn't judge whether you're doing something right or wrong; it only gets faster at doing whatever you repeat. Consequently, some of your worst habits are engrained in your muscle memory. To change this, you have to script for new muscle memories. As you learned in visualization, when you enact scenes in your mind, the stimulation is stored in your body as a procedural memory, the same way it would be if you actually performed the task!

For example, imagine you want to develop more confidence. In your script, you describe the confident person you want to be, visualizing how you stand, move, and express yourself physically. You end with a posthypnotic suggestion that every time you feel insecure, your muscles will remember your suggestion and naturally reflect a confident body image.

Emotional Connection

You know the power of your emotions to keep you engaged in life. When you're happy and curious, life opens for your interest and enjoyment. Synchronicity leads you forward through the gates of significant events as you follow the creative flow of your emotions. In fact, keeping interest in any pursuit requires that you maintain an emotional connection.

Equally, have you noticed when you're discouraged or disappointed, you can't seem to get out of your own way? Activities that should bring enjoyment leave you uninterested. You close the door on opportunity and turn your back on the enjoyment of other people's company.

Emotions provide essential functions that you can use in self-hypnosis. First, they provide information. Second, they provide you with energy and inspiration, a key to writing scripts that fully engage you. And third, they connect you to your spiritual center and higher wisdom.

The Energy Within Your Emotions

The most amazing function of emotions is the energy they provide you. Imagine having no emotion—no excitement over upcoming events, no edge of fear in learning a new skill, no pride in a job well done. How much energy would you have to invest in life? Remember the original *Star Trek* series and the continual argument over whether Mr. Spock was more or less effective because of his lack of emotion? Look at his body posture, facial expressions, and affect compared to Captain Kirk. The greatest difference is the amount of energy Kirk expresses in comparison to the reserved, contemplative Spock. Kirk is energized because he feels emotion!

The energy of your emotions fuels your goals and activities. Things that excite you give you an energy boost, making them easier to achieve. This is important: if the script you're writing doesn't engage your emotions and passion, it won't take you as far as you want to go! When you reach for change, you can go only as far as your emotions will carry you.

 HYPNOTIC CONNECTION

> To master the art of powering your life through emotional energy, check out my book, *The Path of Emotions: Transform Emotions into Energy to Achieve Your Greatest Potential.*

Fortunately, you live within a continual stream of emotions. There is no time when you have zero emotion, and you can rouse emotional energy to fuel your life simply by tuning in. Sound crazy? Think of that last scary movie you went to and how frightened you got watching it. Once you tuned in to fear, all the energy that fear provides in activating the flight-or-fight response flooded your system. Your heart pounded, your palms got sweaty, and you probably squirmed in your seat.

You probably find it easy to tune in and access emotions such as fear or anger because they are familiar and engrained in your muscle memory. You've been frightened and angry and know how much energy these emotions produce. Because you probably don't fully process emotional issues, the fear and anger memory stays right under the surface of whatever else you're feeling. Although fear and anger are essential in countering danger, they move only in one direction. When you use these emotions knowingly or unknowingly to fuel your goals, you create limited outcomes. Fueling your life through the energy of anger and fear brings no lasting satisfaction.

To energize your dreams and create the life you want through self-hypnosis, you need to tune your life script to emotions that open you to flow. They are commonly called *transcendent emotions* and include the following:

- Gratitude

- Awe

- Inspiration

- Reverence

- Appreciation

- Excitement

- Passion

- Belief

When you fuel your life with these emotions, you can go anywhere with your imagination. How do you tune in? You tune in through imagery. Imagine situations, people, places, saints and gurus, actions, and so forth that have inspired one or more of the emotions listed previously and write them into your script. Take the time right now to make a list of all the things that jazz you and open you to flow. This will be an important list in upcoming chapters.

Emotional Access to Higher Wisdom

While the subconscious is the home of your unexamined beliefs, attitudes, and behaviors, it's also the source of your creativity, intuition, and inspiration. It's where your inner knowing resides and is the part of you that understands the interconnectedness of all life.

In many ways, emotions are the pathway to connecting with your spiritual center. When you're in sync with your emotions, you're in touch with what inspires and uplifts you. Through your emotions, you recognize that you're more than a physical substance; you're spirit as well. The connection between your physical and spiritual aspects reflects through your emotion.

This makes emotions central to using hypnosis to access your higher wisdom. Once connected to your own inner spiritual voice, you can use it for guidance in making decisions and choosing directions. It can help you understand your strengths and learn from your emotional discomfort. Instead of thinking of emotions as a secondary impulse, you see they are the key to living fully open, alive, and awake. They are the inspiration for a creatively inspired life.

MESMERIZING MORSEL

"The artist is a receptacle for emotions that come from all over the place: from the sky, from the earth, from a scrap of paper, from a passing shape, from a spider's web."

—Pablo Picasso, artist

When you use self-hypnosis to connect with your inner wisdom, you have a guide in the process. You can retrieve past-life memories or deal with difficult trauma. Emotional wisdom can help you nurture and heal the past.

The Connection Between Mind, Body, and Emotion

According to neuroscientist Dr. Candace Pert, author of *Molecules of Emotion,* the prime function of emotions is communication between the mind and the body. She explains that contrary to popular belief, emotions are carried on molecules that are generated not only in brain cells, but in every cell of the body. Every cell has receptor sites to receive emotional information. Emotions convey essential information between mind and body, intimately connecting the two.

Actually, you already know this is true. You know emotions are generated and received in the body because it's in your body that you feel emotion. In addition, you feel specific emotions in specific areas. You don't say you have a broken foot when you lose a relationship; you say you have a broken heart. Your knowledge of the body-mind-emotion connection is coded in your language. You use body-based metaphors to convey that your emotions are part of your body wisdom and, like your thoughts and beliefs, are reflected in your body language and metaphors.

SUBCONSCIOUS SCAFFOLDING

Consider metaphors such as "heartbroken," "wearing your heart on your sleeve," "chip on your shoulder," "elbowing your way," "standing your ground," "hating someone's guts," "gut wrenching," and as many others as you can. Notice how metaphors link emotions and body wisdom.

Understanding the function of emotions helps you intercept the images and messages coming from your subconscious. As you pursue your self-help intentions, you can interact with deeper aspects of yourself to create life scripts that reflect your path and purpose while creating believable, impactful life scripts that carry you forward on a wave of energy.

Alignment: The Power of Your Mind, Body, and Emotions

You picked up this book because you wanted to create change in some area of your life. Through the third key of engagement, you have access to your three most powerful tools: your mind, body, and emotions. Together, these create the matrix of your life and express your spiritual essence.

You might initiate change because you're running from your inner demons. Old trauma, unhealed hurts, past failures, and imagined slights fuel your worst fears and undermine your confidence. Understanding the dynamics of your matrix allows you to make choices based on a compelling future rather than running from a difficult past. When you begin to see the connection between what you believe, what you envision, what you feel, and what you sense, you begin the journey of living life fully engaged. Nothing is out of your reach as long as you commit to your dreams and are willing to work to achieve them.

The practices in this book repeatedly return to this key. Being able to connect to the matrix of mind-body-emotion, to listen and use the language of the subconscious, and to take action with alignment of all parts allows you unimagined freedom. This means you write your life script based on what you want and choose words that create images, make you feel, and stimulate physiology.

Empowering your life through self-hypnosis requires that you follow the language of your subconscious and give clear unifying instructions. When you do, the sky is your limit.

The Least You Need to Know

- Engagement is using your natural ability to visualize, read body signals, and power your life through emotions.
- Visualization is your natural ability to daydream.
- Your body enacts the thoughts and visions in your mind.
- Your emotions provide you with information and energy.
- Engaging your mind-body-emotion connection aligns you with your goals.
- Congruence among your mind, body, and emotions empowers your life script.

Key 3: Communication with the Subconscious Mind

Communication with your subconscious is twofold: it involves giving instructions to change your programmed life script and listening to your authentic self to uncover and express your path and purpose and develop the innate skills you were born with.

The long-term success of self-hypnosis depends on how congruent the message of your script is with your core beliefs and values. You won't create a change that goes against your beliefs, no matter how nicely you write the script or how much perceived benefit the action will bring you. The third key, which is discussed in this chapter, teaches you how to communicate effectively with your subconscious so you can listen to its messages and create congruent scripts.

In This Chapter

- Learning techniques to talk with your inner mind
- How your body, emotions, and intuition communicate
- Finding the purpose in your negative thoughts
- Positive steps for choosing your words

Developing the Skills of the Finger Lift and the Body Circle

The subconscious program currently running your life does not necessarily reflect your inner self. Usually, this program was never yours to begin with—you inherited it from parents, spouses, society, or other pervasive influences. You have lived by it because your conscious mind rationalized and supported it. Now it's time to restore the deeper, truer voice that reflects your authentic self and live a more meaningful life.

If you want to write a new program that speaks to who you really are, you need to listen to and communicate with your still-small voice within. Using self-hypnosis, you'll hear what is important to your inner mind and obtain information and messages that direct you toward a happy and fulfilling future.

As you create scripts to meet your goals—whether the goal is to lose weight and fit into that great wedding dress, to find confidence, or to develop more intimate relationships—you'll need a simple, direct method to listen to your subconscious and determine whether your goal and script are congruent with your inner self. One way to do this is for you to use techniques that rely on body movements to express yes-or-no answers from your inner mind. This is called an *ideomotor effect*. Essentially, ideomotor effects are movements that reflect your inner psychological states. They are easy to use and very effective.

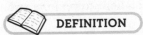 **DEFINITION**

> The **ideomotor effect** refers to unconscious movements that reflect psychological states that can be used to communicate with the subconscious mind. Examples of unconscious ideomotor effects are tears, goose bumps, and muscle twitches.

Ideomotor methods may seem too simple to work, but try them before you judge their value! The preceding chapter explained that your body reflects subconscious messages that are filtered out of your conscious awareness. In fact, the connection between your body and subconscious is so strong that neuroscientist Candace Pert hypothesizes that the body is the subconscious mind. Whether she is correct, dealing directly with your subconscious inner mind through your body signals is fast, easy, and insightful.

Using ideomotor effects begins with the instant relaxation skill from key 1 (see Chapter 3). After entering a relaxed and receptive state, you can bypass the conscious mind by asking yes-or-no questions and waiting for the ideomotor response of a finger raise or body movement. The trick is not to think about it, just notice what you feel.

Here's the finger-lift method:

1. Create a relaxed state by using the key 1 instant relaxation technique (see Chapter 3) or by taking three deep, cleansing breaths, inhaling relaxation and exhaling tension.

2. Rest your nondominant hand on your thigh. You'll most likely receive a response from your thumb, index, and middle fingers. One digit will represent yes, one will represent no, and one will represent all the following: I don't know, maybe, and I don't want to disclose.

3. Ask your body to show you which finger is yes by simply saying "Show me a yes response." You'll know which finger is responding by any of the following: a twitch, tightening, slight movement, lifting, or even just noticing one finger. Whatever your reaction is, that finger is now your yes signal.

4. Ask your body to show you the no signal by saying "Show me a no response" and register which finger moves.

5. Ask your body to show you the third option by saying "Show me a maybe response" and register which finger moves.

6. Now ask yourself a few questions to get the hang of having a conversation with your subconscious. Start with simple, direct questions that don't have a large emotional component. For example, you might start by asking "Is self-hypnosis a useful technique for me?" and then follow with specific questions about what you hope to get from self-hypnosis, such as "Can self-hypnosis help me lose weight?"

 SUBCONSCIOUS SCAFFOLDING

When using ideomotor response techniques, your yes-or-no questions must be accurate, specific, and clear; otherwise the response will be unclear to you.

The body-circle effect is very similar to the finger-lift method and might even be easier than that. For the body circle, you do the following:

1. Relax and sit with your hands in your lap.

2. Ask that your inner mind speak to you by your torso turning clockwise for one answer; counterclockwise for the other; and back and forth for I don't know, maybe, or I don't want to disclose.

3. Record which direction is yes and which is no.

Regardless of which method you use, check the answers you receive with how it makes you feel. Later in this chapter, there are suggestions on how to listen for confirmation from the feeling senses of your body and your emotional wisdom. Using yes-or-no questions along with physical and emotional confirmation provide a way for you to check your self-hypnosis script against your inner values.

As we proceed, you'll be asked to check for congruence by using the previous method that works best for you or one of the alternate methods given at the end of this chapter. It's generally accepted in hypnosis, and I have certainly found it to be true, that you have the best results when your goals are 80 percent or more congruent with your true self. To determine the congruence with yes-or-no techniques, ask "Is this script/goal in 80 percent or more alignment with my core values?" and wait for a yes-or-no response. If it's yes, you're good to go. If it's no, you'll need to rewrite your script or goal to better reflect your inner self.

Listening to the Subconscious

The inner mind speaks to you using a language more complex than yes and no. In Chapter 4, you learned how to send messages to the inner mind with visualization, body sensations, and emotions. This is the same language your subconscious uses to send messages back to your conscious mind. Communication occurs in symbols and images that arrive with specific body feelings and emotions. Your ability to recognize the messages and understand the information depends on your ability to interpret these signals.

The Wisdom of the Body

If you thought self-hypnosis was solely a mental technique, you might be surprised to learn how difficult it is separating your mind from your body. The two are truly interconnected. This knowledge is helpful when writing scripts. To hear messages, you need to be comfortable in your body.

Your body is a master communicator. You communicate with others nonverbally through body language, facial expressions, and gestures. Your subconscious mind uses your body sensations to transmit messages. Physical sensations get your attention. They tell you to stop and attend—something important is happening. They also confirm the intuition you receive from the subconscious.

Here are a few sensations your body may use to get your attention and to validate your inner knowing:

- Tingling sensations along your arms, back, or legs

- Vibration that seems to come from deep within you

- Hot and/or cold passing through your body

- Excitation, such as goose bumps or hair standing on end

- Skin crawling sensations

- Flashes of pain or burning sensations

- Butterflies in your stomach

- A sense of being dropped or of falling

- Your heart racing or pounding

Physical sensations that accompany subconscious messages act as validation. For example, imagine meeting someone for the first time and noticing that you really like him. When your awareness is accompanied by hair rising along your arms and a racing heart, you're more likely to pay attention and possibly believe in love at first sight more than if you simply noticed that the two of you have much in common.

 WISE COUNSEL

Uncomfortable physical sensations without an obvious cause could be an indication of a medical condition. Don't overlook physical causes for your body sensations.

During a self-hypnosis session, you may feel any of the preceding body sensations when you receive information. They usually arise at critical points in your session and increase your believability of your script to convince your subconscious that your goals are possible and beneficial. Imagine reading a script and getting goose bumps. Does it enhance your confidence? Because the information is linked to your body sensation, it's easier to retrieve and act upon after the session is over.

The Insight in Emotions

Emotions are generally classified as good (uplifting) or bad (depleting), depending on how comfortable or uncomfortable they make you feel. Actually, all emotions have a function: they provide information you can use to make your choices. As explained in the preceding chapter, emotions also release energy that powers your life. You don't need to pursue happy emotions or avoid uncomfortable ones; you need to learn how to listen to them all and use them to create a life of self-mastery.

Emotions provide direct and immediate information. They tell you about inner conditions and inform you of external undercurrents. Often, before your mind realizes something, your emotions and body are already responding. Emotions are quick to sense danger, threats, opportunity, and more. Unfortunately, you might have forgotten how to listen to your emotional language. What used to be quite natural is now foreign territory. Check out the following table to see the meaning and function of a few emotions. Take a few minutes to list other emotions and decide what might be the meaning and function of them.

Easy-Access Emotional Dictionary

Emotion	Simple Meaning	Function
Anger	Obstruction; injustice; threat	To generate energy for protection
Awe	Awareness of a larger reality	To renew the spirit and strengthen your connection to life
Boredom	Ability and talents are not being used	To help you connect creatively to the present time, place, people, and activity
Fear	Danger	To generate energy to fight or flee
Guilt	Hurting someone or overstepping another's boundary	To encourage reconciliation
Grief	Loss	To heal through the cleansing of regret
Jealousy	Undervaluing yourself and/or your partner	To instill appreciation
Worry	Unprocessed fear	To encourage emotional processing

 HYPNOTIC CONNECTION

A full compendium of emotions, meanings, and functions can be found in my book, *The Path of Emotions: Turn Your Emotions into Energy and Transform Your Life.*

Gut Feelings and Intuition

Your intuition gives you direct access to the information being communicated from your inner mind. How often do you think one thing, but for whatever reason, feel pulled in another direction? Perhaps you're getting ready to sign a contract with all the job benefits you want, but for some reason you hesitate and instead take a different, seemingly less advantageous job. Later, the company you almost joined folds. If you had taken the job with them, you would be unemployed.

In addition to emotions and body wisdom, gut feelings and intuition help you discern the messages from your inner mind. Intuition speaks through the following:

- Sudden thoughts that have no apparent origin

- Feeling compelled to perform actions, go places, or meet people

- Sudden insights and awareness that arrive with no apparent source

- Knowing the right move to make or direction to go in

- Visions and dreams

Intuition is a faculty you have and use; you just aren't always aware of it. As Chapter 21 reveals, self-hypnosis can create a link to your intuition, making it a major part of your daily life.

Directing the Subconscious

Previous chapters have revealed a number of ways in which you unconsciously direct the programs in your subconscious mind. You know that your repetitive thoughts reinforce existing programs; however, they can also be used to support new ones. You have learned that your language is littered with words that limit you. You know that your mind, body, and emotions create a comprehensive communication system that you can use for your betterment. You know that your emotions fuel your life.

Assembling this information creates a set of tools to rewrite your script (which you'll do in Chapter 7). First, though, you need to look more closely at your negative programming. Remember, you don't take on programs that go against core values, so you might ask "Do negative thoughts have any subconscious value?" The answer is a surprising yes and may explain why simply using affirmations to counter negative thoughts often creates inner conflict and outer chaos.

 MESMERIZING MORSEL

"You use hypnosis not as a cure, but as a means to create a favorable climate in which to learn."

—Milton Erickson, father of Ericksonian Hypnotherapy

To move to a positive framework, you need to understand the function of your self-limiting behavior and negative thoughts. You can then write scripts that will elevate you to higher goals and support you when you arrive.

Self-Limiting Behavior and Subconscious Protection

Many of your self-limiting behaviors were developed to protect you. Past experiences of pain and danger may have occurred at times when you were helpless and couldn't protect yourself or find solutions. Maybe you were too young or too impressionable. The result was a decision, conscious or unconscious, to never be in that position again.

Another source of self-limiting behavior is protection from overwhelming emotions. Trauma—such as physical or sexual abuse, losing a parent at a young age, or living in deprivation—create deep, protective defense mechanisms that direct your self-limiting behavior. While defense mechanisms don't represent your authentic voice, path, and purpose, they do protect them and keep them safe. It's unrealistic to think you can use any technique to override limitations designed for safety. On the other hand, letting them rule your life is equally unacceptable. So what can you do?

The answer is to address the underlying concern. For example, if you want to engage in a loving relationship, it might not be enough to visualize and feel yourself in a relationship. You might be avoiding a loving relationship because you're afraid of abandonment. Therefore, your script must deal with this concern. Finding the underlying issues behind self-limiting behavior is a good place for you to use the yes-or-no ideomotor techniques.

Here's how:

1. Identify a self-limiting behavior you want to change.

2. List the possible underlying fears. For example, possible doubts about relationships include fear of the following:

   - Abandonment and rejection

   - Not being lovable

   - Domination

   - Loss of freedom

3. Use the finger-lift or body-circle method to decide which possibilities are true for you. Ask each fear "Is this fear true for me?" Wait for the yes-or-no response.

4. Write a one- or two-sentence statement that addresses the underlying fear and puts you in the center of the solution. For example:

   - I am strong enough to handle rejection. I stand by myself in all situations, no matter what.

   - I love myself totally and completely.

   - I can be in a loving relationship and be true to myself.

5. Use the finger-lift method to test how well your statement addresses your concern. Ask "Is this statement in alignment with my inner truth?" If yes, you can use it. If no, you'll need to change it or create another.

Breaking Away from Negative Thoughts

Resisting negative thoughts doesn't help get rid of them. The more you resist, the more persistent your thoughts become. Negative thoughts have a purpose: they convey your deeper beliefs behind your self-limiting behavior, express your feelings, and voice the expectation of your past experience. In fact, your negative thinking often originates as self-protection.

The bottom line is that while you need to listen to the underlying fears of your negative thoughts and create scripts to address them, negative thoughts rarely reflect your authentic self. Once you identify and address the message they contain, you need to break the habit of using them.

 MESMERIZING MORSEL

"You cannot have a positive life and a negative mind."

—Joyce Meyer, author and speaker

Here are five steps you can take right now to help break away from negative thoughts:

- **Watch your words.** Pay attention to what you say and the words you use. Do the words you use reflect what you truly believe? Make a decision to only use words that reflect your truth.

- **Monitor self-talk.** Rather than just reacting to your inner dialogue, notice the content and attitude of what you tell yourself. Make the decision to speak only your truth.

- **Use positive reinforcement.** Any behavior that gets positively rewarded will be repeated. Praise yourself when you reach the bottom of a limiting pattern and counter it with a growth-oriented thought.

- **Create rewards.** Think of simple things you love. Make sure to reward yourself whenever you consciously shift an outmoded habit.

- **Choose your friends.** Associate with people who believe in the reality you want to live.

As you start to pay attention, you might find it interesting to self-document using personal media devices to journal your words, self-talk, and feelings.

Furthering the Dialogue

The importance of communication with the inner mind is obvious, and you might be getting really excited to further the conversation. In daily life, you probably take few opportunities to develop your interpersonal communication skills. If the finger-lift method isn't for you, you can try some of the following methods.

In upcoming chapters, these techniques will be used to check scripts and receive communication from inner guidance. However, if you have trouble using them, this doesn't mean self-hypnosis won't work for you. Knowing what you want and going for it are 90 percent of success. Communication becomes clearer when you move forward and use it when it makes sense.

Muscle Testing

Muscle testing is an ideomotor technique developed on the theory that the nerve impulse through your muscles is stronger on a yes response and weaker on a no response. Thus, muscles transmitting yes are stronger than those transmitting no.

Here's how you do muscle testing:

1. Use the instant relaxation skill (see Chapter 3) or take three clearing breaths.

2. Using your nondominant hand, touch the tip of your ring finger to the tip of your thumb to make an "O" shape.

3. Insert the index finger of your other hand through the "O" and hook it around the connection point of your finger and thumb.

4. Apply force to the area where your finger and thumb meet. Resist, trying not to let your index finger break the connection between your fingers.

5. Ask for a yes response and try to pull the "O" open. It should take a fair amount of strength to break the connection open. Ask for a no response and repeat; it should be easy to break the connection.

6. Continue to ask yes-or-no questions that are clear, accurate, and specific. For example, you can pick what color shirt to wear by asking "Is this the best color for me to wear today?" as you touch each shirt.

While this provides a clearer answer than the finger-lift message, the disadvantage is that there is no signal for maybe, I don't know, or I don't want to disclose.

Using a Pendulum

Another ideomotor technique uses a pendulum. In theory, when you dangle an object on a string and ask questions, subtle unconscious, muscular movements make the pendulum swing in different patterns. This technique has the advantage of moving well beyond yes, no, and maybe. Using charts, it can reveal specific answers. In this book, you'll use the chart and a pendulum to find percentages.

Pendulums are made of strings or chains 8 to 10 inches long with a weighted object on one end—perhaps a crystal, copper ball, or sacred object. However, almost anything that makes a balanced weight that you can tie on a string will work, including nuts, washers, and keys. See what is available for you to make one right now. You'll probably want to use it in upcoming chapters.

 HYPNOTIC CONNECTION

The pendulum technique described here can be expanded by using premade dowsing charts. The most comprehensive collection of pendulum charts with clear directions can be found in Dale Olson's book *The Pendulum Charts*.

Here is the technique for using a pendulum:

1. Use the instant relaxation skill (see Chapter 3) or take three deep, clearing breaths.

2. Determine what the pendulum signals are for you. As with the finger-lift method, this step only has to be done once. The next time you look for answers with the pendulum, you can use the same patterns.

   - Hold the end of the chain and let the weighted end swing. Ask for a yes response. After a short while, the pendulum will move from a circular motion to swinging in a straight line from side to side, near and away, or diagonally in any direction. Whatever the movement, this represents your yes response.

   - Return the pendulum to swinging in a circle, steady your hand, and ask the pendulum to show you a no response. Once again, after a few minutes, it will begin to swing in a different, straight line. This is your no signal.

   - Return to circling and ask to be shown a maybe response, which can be another straight line in another direction, a dead stop, or the continuation of a circle.

   - Another technique is to hold the pendulum still and ask for a response. The pendulum will begin to swing and your yes-or-no responses may be clockwise or counterclockwise circles instead of straight lines.

3. Now knowing your yes, no, and maybe response patterns, begin to ask yes-or-no questions. The questions need to be accurate, specific and clear. The faster and bigger the swing of your pendulum, the more emphatic your inner mind feels about the answer.

Another way you'll use the pendulum is to measure the degree of congruence in your scripts. To do this, divide a half-circle into segments with each segment indicating a percentage from 0 to 100 percent in increments of 10. Take a look at the following chart. You can use this chart for upcoming exercises.

To use the chart, start the pendulum circling as you ask "What is the percentage of congruence for this script?" Wait until the pendulum moves into a straight line along one of the segments; this is your answer.

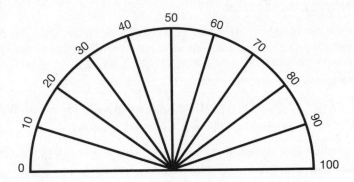

Automatic Writing

Automatic writing is the last ideomotor technique you might employ. Again, your conscious mind relaxes its critical focus on what your muscles are doing. Once in a relaxed state, you automatically write words on a piece of paper, paying no attention to what you're composing. Automatic writing has a long and convoluted history as a means to connect with the subconscious, as well as discarnate spirits, guides, angels, and so forth. This technique takes considerable practice and is more challenging for you to perform than other methods.

At the beginning, the gobbledygook that you write easily engenders doubt. With practice, however, it can develop into an illuminating technique that comes into its own when you're in a full trance and almost oblivious to the muscle action taking place. Its biggest advantage over other techniques is the ability to provide detailed information and fully developed concepts.

There are two ways to perform this technique. In the first, you ask questions and hear words in your mind that you then write down. In the second, you're unaware of the words you write until you read them later. Both methods are useful in questioning your subconscious. Whichever naturally occurs as you try this technique is the method for you. It's fine to use a keyboard instead of pen and paper; however, since this technique is often performed with your eyes closed, especially in the second method, pen and paper is generally easier.

Here are the steps:

1. Find a quiet, comfortable spot with no distractions, such as sitting at a table or desk with pen and paper (or computer) in front of you.

2. Hold the pen in your hand with the point touching the paper or rest your hands on the keyboard.

3. Use the instant relaxation skill (see Chapter 3) to relax and quiet your mind. The deeper you go into a relaxed state, the better your results.

4. Ask your inner self to communicate with you for the highest and best good. Visualize your inner self flowing from your heart into your arm and down into your hand.

5. Try not to consciously write anything; just allow you hand to move. Pay no attention to the scribbles that follow. Keeping your eyes closed is a good idea. At some point, you may notice your hand is moving with greater flow and ease or you're receiving words in your mind that you can write down.

6. Every so often, stop and see what has been written. If you start to see actual words, you can begin to ask questions and wait for answers to form.

7. When it seems to stop, if indeed it happened at all, take a look for any decipherable words, images, or symbols that mean something to you.

 WISE COUNSEL

The types of questions you ask are important in determining the accuracy of results. Make sure the questions are unambiguous and clearly stated. If your questions are an attempt by your ego to increase your self-importance, this technique will not provide useful information but lead you toward delusions of grandeur.

Give a lot of time for each session and practice regularly; this is a technique that requires diligence. Keep the writings, even the first scribbles, to look at later. Over time, patterns might emerge. Try not to place too much emphasis on the automatic part of this technique. Consider it a dialogue with your inner self and allow the thoughts you have to be a reflection of genuine answers.

While elusive, this technique can become a useful tool in maintaining an inner dialogue that builds your self-awareness, confidence, and ability to create the reality you want. Remember, though, the best tools to listening to your subconscious are your emotions, body signals, and intuition.

The Least You Need to Know

- The success of your self-hypnosis depends on how congruent your script is with your core beliefs and values.
- Your unconsciously generated body movements (ideomotor) can be used to talk with the subconscious mind.
- Visualization, body sensations, and emotions can all hold messages from your subconscious.
- While you need to listen to the fears within your negative thoughts and create scripts to address them, negative thoughts rarely reflect your authentic self and should not be allowed to limit your life.
- Self-hypnosis will still work with phenomenal success whether you can use communication techniques or not; knowing what you want and going for it are 90 percent of the success.

PART 2

Designing Your Own Self-Hypnosis Program

Congratulations! With Part 1 accomplished, you have the background tools for creating a self-hypnosis session. Real change begins now as you formulate your goals and see how they fit into the larger picture of your life's mission and vision. Once you know what you really want and where you really want to go, self-hypnosis aligns your conscious and subconscious minds to become your best dream buddies. So dream big! You can accomplish anything you put your mind and heart to!

Mapping for Success

Self-hypnosis is a tool to bring the life you want into reality; however, success takes more than just visualizing yourself in a new future. It takes goals and dedication made easier, more creative, and more effective with self-hypnosis. The first step to craft change is deciding what you want and where you want to go (your goals) and then deciding how to get there (your action steps). If you've been trying to change your life and haven't been able to make the shift, you may have forgotten to create a map.

Self-hypnosis sessions energize and enliven your goals and action steps, becoming support you can use anywhere and anytime to calm the beating heart of anxiety, to confidently engage a new client, or to save yourself from eating the wrong food at the wrong time. You may want to jump straight into using self-hypnosis, and you can, but your efforts will go much further if you first enjoy creating a road map to your future, as I show you how to do in this chapter.

In This Chapter

- Learning to set goals
- Aligning your goals with a larger picture
- Creating a mission and vision statement
- Moving plans into action

Using Your Testing Tools from the Get-Go

As you work through this chapter, you'll develop a wonderful road map full of great goals and action steps. How well they work for you depends in large part on how congruent they are with your inner mind. As you develop your map, use your communication skills from key 3 (see Chapter 5) to test your mission and vision statements along with your goals and action steps for congruence with your inner values.

If you recall, the previous chapter provided several ideomotor techniques so you can communicate directly with your subconscious mind. Use the method that worked best for you to check the level of effectiveness of your mapping components. Ask "How effective is this statement/goal/action step? Ten percent? Twenty percent? Thirty percent?" and so forth. Notice at which percentage point you get a positive response with your chosen technique.

WISE COUNSEL

Don't get hung up on ideomotor techniques. If you're having trouble using them, use your emotions, body, and/or intuition to determine congruence. Does the goal jazz you? Do you feel a sense of opening and flow in your body? Is your gut feeling "yes"? If so, trust that you're congruent and go for it!

In my experience, a goal needs to be at least 80 percent effective to produce a positive result. If it's less than 80 percent, use your communication tools to discover which part of the suggestion isn't effective. Ask yes-or-no questions, such as the following:

- Is my goal congruent with my authentic self?

- Is this suggestion believable?

- Is the timing expressed correctly?

- Is this a realistic goal?

- Does this suggestion fully engage my emotions?

Test until you've identified exactly where your subconscious mind is rejecting the statement. Most often, the problem lies with congruence, believability, or emotional engagement. Once you know which area needs improvement, rework your suggestion until your subconscious mind gives you an 80 percent or better reading for effectiveness. Now everything is ready to support the change your heart desires!

Testing for effectiveness is an excellent place to use a pendulum chart. You can significantly reduce the time it takes to create effective goals by using the chart in Chapter 5 and doing quick checks for effectiveness.

Charting Your Course

I'm sure you know that having goals is important. Have you been avoiding setting them? Maybe you've been meaning to get started but have been sidetracked by the daily grind of maintaining the status quo. Or perhaps you spend hours creating goals and for a while feel really high and excited, but as time passes, lose your enthusiasm and stop acting on your dreams, eventually forgetting about creating them altogether. Goals are important, but sometimes we confuse setting goals with action. In fact, some experts wonder if the very act of goal setting sets you up for failure.

According to the 2011 blog post "Wired for Success" at Psychologytoday.com by Ray B. Williams—one of Canada's top CEO coaches, a certified master coach, a certified hypnotherapist, and a bestselling author—"any goals that require substantial behavioral change or thinking-pattern change will automatically be resisted." Williams also says that to make a change in behavior, we must first make a change in our self.

 MESMERIZING MORSEL

"Despite the popularity of goal setting, there is compelling evidence that regardless of good intentions and effort, people and organizations consistently fall short of achieving their goals. More often than not, the fault is attributed to the goal setter. But the real problem may be in the efficacy of goal setting itself."

—Ray B. Williams, "Wired for Success" (psychologytoday.com/blog/wired-success)

He's right; we do resist making internal change and the truth is, our external circumstances are a reflection of our internal life. So if we resist internal change, we are unlikely to see a change in our circumstances. Fortunately, you have a leg up; you already know the change that's required to embrace a new future is losing your conditioned beliefs and habitual responses. You know what you have to do and how to do it—listen to your inner voice. Once you're listening to and communicating with your subconscious mind, resistance to change decreases.

You have the tools; now it's time to go to work. As you read through the following sections, take time to create your vision, mission, goals, and action steps. Use your ideomotor skills to test how accurately they align with your values. By the end of this chapter, you'll be steamrolling your plans into reality.

Why Set Goals?

Goal setting is creating a map. More importantly, goal setting is transformative; the process of determining your ideal future reveals your values, fears, expectations, boundaries, vulnerabilities, and gifts. It's a great way to really get to know yourself, and guess what, it's fun! Come on, what's not fun about planning the life you've always wanted? A goal is nothing more than a statement of what you want. So what do you want? Knowing the answer—really knowing—is its own motivation to turn your vision into reality.

The degree to which your goals are useful depends on how aligned they are with your inner mind; not your programming or wishful thinking, but your actual, core truth. When you finish creating the map of your goals and action steps, you'll have clear direction for designing your self-hypnosis session. Better yet, your new goals won't dissolve because this time they are supported by the changes you've made in yourself.

The Bigger Picture: Mission and Vision Statements

In order to create supercharged goals, they need to be part of a bigger picture. That's where your personal *vision* and *mission statements* come in. These statements are declarations of your purpose and values. Creating vision and mission statements establishes standards and defines your ideals and principles. They guide what you're willing to do, or not do, to get what you want. And of course, tying your goals to a larger picture motivates you to achieve them.

 **DEFINITION**

A **mission statement** is a declaration of how you intend to enact your values through life. It defines your path and purpose. A **vision statement** is a declaration of your core values and how you fit in the world.

You may be planning to use self-hypnosis for a finite goal, such as losing weight, and don't feel the need to tie such goals to a larger life plan. But how much more motivated would you be if losing weight was part of a larger mission to be a healthy role model for your kids or a fitness plan to climb Mount Everest? Would being part of a larger picture change the method you use to accomplish your goal?

A mission statement defines your purpose and path. What do you ultimately want to achieve in your career, relationships, and so forth? A mission statement is specific, happens within a certain time frame, and has measurable results; it's your declaration of the precise way you'll personally live out your larger vision.

The larger vision that guides you is expressed in a vision statement. What are your core values and beliefs about what matters in life? What is your personal contribution to those values? Your vision statement provides inspiration for daily life and guides strategic decision making.

Creating Your Mission and Vision Statements

Make the creation of your mission and vision statements a sacred and fun time. Sit with pen and paper or computer and use key 1 (see Chapter 3) to relax and tune in. Your mission statement should include what you want to create, when you want to have it done by, and what the desired result will be.

To start, use key 2 (see Chapter 4) and identify your burning passion. What engages your emotional energy: travel, animal rights, medicine, religious practice, teaching others? Next, identify what would be the highest measure of your success: travel the world in five years, establish a cruelty-free educational blog, work for Doctors Without Borders for one month every year, and so on. Because there are many milestones of success, make sure you choose the biggest and most important ones to define your mission. End the statement with your desired result.

Here's a sample mission statement:

> My mission is to decrease cruelty to animals by establishing a blog in the next year that reveals which cosmetic companies avoid testing on animals, allowing women to choose cruelty-free quality beauty products.

This statement precisely defines the enactment of a larger vision. It's specific, time-bound, and result-oriented.

Next is the creation of your vision statement—the inspiration underneath your mission. Pay attention to key 3 (see Chapter 5), asking your inner mind what compels you toward the mission. What value is there in traveling the world? What difference will it make in your life that you do? Listen to your inner mind for answers, merging your emotions, body signals, and intuition with your intellectual thoughts. Write your vision statement in a way that motivates your actions and energizes your choices.

Here's an example of a vision statement that might inspire the previous mission statement:

> The consciousness in all life matters; cruelty anywhere hurts everyone everywhere.

This statement declares the value that inspires the mission and how the value fits into the rest of the world.

As you create and define your mission and vision statements, you may uncover old programing that kept you from moving forward in the past. Maybe you never stepped up to write a blog because you thought "Who do I think I am? No one will listen to me" or "You can't fight city hall." Take the time to identify these limiting thoughts and counter them with an affirmation. (See Chapter 5 if you need exercises to help create an affirmation from your authentic self.)

The S.M.A.R.T. Approach to Setting Goals

The next step in creating your road map is to define shorter-term goals (focusing on only one or two at a time) that serve your larger purpose or mission. One of the most prevalent and used tools for goal developing is the S.M.A.R.T. method:

S: Specific. Make the goal as precise as possible and answer the standard who, what, where, when, and how questions.

M: Measurable. Make sure you can quantify the completion of your goal. Ask the following:

- How much? How many?

- How will I know when it's accomplished?

A: Actionable/attainable. Your goal has to be something you can act on and attain. Ask the following:

- What action steps can I take to achieve this?

- Do I have the necessary resources to act?

R: Realistic/results focused. Your goal has to be something that with hard work is possible to do, and you have to believe that you can do it. Here are some questions to ask:

- Do I believe that this goal can be accomplished?

- Do I have the skills to do it?

- What will be the outcome of success?

- What conditions have to exist to accomplish this goal?

T: Timely/tangible. Your goal needs to be locked into a time line that focuses your action. The more tangible, the more you're fulfilling key 2 and staying engaged. The following are ways to accomplish this:

- Create a reasonable end time for your goal to be completed. Your action steps will tie into this end time.

- Can you taste, touch, smell, see, or hear your goal?

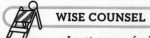

WISE COUNSEL

Anytime you feel frightened, defeated, or diminished as you pursue your goals, use key 1, instant relaxation, and repeat your affirmation. No one but you can make a limitation real, and no one but you can free yourself.

In short, like the mission statement, goals are best when they're specific, measurable, and engaged. Some examples of good and not-so-good goals can be found in the following table.

Okay vs. Excellent Goals

Okay Goal	Excellent Goal
I will lose enough weight to fit into my wedding dress on my wedding day of December 3.	I will lose 2 pounds a week by eating fresh, delicious, healthy foods and exercising 30 minutes every day so I can fit easily into my wedding dress on my wedding day, December 3.
I will be a published author by the end of this year.	I will write a scintillating book proposal following professional guidelines and submit it to five high-powered agents by the end of this year.
I will travel to Costa Rica next year.	Starting this week, I will save $25 a week in a special account for 20 months to buy a ticket to Costa Rica with a comfy hotel and spare money for exploring and having fun.
I will learn to speak Spanish before I go to Costa Rica next year.	I will begin a language course today, using self-hypnosis to learn easily, and schedule 5 hours a week to practice my skills so that I will be able to read road signs, menus, and carry on general conversation when I travel to Coast Rica in 20 months.
I will overcome my public speaking fears in time to speak at next year's convention.	I will enroll this month in a public speaking class and use self-hypnosis to reduce anxiety as I excel in mastering class projects so that I speak confidently and enjoyably, engaging the audience at next year's convention.

Once you've determined your goals, test for congruence using one of your ideomotor techniques. When you have congruent goals, write them down along with your mission and vision statements. Review them daily or better yet, tape them to your bathroom mirror, closet door, or refrigerator. Reflect on them and check in every so often to be sure you're still in alignment with them.

Stepping into Action

Most self-hypnosis programs stop after you've turned your goals into a self-hypnosis script that excites and energizes your passion. However, your dreams will not come to you by magic; your action is required. The final stage in creating your new life is identifying the action steps that will make your goal a reality. You also need a realistic time line and the resources you need to go forward.

It's so much fun to imagine your ideal life and write goals to create it that you might find yourself getting stuck in the planning phase and dragging your feet when it comes to action. You might be afraid to put your goals into action, concerned that you'll fail and have nothing left to excite you. Or you might be afraid that you'll succeed and then not like your dream life or not have anything else exciting enough to pursue. These are resistances. Acknowledge them, ask if they have something useful to offer, and then move on.

 MESMERIZING MORSEL

"It had long since come to my attention that people of accomplishment rarely sat back and let things happen to them. They went out and happened to things."

—Leonardo da Vinci, artist

Self-hypnosis is a tool that propels you into action; your self-hypnosis sessions get you moving forward, and on-the-spot self-hypnosis skills support you through moments of panic when you encounter resistance. Truly, you could not have a better support system than your own subconscious mind. And when you get to your dream life, there is always another vista, another goal to achieve, another exciting adventure to explore.

Defining Your Action Steps

From your mission statement, you created one or more large-scale goals. Each of these goals can envelop several smaller goals. For example, the goal of taking a trip to Costa Rica includes a goal of financial planning, a language skills goal, perhaps a fitness goal to enjoy hiking and surfing, and maybe even a relationship goal. Each of these goals has specific, actionable steps that you can take to achieve them. Now is the time to write down those steps and create a time line. You have the ultimate end time in your larger goal of taking a trip; what is the time line to achieve all your action steps to ensure the final time line is met? Create a one-week, one-month, or one-year plan of action for each goal, with each action step progressing from the one preceding it. Schedule it into your weekly calendar with a daily to-do list.

For example, your first action step for the Costa Rica trip might be gathering material—deciding on what vacation package and language course you want. You might need to read books and talk to other people who have taken a trip to Costa Rica and determine the best places to stay and worthwhile things to do and see. Schedule the research as part of the plan and know that doing it helps improve the realism of your goals and makes them more tangible.

Finally, review your action steps and make sure the overall plan fits the way you want to live your life. This is where knowing your boundaries, values, and past programming is essential. Are you willing to do anything to get your goals met? Really? Let your values guide your action steps and don't do anything that compromises your principles or boundaries in meeting your goal. Otherwise, when you achieve your goal, it won't have any meaning. If you're not sure, use key 3 and employ your communication techniques to test the congruity of your action steps.

Movement and Gain

As mentioned previously, one thing to be careful of at this stage is putting a lot of energy into creating and planning and not enough into doing. Some people call this the difference between being in motion and taking action. Motion is the research, preparation, and planning. It's important, but by itself, it doesn't produce an end result. Action, on the other hand, produces a discernable result. For example, I can read about Costa Rica and learn that the language is Spanish, but in and of itself, this doesn't help me speak Spanish. It prepares me, but action occurs when I start a language course.

You'll never have a perfect mission statement with ironclad goals and action steps. Your mission and goals may change as you start your journey and discover more about yourself than you know right now. You may find some goals that were congruent with your inner voice when you made them have changed as your inner voice reflects deeper inner values. As many vistas as there are to explore in the world, there is an equal number to explore within, and your priorities may change as you discover them. Never be afraid to re-evaluate and reform your plan; just don't give up.

The thing is, you'll never know if there is a deeper voice and more fulfilling mission unless you take action and start the journey forward. Any action is better than no action. You can always revise, reroute, and re-energize as you go.

The Adventure Unfolds

There is a fair amount of controversy over whether or not to share your personal mission, goal, and action plan with others. One viewpoint is that the more you share, the more support you have and the more committed you become. The other viewpoint is that when you share your goals, there will always be some people who tell you your goals are ridiculous and that you're foolish, wrong, or unrealistic. Someone somewhere will try to diminish you and rob you of your energy.

HYPNOTIC CONNECTION

Psychology Professor Dr. Gail Matthews conducted a research study at The Dominican University of California that provides empirical evidence for the increased effectiveness of using three tools for successful goal setting: accountability for meeting your action steps, commitment to another person or group, and writing down you goals. For more on this study, check out dominican.edu/dominicannews/study-backs-up-strategies-for-achieving-goals.

What may be best is to share your goals selectively. Pick people who will be your dream buddies and hold your goals as a sacred trust. Be accountable to them. Send progress reports every time you meet or miss a deadline, share synchronicities, and let them get excited for you! Your dream buddy can be one special person, a group where you all support each other, or even a professional association.

Listen to the advice of your dream buddies, but if they start to drag you down, re-evaluate. Reassess the attainability of your goal and if you believe it's possible, cut your buddies loose. Don't let anyone counter your authentic voice. You're here for a reason, and only you know what it is.

As you begin to take action to fulfill your goals, your inner mind will find ways to communicate with you. Emotions, body signals, and intuition will create a symphony of conversation, as described in Chapter 5. Synchronicity will abound, bringing the right people at the right time. Doors will open, letting you know that you're aligned with your path and the outer world supports the design you came to fulfill. Life becomes magical, not because it's effortless, but because your efforts are rewarded. Now is when self-hypnosis will prove to be the best skill you've ever developed to follow your heart into the life you were meant for.

The Least You Need to Know

- Make your goals congruent with your inner voice to avoid internal resistance.

- Setting goals maps your course and is transformative. You discover your values, boundaries, vulnerabilities, and gifts.

- Goals are supercharged when they're tied to the larger picture of your mission and vision statements.

- To write goals, use the S.M.A.R.T. approach: Specific, Measurable, Actionable/ attainable, Realistic/results focused, and Timely/tangible.

- Action steps tied to a time line make your goals reality.

- Listening to your inner mind ensures congruence among your goals, missions, vision, and action steps with your inner mind.

Creating a Self-Hypnosis Session

Self-hypnosis works because of your desire for change. Remember, all that is required is desiring something new, making the choice to change, 15 minutes a day, the ability to daydream, and the belief that change is possible. Self-hypnosis aligns with your deep inner desire to succeed and supports you in overcoming self-imposed limits. It's time to put everything together to make you the master scriptwriter of your life.

In this chapter, you create all parts of a hypnosis session, beginning with you being induced into a trance, followed by you reading a hypnotic script, and ending with you coming out full of enthusiasm. You also learn to craft a script that visualizes the life you want, encapsulate that life into a one-sentence posthypnotic suggestion, and use that suggestion to reinforce your goals.

In This Chapter

- Learning how to use self-hypnosis
- Practicing an induction method
- Writing a posthypnotic suggestion
- Designing a self-hypnosis script
- Terminating a session

Implementing Self-Hypnosis

Self-hypnosis has two distinct applications. The first is to conduct a complete session in which a full induction takes you into a trance and a script brings your goal to life. A posthypnotic suggestion is introduced in the script that continues to work after the session is over. The second use employs the posthypnotic suggestion as an affirmation anytime you're faced with challenges. You might use your affirmation when plagued by self-limiting thoughts, tempted by an addiction, or facing insurmountable odds.

 MESMERIZING MORSEL

"A #2 pencil and a dream can take you anywhere."

—Joyce Meyer, inspirational author

The best approach to this chapter is to read it and then create your induction and script. When you're ready, speak your session into a recorder and play it back to yourself while you comfortably surrender to relaxation. If that isn't possible, it's okay. Creating your script and reading it out loud while in a relaxed state still instructs your subconscious mind. In fact, simply reading it in your head works, too! Don't worry that you aren't in a deep trance; stay relaxed and focused. When you create images in your mind, your subconscious gets the message.

After the intellectual work of earlier chapters, this process brings everything together with the added benefit of being fun! A secret door is about to open in your mind and allow access to an inexhaustible inner resource.

The Full-Scale Session

A full-scale self-hypnosis session takes anywhere from 15 to 60 minutes, depending on how much time you can devote. Ideally, you might try to put aside 20 to 30 minutes each day. If that isn't possible, decide how many days a week you can dedicate and determine which days you'll schedule your self-hypnosis session. If possible, it's best to try and do the full session the same days of the week and the same time every day. Your body and mind get used to the rhythm and your subconscious prepares ahead for success. In addition, your commitment increases when the session is part of your routine. However, if the choice is to do it at odd times with a catch-as-can attitude or not all, then by all means, do it whenever you can!

The full session is the central hub in your wheel of success. After inducing relaxation, it combines your mission, goals, and action steps into a Technicolor script that engages your mind, body, and emotions and incorporates the wisdom of your inner mind. If your mission statement includes more than one goal, write a script for each one. Choose the script you use on a particular day or week to correspond to the action steps you're pursuing that day. (Chapter 8 gives more suggestions on how to create space and prepare for your session.)

> **SUBCONSCIOUS SCAFFOLDING**
>
> An easy, beneficial, and regular schedule might consist of conducting a full session as a weekly treat and then spending 5 to 10 minutes every morning reinforcing it with your posthypnotic suggestion.

Posthypnotic Suggestions for On-the-Spot Support

If you recall from Chapter 1, a posthypnotic suggestion or auto-suggestion is a direction you give your subconscious mind while under hypnosis about how you want to live. You give the suggestion during your full session while your mind is receptive to new ideas. Would you like to quit smoking, be confident in relationships, or make good on your New Year's resolution to eat healthy foods? Your posthypnotic suggestion helps you achieve your goals.

The posthypnotic suggestion can be reinforced every day with a few minutes of relaxation during which you repeat the sentence to yourself while envisioning its success. Sometimes a posthypnotic suggestion is tied to a specific situation, feeling, or event. For example, the suggestion might be "Every time my boss gets angry, I am serene, focused, and even more effective." This suggestion will take effect when your boss has a hissy fit whether you consciously reinforce it or not.

Posthypnotic suggestions are also used for conscious, on-the-spot support. When faced with temptation, self-doubt, or a challenge, using the relaxation technique from key 1 (see Chapter 3) followed by your posthypnotic affirmation supports you in achieving your goals. The support you need washes through you, providing confidence as you create positive change. You can use your posthypnotic suggestion before or during challenging situations, or anytime you need to shore your flagging spirits.

The Induction

The hypnotic session begins using an induction to enter into a trance. Key 1 gave you a jump-start, and for many people, the instant relaxation skill provides enough of a brainwave shift to receive suggestion. However, a full induction deepens your subconscious receptivity to the hypnotic script.

A common induction is a step-down technique that induces a trance by counting backward from 10 to 1. On each count, phrases are repeated that invite the subconscious mind to relax. A different technique uses guided imagery, and yet another combines basic step-down induction with guided imagery.

When inducing a trance, read slowly and pause whenever you see three dots. Also pause between sentences. Just reading the induction affects your mind, so be sure you're in a safe place to relax. Later, when you're ready, this will be used with your hypnosis script. You can find an audio download of this induction at idiotsguides.com/selfhypnosis.

Phrasing the Induction

As you read the upcoming induction, you might notice that the phrasing is sometimes slightly odd. That's because you're talking to both your conscious and subconscious minds and need two types of phrasing—one to talk with each part. While the subconscious believes what it's told, the conscious mind finds a hundred reasons why self-hypnosis won't work. The phrasing geared to the conscious mind is aimed at occupying its critical and skeptical nature while different phrasing relays messages to the subconscious.

Talking to your conscious mind is like talking to a 2-year-old child. Your conscious mind is oppositional; it doesn't like to be told what to do. Using phrases that are authoritarian will engender a skeptical response, if not out-and-out refusal to comply. Consequently, phrasing that offers suggestions rather than giving directives is best. Also, your conscious mind wants to follow a story, so when phrasing is nonsensical, it gets preoccupied trying to figure out meaning. You might think you want to avoid nonsensical wording, but not so: it can be a useful technique. If your conscious mind is occupied, messages can be slipped under the radar to your subconscious. Finally, asking questions that begin with a statement and end with "Is it not?" is another trick to quiet the objections of the outer mind.

 MESMERIZING MORSEL

"It takes but one positive thought when given a chance to survive and thrive to overpower an entire army of negative thoughts."

—Robert Schuller, inspirational author

Talking to your subconscious mind is much easier since it's more receptive to suggestion. You simply repeat key phrases that lead your body and mind into relaxation and a shift into slower brainwave states. The phrases are laden with images that ensure your subconscious engagement.

Basic Induction with Guided Imagery

Start with your basic instant relaxation. When relaxed, continue to read the following either out loud or in your head; imagine that somebody is reading it to you. "…" indicates to pause in your reading for a short moment. You should also pause for a few seconds at the end of every sentence.

Track 2

Begin:

Now that your body is nicely relaxed, it might be interesting to notice ... or not ... that your eyelids are becoming heavy ... becoming very heavy ... so heavy that it is harder and harder to lift them ... harder and harder ... if you even want to lift them.

And ... if you choose to become more and more relaxed ... you might notice that your breathing is slowed. It's easy to breathe slowly. As you breathe ... more and more deeply ... more and more slowly ... you may notice that as you fill your lungs with fresh, clean air ... part of you might notice that your body feels lighter ... feels so light ... as if you are floating ... as if you are a balloon filled with air.

You might find it interesting ... to notice the odd but comfortable sensation ... that part of you notices your body is heavier and heavier ... yet another part of you feels lighter and lighter ... as you become more and more deeply relaxed ... as you enjoy wonderfully calm freedom ... wonderfully calm relaxation.

As you continue to breathe slowly ... deeply ... as you continue to become more and more deeply relaxed ... you may feel tingling on the bottoms of your feet and palms of your hands .... You may notice the tingling as your eyes get heavier and heavier and your mind feels more and more free.

As you continue to breathe deeply ... you don't have to relax consciously relax. But as you become more and more relaxed ... perfectly relaxed ... perfectly at peace ... you may notice ahead of you the lovely staircase .... In fact, it might remind you of stairs you have seen before.

 SUBCONSCIOUS SCAFFOLDING

A trance occurs more quickly and easily each time you induce it. Increase your ability to quickly enter a trance by inserting a posthypnotic suggestion, such as "Each induction will create a deeper trance with fewer steps." Begin your next session by going down only five steps, and then during the following session, only travel down three steps.

Maybe these are stairs lead down into a garden ... safely leading down a lovely staircase ... to a beautiful garden .... Maybe you can see the soft sunlight reflecting off the grass ... or maybe, taking a deep breath, you might smell the strong scent of flowers.

As you approach the stairs, you might notice a wonderful excitement ... an anticipation that you may soon see someone you know and like .... And as you feel yourself looking forward to walking down these beautiful stairs ... maybe you notice the breeze across your skin ... feeling safe ... feeling free ... feeling alive ... as you move closer ... to the stairs.

Notice your anticipation ... your comfort .... Every sound takes you deeper inside yourself ... where it's really more interesting anyway.

As you approach the stairs, you can see there are 10 steps ... 10 steps going down .... You might find it interesting, or not, to count them as you step down from 10 to 1 ... 10 to 1 .... When you reach 1, you will be perfectly relaxed, perfectly at peace, perfectly open to new thoughts and ideas.

Taking a step down ... ten ... feeling fine ... feeling relaxed ... perfectly safe ... perfectly calm ... breathing deep, surrendering to the wonderful light that is filling your body ... feeling safe ... happy ... moving down ... going deeper and deeper inside .... Don't take the next step ... unless you want to.

Nine ... it's easy to feel yourself becoming more and more deeply relaxed ... more and more perfectly calm ... peaceful, relaxed ... surrendering to the beautiful garden full of color ... that awaits you ... listening to the sound of birds calling you forward ... hearing the wind in the trees ahead ... breathing deeply ... taking the next step ... going deeper down.

Eight ... as you continue to move down the stairs ... feel yourself more and more relaxed ... perfectly at peace ... feeling good ... feeling peaceful ... noticing the warm sun on your face ... more and more deeply relaxed. Notice how heavy your limbs are becoming as you take the next step.

Seven ... as you continue to breathe deeply ... you may notice how deeply relaxed and perfectly calm you feel .... Relaxation fills your muscles ... heavy and comfortable ... perfectly safe and happy ... moving down ... floating up ... going down deeper and deeper ... down the next step.

Six ... every sound takes you further inside to the perfect center of calm ... deeper and deeper ... deeper and deeper into pure relaxation .... Never take the next step until you're ready.

Five ... feeling good ... feeling secure ... feeling safe .... As you continue to breathe deeply, feel yourself filling with light ... surrendering to the deep, warm, comfortable relaxation spreading through your entire body .... You are ready for the next step, are you not?

Four ... with every step ... deeper and deeper .... As you continue to move down the stairs ... feel yourself becoming more and more relaxed ... perfectly at peace ... nicely calm ... stepping onto the next step.

Three ... breathe deeply ... fill yourself with goodness ... feeling fine ... perfectly safe ... perfectly calm ... smelling the flowers ... feeling the breeze ... more and more relaxed .... Have you taken the next step down?

Two ... as you approach the bottom of the staircase, you may notice that your breathing is very deep ... very slow ... very calm .... You may notice how deeply relaxed you feel ... how peaceful ... calm and full of light you feel as you take the last step.

One ... the last step ... breathing deeply ... feeling more and more relaxed ... more and more at peace ... perfectly at ease ... happy and ready for your new life .... You are now at the perfect state of relaxation .... You are now engaging in life's magic.

Personalizing an Induction

Are you feeling relaxed? You may have affected more than you realized or thought you could. Were you able to engage the imagery? There are many reasons to personalize this induction. Perhaps you're allergic to flowers or have a bad memory associated with gardens, so these images don't bring relaxation and safety. To personalize this induction, all you have to do is replace the imagery with something that suits you better. For example, instead of a garden, walk down a flight of stairs into a beautiful, sunlit drawing room or onto a lovely, warm beach. Create whatever scene helps you feel safe, warm, comfortable, relaxed, content, and anticipating something more.

> **SUBCONSCIOUS SCAFFOLDING**
>
> I have three tips for effective induction. First, be repetitive; this seduces your subconscious mind while assuring your conscious mind that it doesn't have to listen. Second, be nonsensical; not making sense gets your conscious mind out of the way of your subconscious as it tries to create order of the mish-mash. Third, engage your mind, body, and emotions; this makes the imagery more real and deepens the induction.

Creating Your Posthypnotic Auto-Suggestion

While in a trance, your subconscious is like a child waiting to be given life-changing instruction. The posthypnotic suggestion is the key lesson. It's an encapsulation of the goal you want to achieve, providing in one sentence the essence of the script. It's your secret weapon in overcoming doubt, worry, and anxiety.

Using hypnotic suggestion is natural. You give yourself auto-suggestions every day. You tell yourself what you can and can't do, judge your abilities, and perhaps even sabotage your success. Remember, if you say something enough and fuel it with your emotions, your subconscious believes it and makes it true, whether it's life affirming or not. Using auto-suggestion with awareness brings what you already do under conscious control, and as you take control of your thoughts, you take charge of your life.

Here are steps to creating your posthypnotic suggestion:

1. Choose the goal you want to work with.

2. Make the suggestion a reflection of either your larger mission statement or one of the smaller goals to attain it.

3. Create a suggestion that meets the recommended criteria for phrasing as given next.

4. Test the effectiveness of your suggestion using the communication skills in key 3 (see Chapter 5).

5. Write a script around the suggestion.

Deciding on your posthypnotic suggestion before writing your script makes the creation of your script much easier. Essentially, the suggestion is based on the goal you set out in Chapter 6, but the phrasing is a bit different. If you remember, your goals are written in future tense: they're what you're heading for, what you intend to achieve. Your posthypnotic suggestion is a declaration of what is. You're telling your inner mind that no matter what it looks like on the outside, no matter what the circumstances are, inside, everything you need already exists.

Your posthypnotic suggestion is an integral part of your hypnosis script where you'll instruct the subconscious mind how to use it. The following phrasing recommendations will help you write a dynamic suggestion to sustain your goals and empower your dreams.

Making Your Suggestions Congruent and Believable

The goals you made are congruent with your values and mission. Now you need to make your posthypnotic suggestion congruent with your goals. Because the authentic self is truthful, it must also be believable. For example, if your dream is to win an equestrian gold medal in the Olympics but you don't have a horse and have little training, the suggestion "I am an Olympic winner" may be congruent but not believable.

However, if winning the Olympics is a desire of your authentic self and you have the raw ability, your suggestion might be "Every day I am stronger and my Olympic goal is closer" or "All my actions bring me closer to my Olympic dreams." These are both congruent with your inner goal and believable. They emphasize action and support the benefit action brings. Using the suggestion as you pursue the action steps to attain your Olympic dream can help sustain your determination and focus your positive, forward direction. As you develop your skill, the suggestion can be altered to fit newly achieved levels of believability.

Positive Scripting in Present Time

Chapters 4 and 5 explained that your subconscious mind communicates in images and the words you speak evoke pictures in your mind. However, you can't see a negative picture. Remember that classic example "Don't think of a white elephant." What are you thinking of right now?

In the same way, if you make the suggestion "Today, I won't eat sugar" or even "Today, I am sugar free," in both cases the picture in your mind is of sugar. Suggestions provide the most positive results when they reflect what you want rather than what you don't want. A more useful suggestion might be "Today, healthy food tastes great" or "Today, I crave succulent fruits and crispy vegetables." Then, when you're in the store, instead of resisting buying the sugar, your body will be reaching for the fruits and veggies.

HYPNOTIC CONNECTION

Start paying more attention to food commercials. Can you pick up the crafted suggestions that make viewers desire the product?

You might have noticed that suggestions are written in the present tense. Images can be viewed only in the present, so the present is where the subconscious mind lives. Your ability to act is also a present-time event. You can't change the past or act in the future; the point of action is always the present moment.

It's common to see suggestions poorly written in the future tense, such as "Tomorrow I will wake up refreshed and ready to go." The problem, as the musical *Annie* tells us, is that "Tomorrow is always a day away." With future wording, the program is always set for the future. A better suggestion is "I wake refreshed and ready to greet the day."

Engaging Your Mind, Body, and Emotions

Making your suggestion congruent, believable, positive, and written in present time links your new script to the inner mind. Now use key 2 (see Chapter 4) and make sure the suggestions create a powerful image, are grounded in your body, and are fueled with emotion.

To ground your suggestion in your body, link it with a body action or sensation. The easiest way to do this is to couple the suggestion during the self-hypnosis session with your breath. Say the words of your suggestion with a conscious breath. For example, you might inhale on the first half of the phrase and exhale on the second. Another technique is to make some sort of gesture, such as pressing your thumb to your index finger, as you make the hypnotic suggestion. Then, when you use your suggestion for on-the-spot support, taking a deep breath and/or making the gesture activates the suggestion.

Here's an example of how it works: Let's say the goal of your self-hypnosis session is to gain enough confidence to ask your boss for a raise. Your suggestion is "I greet my boss with confident assurance as I calmly ask for all that I deserve." As you head to the meeting, a few deep breaths bring you into a state of calm confidence and while you talk, pressing your thumb and fingertip together keeps the suggestion active. By grounding the suggestion in your body, it's easier to retrieve after the self-hypnosis session is over, thus producing more reliable results.

Fueling your suggestion with emotion requires making pictures that engage your emotional energy. You can do this by how you choose your words. Use words that evoke pleasing pictures that make you feel good. Describe both the quality of what you want and the pleasure you'll feel. In the two suggestions in the last section, the second one that reads "Today, I crave succulent fruits and crispy vegetables" provokes more positive emotion and is therefore more effective. The following table illustrates the difference between less-effective and more-effective suggestions.

Effective Suggestions

Less-Effective Suggestions	More-Effective Suggestions
When the session is over, my backache will be gone.	Every day my back is stronger, healthier, and more relaxed, with greater and greater comfort.
I am an ex-smoker.	I breathe freely; each breath calms, soothes, and fulfills me.
I am reliable and capable and deserve a raise.	I am reliable and capable, and my full worth is recognized and financially supported.
My knee pain is less every day.	Every day, my knee has greater freedom, movement, ease, and comfort.
I am worthy and love myself.	I am worthy. I love myself and feel welcomed, accepted, and supported in the world.
Every day, I am stronger and enjoy exercising.	Every day, I enjoy the increasing strength in my muscles and delight in effortless, fun exercise.
I have all the money I need.	I am a money magnet, attracting all the money I can use and more.

 MESMERIZING MORSEL

"Your subconscious mind has three key attributes: it believes whatever you tell it; it doesn't understand negatives; if you keep on telling it something that isn't true, it will make it true for you."

—Michael Hadfield, author and hypnotist

Using Your Posthypnotic Suggestion

You can make your posthypnotic suggestion a reflection of your larger goal, one of the smaller goals that gets you to the larger goal, or a combination of both. Let's take an example from Chapter 6. The larger goal is to broaden your cultural perspective through travel, starting with a trip to Costa Rica. To support the larger goal, two smaller goals created the financial path and broke the language barrier.

Here are the two goals:

- Starting this week, I will save $25 a week in a special account for 20 months to buy a ticket to Costa Rica with a comfy hotel and spare money for exploring and having fun.

- I will begin a language course today, using self-hypnosis to learn easily, and schedule 5 hours a week to practice my skills so that I will be able to read road signs, menus, and carry on general conversation when I travel to Coast Rica in 20 months.

Your posthypnotic suggestions for these might be the following:

- I easily and effortlessly earn vacation money and watch my savings grow.

- I confidently enjoy talking to others as my mind easily learns, understands, and remembers Spanish words and phrases.

The script that you write will be designed around either or both of these suggestions. It will bring the larger goal to life with imagery that absorbs the imagination and inspires the completion of your goals.

Writing a Full Session Script

Your script is your opportunity to show the subconscious what you want and how super cool it will be to have it. You introduce the script right after you finish the induction, while you're relaxed and receptive. Your script can include your mission, vision, goals, and action steps.

Remember from Chapter 1 that the conscious mind will rationalize anything the subconscious mind presents as true. The hypnotic script is your opportunity to present the subconscious with a belief that you want your conscious mind to accept. Every time you reinforce the belief with successful outcomes, you then give your conscious mind proof, helping to support your subconscious belief.

Here are the rules for script writing:

- Talk to your subconscious mind, not your conscious mind.

- Focus on your dream—the desired outcome you're after.

- Write in present tense; be congruent with your mission and vision statements; and engage your mind, body, and emotions.

- Stretch believability; after all, this is your dream! Go for it!

- Include antidotes to your self-limiting talk.

- Once written, test your script's effectiveness using your communication skills in key 3.

> **SUBCONSCIOUS SCAFFOLDING**
>
> Remember that communication through your body senses and/or emotions are equal to ideomotor skills in creating effective scripts.

Handling Self-Limiting Thoughts

As you write your script, you may encounter beliefs that rise up to tell you how impossible your dream is. If you've been doing the exercises in previous chapters, you might already have a list of self-limiting beliefs and self-talk. The script is a good place to address these and nip your doubts in the bud.

When you have a self-denying thought, how does it make you feel? The feeling is the key to changing your conditioning. When you think "There's no use, I'll never be good enough to win an Olympic medal," the feeling may be futility, despair, or even self-pity. Rescript your thought by addressing your feeling.

For example, can you imagine, even while feeling futile, being supported? Can you picture a support team cheering you on and really feel your inner power as you head toward your goal? Be sure to write scenes into your script that provide such antidotes to your self-denying thoughts. When your script engages your emotions, you activate your power to its fullest potential.

When creating a self-hypnosis script, feel free to incorporate any intuitive insights that will help you engage your inner mind. You can also use intuition to check your script for alignment with your vision statement. Intuition helped you decide on your goals and determine your action plans; now use it to guide the creation of a successful script.

Sample Script

Every chapter in in the next few parts provides sample scripts for meeting specific goals and overcoming self-limiting beliefs. The exercise here is an example of how to do it, continuing with the previous goal of travel and the posthypnotic suggestions already developed in the script. Perhaps one self-limiting thought relates to fear of embarrassment over not being able to speak a foreign language. The underlying belief might be "I'm no good with foreign languages." Start this script where the earlier induction left off.

Begin:

Now that you've reached the bottom of the steps ... a whole new world opens. Your heart expands ... and you smile ... as your attention is drawn forward. As you walk along a flower-bordered path ... you hear people laughing and calling out to you ... you hear them just beyond the bend. Do you hear your name being called? Your heart races with excitement ... and you quicken your pace toward the happy sounds. Rounding the bend ... you stop short in surprise ... as you stand on a mountain plateau overlooking a sandy beach. You recognize where you are from a travel brochure: Costa Rica. A smile spreads across your face.

The sun sparkles on the waves ... crashing on the shore ... as seagulls circle ... and call overhead. The crashing of the waves ... matches the pounding of your heart. Listen to the seagulls calling. Children scream and laugh ... as they race to stay ahead of the water ... rushing toward them from the wave ... coming out of the sea. On the beach ... you see a hut renting surfboards. Moving quickly along the path ... you're excited to be where you've always wanted to be ... exploring new places and meeting new people ... spreading goodwill around the world one person at a time.

SUBCONSCIOUS SCAFFOLDING

During a self-hypnosis session, read the script you've developed after you've read the induction and are deeply relaxed. It's okay that your eyes are open and you're conscious. Isn't that how you daydream, too? Remember to read slowly and rhythmically, but try and avoid a monotone. Be interested in the scene you're describing.

You arrive at the hut to find a group of people laughing and joking. A man gestures to you to join them. You hesitate ... embarrassed by your poor language skills. As you start to pull back ... you notice you understand what everyone is saying ... and all your concerns melt away. You pinch yourself so that you'll never forget that you confidently enjoy talking as your mind easily learns, understands, and remembers Spanish words and phrases.

Picking up the surfboard ... you run into the waves. Cool water splashes across your skin. Jumping on the board ... you paddle out ... catch a wave ...balance on your board ... and ride the wave ... toward shore. Your muscles flex ... you balance on the board as though on top of the world. The sun is cresting on the water line ... ahead of you ... brilliant rays ... turning the sandy shore pink and gold. You inhale the crisp, clear air ... and speed along the top of the water toward the shore.

You laugh as you jump lightly off the board ... onto the warmth of the beach. Sand sifts between your toes. It is time to go home. You return the board and say good-bye to your new friends. At first you feel sad ... then you smile. Clapping your hands, you know you will return as every day you easily and effortlessly earn vacation money; every day you watch your savings grow.

Sprinting easily up the mountain path to the garden on the plateau, you begin your climb up the staircase.

Can you identify the different principles and how they're used? Now, every time you feel frustrated with the difficulty of learning a new language, pinch yourself and repeat your posthypnotic suggestion. Every time you wonder if you can keep to your goal of saving $25 dollars a week, clap your hands and repeat your suggestion. As you learn and use Spanish and as your savings grow, you'll prove to your conscious mind the reality of your subconscious belief. Soon your conscious mind will be your greatest ally in making your dream come true.

Awakening Relaxed, Refreshed, and Renewed

The final stage of the hypnosis session is every bit as important as the earlier two. Remember, you're always in control of the session, so there's no chance you won't come out of a trance. The only question is what suggestions you want to give yourself on the way out.

 WISE COUNSEL

If you're concerned with falling asleep during hypnosis or not coming out of a trance easily, you might want to start your hypnosis session with the suggestion that you'll wake easily into full consciousness, alert and relaxed, within the time frame you set aside for your session.

The following is a hypnosis termination script that uses the imagery of the induction to bring you back out. You don't need to return to the induction imagery; you can simply count your way back up.

Begin:

As you pass through the garden and approach the stairs, know that you will soon return to normal consciousness. Run up the steps, taking them two at time and counting as you do so. At the count of five, you will be awake, refreshed, renewed, and happy to be you.

One ... coming back, feeling fine, feeling happy.

Two ... lifting up, coming back to the present moment, present time.

Three ... hearing the sounds of the room, the clock, the traffic.

Four ... I am coming out of hypnosis, fully aware, fully alert, refreshed, and renewed.

Five ... my eyes are open and I am now fully awake, fully aware, fully alert, and happy to be me.

Wiggle your toes, stretch your legs, open your eyes, and sit up. Take a deep breath and a sip of water. If you're journaling your experience, this is the time to write things down.

Congratulations! You've accomplished a complete self-hypnosis session! Remember, start every day with key 1, instant relaxation, followed by one or more of your posthypnotic suggestions. You can then feel free to use the suggestions with your physical cue anytime during the day when you feel the old self-denying mindset slipping in.

The Least You Need to Know

- Self-hypnosis has two key applications: the full session and on-the-spot support.
- Your induction needs to be phrased in order to speak to the conscious and sub-conscious mind.
- The conscious mind dislikes authority; use words like *might, may, possibly,* and so forth.
- The subconscious speaks in imagery. Make suggestions positive, congruent with your values, in present tense, believable, and constructive.
- Base your suggestions and script on your mission and vision statements, goals, and action steps.
- Terminate the session with suggestions to leave you refreshed, aware, alert, and happy to be you.

Fine-Tuning Your Session

The previous chapters covered an amazing amount of information, with techniques that can truly change your life. Just being receptive to the possibility of the different concepts creates openings in your subconscious mind. It might seem like a lot of work—and there is work involved. However, your subconscious mind is already implementing the ideas you've connected with. Without doing any more than reading the scripts, you've planted seeds of change and begun to employ new skills.

Before getting into the scripts for specific issues, though, I'd like to go over a few remaining details to help you fine-tune your self-hypnosis sessions.

In This Chapter

- Creating the perfect ambience for a session
- Implementing additional support for your self-hypnosis session
- Overcoming common problems when using self-hypnosis
- Self-hypnosis session FAQs

Session Preparation: Conductive Ambience

In the early stages of using self-hypnosis, the ambience you create for a session is important to your success. In the first few sessions, you'll be juggling scripts while trying to keep guidelines in mind. The more support your environment provides, the better you'll be able to focus.

As you use self-hypnosis, you'll likely find your ability to tune out surrounding distractions becomes so acute that it won't matter where you are. You'll be able to conduct a successful session in almost any surrounding. This is useful; it means there will never be wasted time in your life again! Do you have an hour's commute on the train every day? That's an hour a day of self-hypnosis. With practice, you'll literally be able to conduct a session almost anywhere: trains, planes, and automobiles (as a passenger, of course!); boring lectures; at night when you can't sleep; and busy terminals when planes are delayed. The list of possible sites and conditions is endless. From now on, it's your choice whether stalled time is wasted or spent creating your dreams.

 MESMERIZING MORSEL

"I can't change the direction of the wind, but I can adjust my sails to always reach my destination."

—Jimmy Dean, country singer and businessman

Removing Distractions

Distractions during a self-hypnosis session certainly provide the biggest obstacle for beginners. Eventually, you'll tune them out. However, ringing cell phones, beeping text messages, barking dogs, and your grumbling stomach will certainly pull you out of relaxation. So be sure to turn off phones, put a do-not-disturb sign on the door, eat your breakfast, and put the dog in another location.

A self-hypnosis session is your "me time." Take an inventory right now of all the typical distractions that occur when you're taking time out for yourself. Which ones do you have control over? Before starting your session, address and remove everything you have control over; make yourself the priority.

However, there are some interruptions you won't have control over. Distractions are diverting because your mind is programmed to respond. The text message beeps and immediately you're preoccupied with who wants you and why. Reprogramming your response early on will help you learn to use hypnosis in any location. If you're in a situation where you can't rid the ambience of distraction, immediately employ a spontaneous addition to your script to counter it.

Here are some examples:

- Every sound I hear takes me deeper inside, where it's really more interesting anyway.

- Sounds travel from outside to inside and take my mind deeper and deeper inside, further and further into relaxation.

- Everything and everybody carries on without me as I move deeper and deeper into relaxation.

- All the world is fine. Every minute, in every way, I become more and more relaxed. Only true emergencies can bring me out of relaxation.

You may be surprised at how easily you can decondition your mind!

Physical Comfort

The second consideration to easy self-hypnosis is comfort. It's difficult to stay focused when your back hurts, your legs are going numb, or you're freezing. Upcoming chapters focus on creating physical comfort even while in pain. Spending time and energy countering physical discomfort can be draining.

Think ahead. Situate yourself on a soft bed or comfortable chair. The more relaxed you are, the slower your metabolic rate becomes, so cover yourself with a blanket or have one handy that you can pull on if you get cold. Go the bathroom beforehand, eat a snack, light some incense, and enjoy a comfortable time-out. Of course, if you encounter physical discomfort in your session, do what you need to adjust your position, and then add a counter in your script like the following:

> All physical sensation makes the reality of my _____ (name the location, activity, or so on of your hypnotic script) more real.

You can be as specific as you want, writing the physical sensation you're having directly into the action of the script.

 WISE COUNSEL

If you have unusual and/or unaccountable pain during a self-hypnosis session, investigate it. It might be a minor discomfort. However, it could be your body asking for recognition of a problem that you've been ignoring. Your session might provide the only time it can get its message heard through your automatic disregard of its signals.

Timing

As a self-hypnosis beginner, the timing of your full sessions can be critical. It's more difficult to concentrate when you know that in 10 minutes your kids will be home from school or you have a big job needing your attention. If you find yourself with 5 or 10 minutes to spare before such events, by all means practice some on-the-spot hypnosis. But for your full sessions, try to set the time aside when you're not too tightly bound by obligations.

As mentioned in Chapter 7, it's a good idea to schedule regular full sessions at the same time of day and same day of the week. Think of it as self-therapy, and if you don't do it, you'll have to pay for the session! You can make yourself pay by volunteering time to a worthy cause or doing a job around the house that you've been putting off. It may end up that your payment becomes a reward, but you get the general idea!

Eventually, you'll be able to employ self-hypnosis with easy cues and use any amount of extra time, anywhere, under any conditions for a self-hypnosis session. The only limit is your desire.

Creating an Outer Sacred Space

Conducting sessions repeatedly in the same special spot is very beneficial for increasing effectiveness. As soon as you enter the space, the ambience creates relaxation and supports you in engaging an altered state. If you do not have a room you can set aside just for meditation, prayer, or self-hypnosis, create a sacred space wherever you are.

One good way to signal to the body that you're creating a sacred spot and ready to enter a session is with a special scent. This can be an essential oil, a scented candle, or incense. Just be sure to use the same scent every time you have a session. The smell will stimulate the brain and re-create past feelings of relaxation.

Here are some additional suggestions for transforming your space:

- Bring one or more objects that have meaning for you, such as crystals, pictures, meditation beads, and so forth.

- Use a prayer shawl or unique blanket that signifies the special nature of the event.

- Play relaxing music.

- Start and end the session with the sound of a bell, gong, or other audible cue to train your subconscious.

 WISE COUNSEL

A candle is an excellent way to create sacred space. However, be careful not to start a fire. Be sure the candle is placed in a safe, stable location and surrounded by a protective glass shield.

Creating an Inner Sacred Space

Inner sacred space is an internal imaginary power spot that gives you access to higher levels of energy. Focusing your mind, you can use this energy to augment an inner resource you're developing. In some traditions, sacred spaces are physical locations that are believed to have extra doses of Earth energy (such as Niagara Falls and Sedona, Arizona) or where man-made structures have enhanced Earth energy (such as Stonehenge in England or the Great Pyramids in Giza). However, you don't need to believe in Earth energy to use the concept of a power spot to enliven your self-hypnosis practice. Having a place in which you feel supported automatically increases the amount of energy and attention you have available to pursue your goals.

Internal sacred space also facilitates self-hypnosis through the attitudes you hold. The attitudes brought forward in sacred spaces include relaxed nonjudgment with self-acceptance and self-compassion. How effective are you when your conscious mind is criticizing everything from your script to your space? Finding nonjudgment might be the focus of an entire session, as self-love is something that is generally lacking. (You might look at exercises in Chapters 12 and 20 if this is something you want to pursue now.)

It's also a wonderful experience to create an inner sanctuary that is a retreat for doing this work. For some, the space becomes an inner garden, while for others, it's a library or church. The sanctuary is found in a specific location in your body and can be accessed simply by placing your hands on the spot and using key 1, instant relaxation.

The following is a script to get you to your sacred spot for the first time. Remember to read slowly and rhythmically, allowing time to create images. Afterward, whenever you use a relaxation technique, visualize yourself in this scene and place your hands over your designated body area to facilitate access.

To start, use your instant relaxation. Now, take your awareness inside and slip deeper into your body. Ask yourself, "Where is my sacred center?" Notice where your attention is drawn. Maybe you're drawn by warmth in your heart or an opening in your solar plexus. Wherever your attention is drawn, place the palms of both hands over the area. Allow your awareness to drop even deeper into this spot. Breathe deeply into this area. As you explore the area, you may notice that you're walking along a path through the forest, a gently winding path with a soft breeze brushing over your skin. Notice how happy, calm, and peaceful you feel as you move deeper into this special place inside you. Feel the area opening inside you. Rounding a corner, you see the heart of your sacred space. Maybe you see a stone circle, a cathedral, or a lovely forest thicket. Pause a minute and take in every detail of this sacred space. When you're ready, move inside the sanctuary. What does it feel like? What does it look like from the inside? Look around and find the seat that is made just for you. Sit and settle into the warm embrace of this sacred place. Feel perfectly supported, perfectly safe, perfectly focused, calm, and alive. Take a few minutes to let your soul receive whatever you need right here, right now—maybe rejuvenation, healing light, or a word of wisdom. Sit silently and receive.

When you're ready, count to three and awake fully refreshed, fully aware, and fully awake. Know that you can return to this space anytime for any reason. It's your space and you carry it with you everywhere you go.

Additional Tools and Support

The induction, script, and posthypnotic suggestions are all that you need to practice self-hypnosis. After that, any tools you use are devices to help you focus and train your mind. Prayer shawls, candles, crystals, and so on are for psychological support. In and of themselves, they are not necessary.

You might remember old movies that showed people succumbing to a trance while staring at a swinging pendulum. Devices to focus the gaze—such as rotating discs, pendulums, or alternating light machines—used to be very popular. Some people still use them to induce a trance, but many people find them a distraction with little benefit.

 HYPNOTIC CONNECTION

A 2002 study reported in *the American Journal of Clinical Hypnosis* tested many devices and concluded that "such devices proved to have no inherent facilitating properties other than a general placebo effect."

There are a few tools, however, that can enhance your session. They are not gimmicks; instead, they support you in achieving your goals.

Self-Recording Your Script

Prerecording your own voice reading your induction, script, and termination is a powerful tool. You can use an MP3 device, a cell phone, or just a plain old-fashioned tape player. Self-recorded scripts help you relax and stay focused. In addition, they train your inner and outer mind to pay attention to your own directives. This method has the added benefit of allowing you to use a personalized script over commercial CDs and downloads.

When you're moving into a trance, you're hyperalert to sounds and influences around you. Therefore, when making your recording, be sure that external sounds are minimized. Also, try to limit the number of times you start and stop the process to avoid the clicks of the device. Of course, you can always write into the script a line such as "The sounds of clicking powerfully enhance my calm, relaxed state."

Because you're reading your script to yourself, it's more authentic to write in "I" statements versus "you" statements. For example, "I'm becoming more and more deeply relaxed" versus "You are getting more and more deeply relaxed." Your subconscious is acutely aware of authenticity, so this is important.

The induction and scripts written in this book use "you" because I am essentially reading them to you in your voice. Get it? In addition, since some are on the website (idiotsguides.com/selfhypnosis) as downloads, you'll be hearing them in my voice. If you personalize the scripts in this book, rewrite them in "I" statements. If you leave them in "you" format, make sure to add your name every once in a while. For example, add comments such as "Okay, Richard, now you are becoming more and more deeply relaxed."

Downloads and Commercial CDs

Like prerecorded self scripts, downloads allow more complete relaxation and enjoyment of the process of self-hypnosis. The downside is that they limit spontaneous, creative input from your inner mind.

For this book, the website (idiotsguides.com/selfhypnosis) has downloads that include a relaxation exercise, induction, and several scripts. Tracks are designed so you can switch from one to the other using your chosen script to immediately follow the relaxation and induction and end with the termination track.

 HYPNOTIC CONNECTION

> A great company for buying CDs and downloads is The Monroe Institute. They use state-of-the-art technology and are very effective. You can find a listing of products at monroeinstitute.org.

An internet search will reveal many sources of guided imagery CDs and Hemi-Sync tapes. Hemi-Sync is a technique that gives different directions to each side of the brain, confusing the conscious mind and speaking directly the subconscious. There are many reputable companies that make excellent products of this nature. You'll also find free downloads, but watch out—free downloads almost always have a catch. They may want your email address for building a public platform or sales effort, or they may want to use you as a test market for the product. There's nothing wrong in any of this; just know you're subscribing to a larger interaction than the download.

Make sure when you look into commercial products that you buy the one that matches your core spiritual or philosophical beliefs. If you belong to a particular religious group, you'll want wording that is consistent with your beliefs. This is one strong reason why many people prefer to make their own recordings.

Musical Magic

Like scent, music can stimulate the *limbic system* of the brain, which is the part that differentiates among emotions and manages emotional memory. Using the same or similar type of music for your inductions supports a faster response. In addition, some music is designed using specific tones and measures to induce relaxation. You can find relaxation music on the internet. Sometimes you can listen before buying.

 **DEFINITION**

The **limbic system** is the part of the brain that manages emotional memory.

You can either play music as you record your script or play it on another device in the background as you listen to your recording. The second has the advantage of you being able to change the music if it starts to be too predictable or you get tired of it. You might want to try nature sounds, if you don't already have a favorite music. You want to avoid playing music with lyrics, as the tendency is to follow the lyrics when you need to follow the script.

Journaling

During a session, you might receive insights and may be inspired in new directions. Give yourself time to write your observations and thoughts after your session is over. Use pen and paper, a computer, a tablet, or whatever is most conducive to creative writing. Here are a few tips for journaling:

- Be brief. Write bullet points rather than sentences.

- Put the notebook or journaling tool near you before you start the session. If you have to look for it, you probably won't journal or will forget important points.

- Be consistent. If you journal after every session, you'll start bringing back more and more significant detail. You'll be telling your inner mind that what it has to say is important.

- If you're committed to electronic media to record your observations, so be it. My experience, however, is that it's easier to get distracted on electronic devices. Incoming email and the multiple functionalities of these devices have an interesting impact on focus.

- Keep your session notes in a separate notebook or computer file and be sure each is dated and the script goal is noted.

- Maintain your notes as a record and look back through them for emerging patterns.

At first, you may have overwhelming amounts of seemingly unimportant details that bog you down. Your subconscious then will become more selective and provide only pertinent details. Eventually, you'll notice deeper insights emerging.

> **HYPNOTIC CONNECTION**
>
> There are many online sites that support the important tool of journaling. Penzu (penzu.com) is a free service that allows you to store journaling notes online and also offers mobile apps for iOS, Android, and Blackberry.

Troubleshooting Common Session Problems

It's nice to think that self-hypnosis is so natural (which it is) and so accessible (also true) that you won't have any difficulty getting started or staying on track. Well, that's not quite the way it always works. At some point, you'll probably have trouble and won't stay on track. That's just the nature of change. In fact, the more you internally resist the change you're after, the more trouble you're bound to have.

Some issues are more common than others. Let's say you've started your self-hypnosis sessions and can't relax in the induction or stop the mental chatter of your critical mind. Or maybe you want immediate results and become frustrated when life events don't change as fast you'd like. Here's the bottom line: these techniques work, and they can work for you. Difficulties are usually messages from your subconscious. So let's take a look and see what might be going on.

Self-Sabotage

Self-sabotage is a common way to stop forward movement. You can sabotage yourself by doing the following:

- Choosing unrealistic goals that don't have a chance of being fulfilled
- Creating a lot of drama so that you're consumed with emotional diversions
- Ramping up old defeatist programming

In whatever way you're self-sabotaging, the bottom line is that you're resisting the change you want. Resistance is a message from the subconscious. Usually it means one of two things: either you aren't paying attention to some important internal part of yourself that will be adversely affected by the change you're seeking, or you're afraid of success. Sometimes success means you might lose someone or something in the change or have to redefine yourself in a way that is uncomfortable. In all cases, the way to understanding is to go back to your mission and goals and find out what isn't congruent with your inner voice.

Often, just posing the question will give you the answer in a flash of insight. If not, use your key 3 ideomotor skills in Chapter 5. Ask yes-or-no questions until you've narrowed the issue, and then rewrite your goals and script to reflect what you've learned.

Overthinking and Trying Too Hard

These are two common problems everyone falls prey to at one time or another. Overthinking and trying too hard are aspects of expectations. When your experience doesn't match your expectation, it leaves room for doubt and fear of failure. Once again, expectations are an opportunity to talk with your subconscious about where your doubts and fear of failure come from.

Were you raised to be afraid of making a mistake or of not measuring up? Are you anxious about looking foolish if you try something and it doesn't work? Or are you so desperate for change that the idea your expectations won't be met is terrifying? This is another good opportunity to talk with your inner mind and find out what is driving your self-doubt.

In the meantime, see if you can simply enjoy self-hypnosis for the fun of a creative time. Let go of any expectation of what a trance feels like, what will happen in the session, or how quickly your goals will manifest. The best way to invite change is to find gratitude in what you already have. Remember the transcendent emotions discussed in Chapter 4? Tune in now and experience real gratitude for all that life is. Be present and allow life to unfold. Your goals are a done deal. Enjoy getting there as much as being there.

> **SUBCONSCIOUS SCAFFOLDING**
>
> Transcendent emotions are ones that elevate you above self-interest. Common ones are admiration, awe, compassion, gratitude, and unconditional love. Tuning into these emotions can shift stuck emotional energy.

Control Freaking

The need to be in control of every detail and eventuality of your mission, goals, and script might be keeping you locked in motion instead of action. Are you spending time you don't have planning instead of jumping straight in? What would happen if you just wing it? Or is overcontrol showing up as a fear of relaxing during the session? Does your mind have to actively create each aspect of your experience?

Overcontrolling your self-hypnosis goals and sessions blocks serendipity and the spontaneous fulfillment of your dreams. You literally short-circuit synchronicity and limit the possible ways that change might come to you. Creative inspiration during the session is curtailed. What is missing here is trust.

Use your communication skills to find out what you're afraid of and discover what you need in order to be able to trust the process. Try and believe you're not here by accident—there is a plan and purpose that is beyond your current control. Relax, hold your intent, and let life unfold.

Falling Asleep

If falling asleep in a session is something that happens only once in a while, you probably need to be careful to get more sleep beforehand. If you know you're tired but still want to have a session, try sitting up for the session instead of lying down. Make the session short and add suggestions to your script that direct you to stay in an alert and awake state of relaxation.

On the other hand, if you're falling asleep every time you sit down for a session, is there something you're trying to avoid? Is there something your subconscious wants to discuss that you're afraid to know? Sit down right now and have a discussion with your subconscious mind using ideomotor techniques to find out what it is. Otherwise, you'll continue to find it difficult to get your session completed or your dreams to manifest.

Lack of Commitment

One of the most unfortunate misconceptions about self-hypnosis is that change happens magically without any work. This is simply not true. Anything of value takes work. Self-hypnosis makes sure your work brings the best possible result. If you're having trouble staying committed, does your mission, goal, and script jazz you? Are your emotions engaged, or are you just writing something that sounds better than what you have right now?

Your vision of what you want has to get your heart pounding with excitement. That is the energy that will flow from you and into the world to create what you want. If you don't have a vision that pumps you up, it's time for another chat with your inner mind. Use the communication skills and uncover the dream you're afraid to share or don't think you deserve to have.

 MESMERIZING MORSEL

"Without leaps of imagination or dreaming, we lose the excitement of possibilities. Dreaming, after all is a form of planning."

—Gloria Steinem, political activist and author

Frequently Asked Questions About Self-Hypnosis

You now have all the information you need to conduct a self-hypnosis session. Hopefully you've been working with the exercises in each chapter and have conducted at least one full session. At this point, you may have questions that weren't fully answered. Most of them are likely discussed in upcoming chapters, but here are answers to some of the most commonly asked questions.

How is daydreaming different than hypnosis? This is a good question; they are similar and both engage alpha brainwave states. Remember from Chapter 3 that alpha waves are the gateway between the conscious and subconscious mind. The biggest difference between them is that daydreams lack the power and focus of self-hypnosis. Daydreams are fun fantasies; self-hypnosis is the same state of mind turning goals into a powerhouse of intent.

Is the trance state sleeping? No. A trance is not the same as sleep. At various stages, sleep, meditation, and self-hypnosis all pass through alpha, theta, and delta brainwave states. The difference is that while in sleep, you move through those stages without conscious awareness. In meditation and self-hypnosis, you are awake, alert, and aware throughout.

Are drugs ever involved in hypnosis? No. They simply have no place in any type of hypnosis. A trance is obtained through natural, internal processes of intent.

If I can't record my session and have to read it, will I still get the same benefit? It's more fun to be able to let go and fully relax, enjoying the direction and unfolding of a session. However, reading the script gives you every bit as much benefit. Do it slowly and consciously, envisioning all the suggestions in your mind's eye as you read.

I have one of the contraindications in Chapter 2. Can I still use self-hypnosis? It's very possible self-hypnosis can be a wonderful tool for you. However, it's best if you first have several hypnosis sessions with a qualified hypnotherapist who is also a psychotherapist. This will help you identify the difference between a hypnotic trance and a psychological state. Experiencing the trance state in a protected setting will also help you determine if it's safe for you. A therapist can guide you in understanding the limits and uses of the technique in your situation.

Can I work on more than one goal at a time? Yes, you can work on several goals; however, it is best not to work on them in the same session. Have independent sessions at different times. You can do as many as two scripts in a day, but it's best if they are related to different aspects of the same goal.

How many times do I need to repeat a session for each goal? Continue to repeat the session until you have achieved the goal. As you move toward success, you may want to alter the script to reflect what you have achieved and to focus on where you now want to go.

Is there a best time of day to do hypnosis? There is a best time of day for you; only you know when you will be least disturbed and have the most amount of focus.

Does it matter if I lengthen or shorten the scripts in the book? No. There is no real benefit in a long script over a short one. Adjust the script to fit the amount of time you have, keeping the elements that most resonate with you in the script.

Does it matter that the scripts are repetitive? No. Hearing the same repetitions conditions the mind to move into a receptive state more quickly each time. However, if the scripts begin to bore you so that you stop paying attention, then by all means alter them.

How are hypnotists trained? Hypnosis training is self-regulated, which means there is no standard criteria. There are several guilds and associations that supply training and certification, such as the National Guild of Hypnotists, the American Hypnosis Association, and the Hypnotherapy Academy of America, among others. There are also several similar-type trainings that don't call what they do hypnosis, such as Silva training and neuro-linguistic programming.

How do I choose a therapist? To choose the therapist with the training that's right for you, first decide what kind of hypnosis you want to receive—overcoming addictions, weight loss, trauma, and so forth. You can then compare what you're looking for with the goals and training of area hypnotists. If you're working on psychological issues, such as trauma recovery, you'll want a psychotherapist with hypnotherapy certification.

The bottom line in finding the right therapist is word-of-mouth recommendation. Find out what people are saying, make a consultation appointment, and then trust your gut. If you feel drawn to the person and technique, go for it. If you're not, honor that, too.

In the meantime, enjoy the upcoming chapters and create the best scripts for the dynamic life you're creating.

The Least You Need to Know

- The ambience you create can help induce your trance. Remove distractions, making yourself comfortable, and create inner and outer sacred spaces.
- You can help your session be more effective by using audio downloads or making your own recordings. In both cases, you can incorporate music into the session.
- You'll get the most of your sessions if you keep a journal of your experiences.
- The most common problems in using self-hypnosis are due to subconscious messages you're not listening to.

Taking Charge!

Self-limiting behavior may have kept you locked in place and unable to make life-enhancing change. But that doesn't have to be your future! Now you have the tools that unite your mind, body, and spirit to create positive life changes that your conscious and subconscious minds can support. Taking charge of your life entails taking charge of self-limiting beliefs and behavior while letting your inner dreams fly.

As you engage the scripts in this part and the rest of the book, be sure to use the induction in Chapter 7 at the beginning of each hypnosis session. And remember, you will find hypnosis downloads at idiotsguides.com/selfhypnosis.

Solutions for Negative Thinking

Psychology studies estimate that the average person has up to 60,000 thoughts a day and as many as 80 percent of them use words like *can't, never,* and *should*. Of course, everyone has negative thoughts; they can actually serve a useful purpose. When negative thoughts lead to defeatist thinking, however, they undermine confidence and limit potential. The truth is that both positive and negative thoughts can become self-fulfilling prophecies. What you expect in a venture often predetermines the outcome.

Resisting negative thoughts doesn't help you get rid of them. Have you noticed that the more you resist a negative thought, the more persistent it becomes? In this chapter, you learn how to use the function of a negative thought while eliminating the destructive qualities of negative thinking that can sabotage you when least expected.

In This Chapter

- Learning the function of negative thoughts
- Determining if you're a negative thinker
- Discovering the positivity ratio
- Scripting for constructive change

Safely in a Box

Negative thoughts are normal and natural. You might know people who try to banish every negative thought and replace it with an affirmation or consider that stating the existence of a problem is being negative. Unfortunately, they have confused the constructive function of a negative thought with the destructive power of negative programming. Does that sound confusing? Let's take a look.

 WISE COUNSEL

If you're plagued with negative thoughts that undermine your ability to function, or you can't see any light at the end of the tunnel, you may be experiencing depression. Take the time to find professional help, call a crisis hotline, or log on to a depression chat room. Despite what you may be thinking, *you have value and are worth love!* Here are two great links to get you started: crisischat.org/chat/ and beyondblue.org.

Negative thoughts rise, give their message, and retreat. They often reflect where you've failed or have been hurt in the past and are trying to protect you from the same thing happening again. In and of itself, a negative thought has no power; it's just a messenger.

A negative thought becomes powerful when you create a belief around it: "I failed this project, so I must not be good at my job." The belief extends beyond the actual event and becomes a far-reaching generalization.

The next time you're asked to do a job, this belief causes your heart to pound, and you immediately feel unsure of your ability. Because it's impossible to do a good job when you're second-guessing yourself, you fail again and cement the belief into a negative program.

If you let your negative thoughts define you and create the program you live by, they've moved beyond function; they've become auto-suggestions supporting a subconscious program that undermines and limits your potential. The auto-suggestions of a conditioned mind sound something like this:

- I'm not good enough.

- I can't do anything right.

- Nobody will ever love me.

- Who do I think I am?

- I can never win.

- I'll never be anything but a failure.

Do you recognize any of these? Don't worry, everyone has a few of these thoughts. But if you continually talk to yourself this way, you quite literally hypnotize yourself into a life that offers less than you deserve. A thought that started as protection is now a box that confines and limits you. The good news is *you can rescript your life!*

The Purpose of Negative Thoughts

Despite their bad rep, negative thoughts actually have a function. They identify problems and warn you to take realistic precautions. They function as an alert system, cautioning against over-reach and making suggestions for where you need more support, better training, or more time. In effect, negative thoughts keep things real. People who refuse to harbor a negative thought often have trouble averting calamity because they don't react to problems everyone else sees coming. When you talk to these people, you might feel aggravated by their fantastical approach to projects or goals.

When you have a negative thought, you have a choice: you can listen to the problem being presented and be motivated to find solutions, or you can let the thought deflate and limit you. Letting a negative thought limit you is how a negative thought becomes the basis of a negative program. It occurs when your experience of past disappointments is transferred into expectations for future disappointment. Negative thinking rarely reflects your authentic self; the purpose of self-hypnosis is to write a script that aligns with your true self.

SUBCONSCIOUS SCAFFOLDING

Sometimes a negative thought is not telling you about a current problem but one you never got over in the past. You can find more tips about dealing with this in Chapter 11.

Constructive or Destructive Reactions

The problem with negative thoughts isn't that you have them; it's what you do with them. Let's look at a situation and see how three different perspectives handle the same negative thought.

Imagine your boss comes to your office with an armload of papers. Dumping them on your desk, he tells you that if plans for this project can be drawn up in two weeks, the company will gain an influential new client. He adds that the additional income to the firm will provide the money for the promotion and raise you want, both of which are guaranteed if you succeed. However, if the plans aren't ready in two weeks, the client will sign with another firm and the funds won't be available for your raise.

You look at the papers and realize the scope of the project. Your first thought is "This is impossible. It can't be done. I don't have the time or material to do this. I just can't do it." Adrenaline pours through your system and your muscles shake with pent-up energy.

In response number one, the negative thought galvanizes you into action. You start leafing through the project, making lists of what needs to be done, putting it against a time line, and determining how it might be possible. Maybe you decide you can do it and throw yourself full throttle into the project, getting it done and getting your raise. It's also possible after looking at it, you know it can't be done and offer an alternate plan to your boss or choose to pull out altogether. Whatever you do, it's an informed decision that you feel good about.

In response number two, the thought of the project's impossibility galvanizes your anger and puts you in a tailspin. How dare your boss give you a job like this and hook your well-deserved raise to an impossible feat! Clearly your boss has purposefully set you up to fail; he obviously wants to get rid of you. In frustration, you dump the work back on your boss's desk and quit.

In response number three, your thoughts galvanize your poor self-esteem. You look at the job and imagine that other people in the office would be able to do it. Clearly there's just something wrong with you that you can't. Obviously you're a failure and a disappointment to your boss.

In response number one, your negative thought galvanized action and motivated you to problem-solve the situation, making the negative thought constructive. In the second, your negative thought galvanized anger and motivated a victim mentality. In the third, your negative thought galvanized defeat and motivated failure. For the second and third responses, the negative thought became destructive.

 MESMERIZING MORSEL

"Read it with sorrow and you will feel hate.
Read it with anger and you will feel vengeful.
Read it with paranoia and you will feel confusion.
Read it with empathy and you will feel compassion.
Read it with love and you will feel flattery.
Read it with hope and you will feel positive.
Read it with humor and you will feel joy.
Read it with God and you will feel the truth.
Read it without bias and you will feel peace.
Don't read it at all and you will not feel a thing."

—Shannon L. Alder, inspirational author

The problem isn't the thought; the thought is a normal and natural reaction to a request that required a superhuman effort. How you respond depends on your programming. Fortunately, that can be changed!

Critical Positivity Ratio

Some physiologists propose that having negative thoughts is healthy and natural as long as you have more positive thoughts than negative ones. The concept is that there is an ideal ratio of positive to negative thoughts that determines whether or not a person is able to attain his goals and flourish in life.

Mathematician Marcial Losada applied mathematics to emotions and determined the ratio of positive to negative thoughts that are required to flourish in life with successful outcomes (known as the *critical positivity ratio*) is 3:1.

In other words, you need to have three positive thoughts to each negative thought in order to disable a negative program and ensure the success of your goals. Remember, negative thoughts are not bad; you can't fix a problem you don't see, so you're not trying to suppress negative thoughts. Instead, you want to find three positive ways to address the negative thought and move on.

For example, in the statement "My dream is impossible; it will never come true," the first part of the statement is a negative doubt, while the second part is a negative program. Respond to it by immediately looking at how your dream might be possible and what you will need to make it possible. Be specific with your positive responses. For example, you could say "My dream is supported with good data; it is a realistic and desirable possibility for everyone involved. Expressing my ideas with confidence encourages support for my effort. I have everything I need to make this dream come true."

 HYPNOTIC CONNECTION

Marriage psychologist John Gottman was over 90 percent successful in predicating whether newlywed couples would stay together based on the ratio of positive to negative expressions they used during the early days of their marriage. He found successful partnerships needed at least a 5:1 ratio of positive to negative expressions.

As you see, the positivity ratio doesn't mean replacing a negative thought with three positive affirmations; it means you find three ways to positively reframe one problem-oriented, negative thought. Your response has to be realistic and believable or your subconscious mind will reject it.

The biggest challenge is recognizing a negative thought and then believing that change is possible. As in the previous example, the situation may look and feel impossible, but can you find a place inside that believes it might be conceivable? Can you look for three positives to each negative? If you can't believe in possibility, your responses won't be believed by your subconscious.

Are You a Negative Thinker?

Maybe you have negative thoughts but don't consider yourself a negative thinker. Rather, you see yourself as a realist. Because negative thinking creates a self-fulfilling prophecy, you'll never know if you're a realist or creating your own problems unless you're willing to shift your reality.

If you're wondering whether or not you're a negative thinker, take this quick quiz and see how many yes responses you have. The more yes responses, the more your negative thoughts have become ingrained as negative programming.

The Negative Thinking Quiz

1. When you're called to the supervisor's office, do you automatically assume you're in trouble?

2. When you make a mistake, do you feel like a failure? ("I never do anything right.")

3. When you don't succeed, do you imagine you will never succeed?

4. When you don't have the skills for a job, do you imagine that you're not good enough to learn the skills?

5. Do you take other people's bad moods and actions personally? ("My boss was in a bad mood; I must have upset him.")

6. Do you make general assumptions based on personal discomfort? ("My boss doesn't support me because bosses don't care about the people who work for them.")

7. Do you diminish your success and agonize over your failures?

8. If something good happens, do you tell yourself not to get too excited?

9. Do you have trouble celebrating your successes?

If you've identified yourself as a negative thinker, congratulations! You can't change a pattern until you're willing to look at it. If you've determined you're not a negative thinker, congratulations! You've learned well from your disappointments in life.

 SUBCONSCIOUS SCAFFOLDING

If you're a negative thinker, you project a failure in one area of your life onto all areas; in other words, you make unfavorable outcomes global. When you don't have what you need, you assume you'll never be able to get what you need, which makes the problem permanent in the future. You look at obstacles and take them as personal judgments against you. Rather than problem-solving when things go wrong, you blame yourself or others.

Rescripting Your Program

There's no doubt that negative programs come from past experiences. Perhaps you were hurt and never fully processed the pain or forgave yourself or others. Each negative program is a reflection of an unprocessed event or emotion. However, trying to track down and clear the source of every one will take the rest of your life. The truth is, you don't need to know where your negative program came from in order to deactivate it. All you need do is accept that it's not an accurate view of reality and be willing to change.

As you use the hypnosis script, you may find that long-forgotten memories surface. They may even reveal the source of your negative programs. If this happens, it means you're ready to let them go. Thank the experience for everything that you've learned. Forgive everyone involved and choose to move on.

How to Rescript

The following script can be modified for any negative programs you're trying to overcome. First, you'll need to identify a negative thought that often plagues you. If you've been following the exercises in earlier chapters, you may have already pinpointed one or two that cause you the most trouble. If not, watch everything you say for one entire day. Try to notice the negative thoughts, especially the ones that undermine your happiness.

Name the main thought that plagues you the most and find three positive thoughts that respond to this one negative. Before you start reading, use the induction in Chapter 7. Remember, as you read, pause for a second or two when you see an ellipsis or reach the end of the sentence, even when you're reading in your head.

 MESMERIZING MORSEL

"Every problem has in it the seeds of its own solution. If you don't have any problems, you don't get any seeds."

—Norman Vincent Peale, motivational author and speaker

Elegant Solutions Script

Now that you've reached the bottom of the steps and are deeply ... totally ... relaxed ... you may notice the soft ... comfortable armchair ... that is positioned on the edge of the garden. You may notice your heart leaps at the idea of escaping into this soft, comfortable chair ... sinking into its warm support ... being totally ... held in comfort. As you descend into the cozy ... soft cushions ... you are aware that you can relax even more. In fact, every time you enter a trance ... you discover you can let go of one more tension ... one more distraction.

See your tension dissolve ... as you melt into the chair ... and notice the soft ... comfortable glow in your body. Allow distracting thoughts that come into you mind ... to go out right out the other side. See your thoughts as birds, soaring away on the horizon. You may notice how completely supported you feel ... how every part of you is cradled in support ... how you feel able to let go even more.

Gazing contentedly around ... you might enjoy noticing ... the abundant blossoming ... of beautiful flowers ... attended to by busy bees ... droning in the background ... droning in your mind ... taking you further down into relaxation. Next to you is a fountain, and you watch the water sliding down and slipping away.

In this relaxed, alert state, you reminisce over the day ... or week ... or event ... you just experienced. In this state, you may notice the negative thoughts you had and see clearly how they held you back. In this relaxed state, you see ... your negative thought really doesn't matter ... because you know ... and say to yourself ... "I see problems clearly and find elegant solutions." You watch as your negative thought soars away into the sky ... only solutions remain.

Now ... you notice ... the profound enjoyment you have in life. All the unhappy feelings you have experienced ... due to this old thought ... are washed away ... floating away in the water fountain ... as you hear the musical ... soothing sounds ... of the beautiful flow ... washing your old feelings away. The sun warms you ... filling your heart ... expanding your heart ... allowing your heart to glow ... with gratitude. Gratitude fills your whole body ... with gratitude comes determination to succeed. You know and say out loud as you make a thumbs-up gesture "Every time I have a negative thought, I see problems clearly and find elegant solutions. I have everything I need to succeed and am filled with gratitude. I appreciate my gifts and am thankful for my abilities."

Suddenly, as you watch ... all the problems you had ... in this day ... in this week ... in the event ... disappear in the face of elegant solutions. Problems are washed away ... only solutions remain ... old frustrations soar off into the sky ... only gratitude and determination remain.

Take a few minutes to enjoy the garden ... the armchair ... and to visualize your new life ... based on solutions and gratitude.

When you're ready ... no need to get up ... taking your comfortable support ... bringing your elegant solutions ... bringing your feelings of gratitude with you, count from one to five. On the count of five, you will be fully awake, fully aware, fully restored.

One, coming up.

Two, becoming more awake, more alert, more aware.

Three, feeling fine ... eyes start to flutter.

Four, feeling great ... toes start to wiggle.

Five, feeling awake, aware, and fully restored to normal consciousness.

As you continue your day, know that every time you encounter a negative thought, with a simple thumbs-up gesture, you shift your reality to accept the presence of an elegant solution and fill with gratitude and determination.

Enjoy your day!

The Least You Need to Know

- Negative thoughts are normal and natural.
- The function of a negative thought is to show you problems and help you find solutions.
- Negative thoughts turn into negative programming when you focus on the problem and think it means more than it does.
- The critical positivity ratio implies that three positive thoughts are needed for every negative thought you have in order for your dreams to flourish.
- Negative thinking makes obstacles permanent. Negative thinking takes failure in one place and reflects it in all places. Negative thinking takes life personally.

Freedom from Addiction

If you've turned to this chapter first, good for you! You've already identified that something you enjoy doing is causing you harm and have decided to make a change. The truth is that everyone has addictions, but not all addictions carry the same degree of harm—or the harm they carry is more socially acceptable. Having an addiction doesn't mean you're a horrible person; it means you're hurting yourself and want to stop.

You can be addicted to things you ingest (such as alcohol, tobacco, and drugs), actions (such as gambling and sex), or thoughts that are self-denigrating or critical of others. More acceptable addictions include sugar, coffee, personal drama, work, and even hobbies. Have you heard the terms *workaholic* and *sports addict?* These labels carry an element of heroism but convey just as devastating a price tag as other more criticized addictions.

Now that you've decided to end an addictive action or behavior, you can use self-hypnosis to support your goals. This chapter gives you sample scripts to use or adapt so you can work toward freeing yourself from an addiction.

In This Chapter

- Identifying your addictive behavior and the need it fills
- Creating a plan for success
- Learning self-hypnosis scripts for overcoming addictions

Releasing Addiction

Anything that becomes a compulsion and has a destructive impact on your life is an addiction. Some addictions are easier to live with than others, yet wouldn't you prefer to be in control of your actions and decisions rather than be at the mercy of a pull that is hard to resist? The first step to break addiction is acknowledging that it's a problem. Until you do that, nothing can change.

 WISE COUNSEL

Remember, while self-hypnosis is an exceptional tool for overcoming addictions, it's not a replacement for professional or medical care.

Do you judge yourself harshly each time you succumb to temptation, berating yourself every time you give in? You've probably tried to give up the habit before. Each time you succumb, your self-blame increases along with your self-condemnation. But you can break the pattern; you can find the parts of yourself that you admire and finally enjoy being you!

Acknowledge the Need; Change the Behavior

Many psychologists believe that addictions are an attempt to fill unmet needs. Perhaps the love and support you didn't get as a child is being supplied through the rush of enjoyment an addiction provides. Maybe constant criticisms from your past are quieted in the thrill of being a big-time winner at the poker table or at the prospect of landing another huge client. Most of the time, addictions are speaking to your lack of self-worth and asking you to develop a stronger sense of your authentic self.

The first step in deciding to eliminate an unhealthy behavior is to find out what you need that you're not getting. Could it be respect, love, admiration, acceptance, or some other intangible emotion? Or are you running from something you're afraid of, such as failure, self-hatred, or criticism? Acknowledging the emotional need is essential to changing it.

Once you understand the need, is there a better way to fill it than the way you have? If you spend excessive time at work in order to feel successful and make a lot of money, can you redefine success to include personal relaxation, family time, and happiness? If you drink to numb the pain of rejection, are there other ways to feel the warm glow of acceptance outside of the bar? Now is the time to acknowledge what you need and look for other ways of getting that need filled, because if you keep on as you are, eventually the negative side effects of your behavior will catch up with you. Besides, you deserve to be happy. Can you honestly say that engaging in addictive behavior makes you happy?

MESMERIZING MORSEL

"Remember, you don't ever break a habit. If you want to get rid of bad behavior, you have to replace it with something positive; something that will make you stronger instead of weaker."

–Dr. Phil, psychologist, author, and television host

The Freedom Plan

Accepting that your habit is not meeting your unfilled needs is the first step to changing the pattern. Now you can use self-hypnosis to support feelings of self-acceptance and respect, along with the unmet needs you would like to fill. In addition, you might consider making a plan to guide the changes you seek. It will help you look ahead and address obstacles before they happen. If you've tried to overcome this addiction before, you know just what these obstacles are: people, places, and situations that enable addictive activity.

The best move you can make at the start of any endeavor is to enlist support. Don't wait until you're in crisis to get help. Go online for support groups in your area or professionals who work with the addiction you're trying to break. A good professional can help you identify inner needs and resources. In some cases, unpleasant withdrawal symptoms may require medical assistance. Twelve-step groups, online chat rooms, and other supports can be lifelines when your inner resources are floundering.

The following tips may help you create a plan, but if you can't make a concrete strategy, don't worry. Make the choice and get started with self-hypnosis anyway!

- **Face your problem.** Write down all the harmful effects your addiction has on your health, your self-esteem, your family, your finances, your love life, your career, your creative expression, and so forth.

- **Write down the benefit you want by stopping.** That could be better health, more energy, more freedom, more money, more love, and so on.

- **Create your future.** Write how your life will change. What will your life be like? What will you feel? How will you look? What dream do you hope to fulfill? Imagine yourself proud, confident, and free.

- **Pick a strategy with a reasonable time line.** Do what works best for you, whether it's cold turkey or ramping down your addictive behavior.

- **Know your triggers and try to avoid them.** What makes you want to engage the addiction? Plan for ways to avoid or deal with them.

- **Change your environment to reflect your new goals.** Remove paraphernalia, contacts, and enablers from your life.

- **Support yourself with reminders of your goal.** Put pictures of the addiction-free life you're creating on your refrigerator or bathroom mirror or in your car, wallet, purse, computer, and cell phone.

- **Act "as if."** Behave as if you already have exactly what it is you want. This is not pretending; it's owning the positive feelings your success brings and changing your identity from someone who is quitting a bad habit to someone who doesn't have the habit at all.

- **Form new patterns.** At first, you'll be at a loss to fill the time you spent with your old habit. Find new things to do—pursue old interests you left behind, start a hobby, feed your curiosity, and replace your old habits with healthy new ones.

Supporting You!

Okay, you have a plan and a support group; now you need to find ways to support yourself. The biggest mistake you can make is to assume you're strong enough to be in the same environment without being triggered. Sure, you can go to the bar or the bakery and not have a drink or eat a pastry, but what are the chances you'll be successful? The best strategy is to avoid your triggers, which include places, activities, and people that you associate with the habit. It may feel like you're abandoning friends, but think of being in an airplane when the oxygen masks come down. You have to save yourself before you can help the person next to you.

Remember, your conscious mind is an amazing rationalizer. If you subconsciously believe that you need the addictive behavior, your conscious mind will find a dozen reasons why you should go to the casino, have a drink with a buddy, or enjoy that chocolate cake. After all, "We all die sometime." Don't give your conscious mind a chance. Make a posthypnotic suggestion and use it every time your conscious mind offers a rationalization for why what is hurting you is okay to do.

> **SUBCONSCIOUS SCAFFOLDING**
>
> One of the best auto-suggestions to use in any situation was developed by French positive psychologist Émile Coué de la Châtaigneraie. It is: *Every day, in every way, I am better and better.* Change the word *better* to *stronger* or *freer* if that fits your situation more closely and use it whenever you're challenged by temptation.

Don't forget to celebrate your accomplishments and enjoy your success. What you're doing is a challenge and deserves recognition. Every day free is a celebration! Find ways to celebrate that feed the inner you struggling to break free. Get a massage, go to a sauna, or see a movie with a friend. Do something kind for yourself! And if you backslide, get up, wipe the dust off your pants, visit your support group, do a self-hypnosis session, and keep right on going.

Addiction Scripts

The following scripts can be adapted to fit your particular need. Simply personalize the one you choose with new wording to reflect your issue. Each script begins with a list of suggested posthypnotic suggestions, many of which are woven into the script. Use one or all of these or substitute your own. Try to include in the script the feelings or needs that you want to have, along with new ways of getting them met.

Before using the following scripts, be sure the imagery sparks positive associations. If you're allergic to flowers, cut those references from the script and replace them with images you find relaxing and enjoyable, such as birds, trees, waterfalls, and so forth. Another approach might be to add a sentence that addresses your difficult association, such as "While you might be allergic to pollen, you may be surprised and delighted to find that you've left your allergies behind. You happily say to yourself, 'I am allergy free and enjoying the flowers.'"

Remember to precede each hypnosis script with the induction in Chapter 7. Have fun, enjoy yourself, and know that your subconscious mind powerfully supports you in the change you're making!

Freedom from Alcohol and Drugs

Posthypnotic Suggestions

- My subconscious mind powerfully supports me. I am free of desire for any substance that doesn't serve my body, mind, and spirit.

- Withdrawal effects and cravings disappear before the power of my subconscious mind.

- My subconscious mind powerfully supports me. I overcome cravings with ease. My body balances withdrawal effects.

- I crave and enjoy only healthy, sustaining substances.

- I forgive myself for any and all the mistakes I've made. That is the past. I go forward with love, powerfully supported by my subconscious mind.

- My body, mind, and spirit are healing. Every day, in every way, I am better and better.

As you step off the last stair and sink into the soft, grassy soil … notice the deep peace … total contentment … that sweeps through you …. Breathing deeply, filling your lungs with clear, fresh air … walk along the garden path … and say "I leave behind all substances that don't serve my well-being." Your whole body fills with relief … fills with pride … swells with joy. Every cell rejoices in healthy vibrancy. You say "I am free. I crave and enjoy only healthy, sustaining substances."

As you move into the warmth of the sun … feeling the warmth spread over your face … your throat, your chest … warmth moving through your whole body … you smile, recognizing the garden … and anticipating enjoyment.

Walk among the flowers … looking at the purple, white, pink, yellow, and bright red blossoms …. You notice a fresh breeze … a cleansing breeze …. Feel it brush across your skin … sending shivers down your spine … enlivening every cell. You turn your head into the breeze … and notice that ahead of you … is a boardwalk along a cliff …. Walking toward the cliff … you see it overlooks the ocean …. You can see the brilliant water sparkling in the warm sun.

 HYPNOTIC CONNECTION

If you don't have a support group, online chat rooms are a great resource for help in overcoming temptation. An excellent site you might want to check out is drugandalcoholhelpline.ca.

Standing at the cliff's edge … the ocean spreads out away from you …. Breathe deeply, filling your lungs with oxygen … feeling alive … happy to be you …. You hear the seagulls call as they glide on the breeze … hear the waves crashing on shore … feeling alive … feeling grateful … absorbing the raw power and beauty before you. You say "With every breath I take, my body is alive, healthy, and free of any desire that doesn't serve my body, mind, and spirit."

Open … your arms wide before the magnificent vista …. You delight in realizing … that you left your unhappiness behind … left your challenging habit in the past. Spreading your arms … leaning back … you open your chest wide to the elements. The sun warms and enlivens your chest …. The wind cleanses your cells and soul …. Breathing deeply … you are free …. Oxygen fills your lungs … you are free …. Exhale … inhale … each breath fills you with life …. You feel alive like you've never felt before.

Seeing a rock outcropping, you sit …. In your mind's eye, images pass by … images of you with your habit … and rather than engaging these images … you see into them … see the pain you've been running from … and beneath that … you see your pure soul … see that you are wanting to be loved … you see your past and let it go … saying "I forgive myself for any and all mistakes I have made. That is the past. This is a new day. I go forward with love, powerfully supported by my inner mind." You resolve to face anything you have been hiding from.

Breathe deeply …. Light fills your lungs and spreads through your whole body. Seagulls call as they swoop by … they seem to be cheering you on …. You call out to the universe "I am transformed. Every day, in every way, I am freer and freer."

Breathe and be transformed by bright, warm light …. You are free … nothing holds you back …. In your mind's eye, you see your friends, your family, all the people who love you … clapping … see them jumping up and down … hear them calling your name …. Even the waves clap and exalt you …. You are free … your lungs are clear … your breath is full and sweet. You say "I am in control of my life."

Just for a moment, remember the many benefits you receive from quitting … financial … friendships … family. Imagine your life free of your challenge.

Walking along the cliff's edge … you feel strong … and alive in ways you haven't felt in a long time. Your body is strong and healthy … your eyes are clear, your posture is straight and proud … all parts of you feel healthy. With every breath … you release old cravings. With every breath, your body is clearer … healthier. With every breath, you know … your body, heart, and soul are healthy and free. You know that no matter how tempted you are, you're in control. You say "My body, mind, and spirit are healing. Every day, in every way, I am better and better."

Turning a corner, you see a group of people … they gesture you to join them …. You hesitate … then, standing straight … you walk over …. You are happy to feel accepted … welcomed into the group … happy to feel a healthy appetite for good food and beverages. You feel proud of your decision to live free of your addiction. As you eat healthy food … you're happy to notice that you're satisfied … all you want is here. Smiling, you clasp your hands together and say "My subconscious mind powerfully supports me. I am free of desire for any substance that doesn't serve my body, mind, and spirit."

As you enjoy good company and good food … you begin to remember things you enjoyed in the past … activities you pursued before you got sidetracked by addiction. Remembering what used to bring you joy … starts your heart pounding in excitement … your mind becomes curious. A gentle wave of happiness spreads through your body as you realize … there are so many things to enjoy … so much to look forward to …. Right now, you decide you will pursue one of your early enjoyments again … starting right now …. You find so many things to be interested in … so many avenues worth exploring.

Feeling proud, feeling happy … heading away from the cliff … walking back through the garden … you know you are healing …. Your memory is returning … your mind is clear … your body is healing … your mood is balanced … your healthy appetite is restored … your sexual drive and function are restored …. You say "My body, mind, and spirit are healing; every day, in every way, I am better and better."

 MESMERIZING MORSEL

"Power is the faculty or capacity to act, the strength and potency to accomplish something. It is the vital energy to make choices and decisions. It also includes the capacity to overcome deeply embedded habits and to cultivate higher, more effective ones."

—Stephen R. Covey, author and leadership authority

*Moving toward the stairs … you are overwhelmed with happiness … contentment explodes in every cell ….
Feeling grateful … you give thanks to the elements … the wind, the sun, the ocean, the garden … for supporting
you in your healing … knowing you can return to this garden, anytime, anywhere …. Reaching the stairs, you
take a deep breath and begin to step up.*

Smiling, you start up the stairs and on the count of five are awake, alert, and happy. Life is good.

One, coming up.

Two, becoming more awake, more alert, more aware.

Three, feeling fine … eyes start to flutter.

Four, feeling great … toes start to wiggle.

Five, feeling awake, aware, and fully restored to normal consciousness.

Every time you are challenged by temptation, clasp your hands and say "My subconscious mind
powerfully supports me. I am free of desire for any substance that doesn't serve my body, mind,
and spirit."

Ceasing Smoking Now

Posthypnotic Suggestions

- I am a nonsmoker.

- With every breath, my lungs are cleaner, stronger, and healthier.

- Every day, in every way, I am freer and freer.

- As light and air enter my lungs, all cravings subside.

- I am in control of my life.

- My subconscious mind powerfully supports me, overcoming cravings and eliminating
  withdrawal effects.

- My subconscious mind powerfully supports me. I am free of desire for any substance
  that doesn't serve my body, mind, and spirit.

*As you step off the last stair and sink into the soft, grassy soil … notice the deep peace … total contentment
… that sweeps through you … breathing deeply, filling your lungs with clear, fresh air … walking along the
garden path … and saying "I am a nonsmoker." You whole being fills with pride …. Your whole being swells
with joy. "I am a nonsmoker."*

As you move into the warmth of the sun … feeling the warmth spread over your face … your throat … your chest … warmth moving through your whole body … you smile, recognizing the garden … and anticipating enjoyment.

Walking among the flowers, you notice a fresh breeze, a different breeze … and feel it brush across your skin, sending shivers down your spine …. Turning your head into the breeze … you notice ahead of you … is a cliff …. Walking toward the cliff … you see it overlooks the ocean …. You can see the brilliant water sparkling in the warm sun.

HYPNOTIC CONNECTION

Support for quitting smoking can be hard to find. One online resource that offers many support services and a live chat room is smokershelpline.ca.

Standing at the cliff's edge … the ocean spreading out away from you … breathing deeply, filling your lungs with oxygen … feeling alive … happy to be you … you hear the seagulls call as they glide on the breeze … hear the waves crashing on the shore below … feeling alive … feeling grateful for the raw power and beauty before you. You say "With every breath, my lungs are cleaner, stronger, and healthier."

Opening your arms wide before the magnificent vista … you delight in realizing … you left your smoking habit behind. Spreading your arms … leaning back … you open your chest wide to the elements. The sun warms and enlivens your chest …. Breathing deeply … you're free …. Oxygen fills your lungs … you're free …. Exhaling … inhaling … each breath fills you with life …. You feel alive like you never felt before.

Seeing a rock outcropping, you sit …. In your mind's eye, images pass by … images of you as a smoker … going outside on your break … hiding your habit from children or other people … wasting time … wasting money … isolating yourself … hurting yourself … acting as though hurting yourself is fun. You see images of yellow stained fingers … overflowing ashtrays … burn holes in clothing. As all these images pass before your inner eye … you breathe deeply … light fills your lungs and spreads through your whole body. You call out to the ocean "I forgive myself. Every day, in every way, I am freer and freer."

Breathe and be transformed by bright, warm light …. You are free … nothing holds you back …. Before your mind's eye, you see your friends, your family, all the people who love you … clapping … see them jumping up and down … hear them calling your name … Even the waves clap and exalt you …. You are free … your lungs are clear … your breath is full and sweet. You say "I am in control of my life."

Walking along the cliff's edge … you feel strong … and alive in ways you haven't felt in a long time. Your body is strong and healthy … your eyes are clear, your posture is straight and proud … your breath is fresh and clean … you express yourself with perfect ease … all parts of you feel healthy. With every breath … you release old smoke from your lungs. With every breath, your lungs are clearer … your lungs are healthier … your body, heart, and soul are healthy and free. You know that no matter how tempted you are, you are in control. Making a thumbs-up gesture, you say "As light and air enter my lungs, all cravings subside."

Just for a moment, remember the many benefits you receive from quitting ... financial ... friendships ... family. Imagine your life free of your challenge ....

Turning a corner, you see a group of people ... they gesture you to join them .... You hesitate ... then, standing tall ... you walk over .... You are happy to feel accepted ... welcomed into the group ... happy to feel a healthy appetite for good food and beverages. You feel proud of your decision to live smoke free. As you eat healthy food ... you are happy to notice that you are satisfied ... everything you want is here. Smiling, you say "My subconscious mind powerfully supports me. I am free of desire for any substance that doesn't serve my body, mind, and spirit." You know you can be with people and stay smoke free.

Feeling proud, feeling happy ... heading away from the cliff ... walking back through the garden ... heading toward the stairs ... giving thanks to the elements ... to the garden ... for helping you heal ... knowing you can always return. Reaching the stairs, you take a deep breath and, smiling, you start up the stairs. On the count of five, you are awake, alert, and happy. Life is good.

One, coming up.

Two, becoming more awake, more alert, more aware.

Three, feeling fine ... eyes start to flutter.

Four, feeling great ... toes start to wiggle.

Five, feeling awake, aware, and fully restored to normal consciousness.

Every time you are challenged by cigarettes, give the thumbs-up gesture and say "As light and air enter my lungs, all cravings subside."

Denying Drama

Posthypnotic Suggestions

- I think and speak only positive and truthful statements about myself and others.

- Gossip holds no interest to my evolving mind.

- I enjoy enriching, fulfilling relationships based on mutual respect.

- I control the words I speak.

- I am content and happy with myself and my life.

Now that you're at the bottom of the stairs ... see the garden inviting you forward ... and notice the warm glow of delight spreading through your body ... as you recognize where you are ... and anticipate enjoyment.

SUBCONSCIOUS SCAFFOLDING

Drama raises energy, puts you in the middle of attention, and keeps life exciting. If you're addicted to drama, you may need to find exciting and energizing events to become involved with and find people who like you for you!

As you move forward onto the garden path … you hear the call of birds as they fly past … and the buzz of bees gathering nectar in the blossoming flowers. You feel the warm sun on your head … your face … your chest. Warm, relaxing energy spreads through your body … helping you feel even more alive … more vital. Notice how strong and happy you feel … notice how nice it is to be you.

As you continue meandering among the flowers … no place to go … nowhere you have to be … nothing you have to do … notice the alluring smell of jasmine and honeysuckle. Feel the breeze across your skin. Notice the soft grass under your bare feet.

Walking, you enjoy positive, happy thoughts …. Feeling happy, feeling proud … notice how comfortable you are being you …. Feeling happy … say to yourself "I am content and happy with myself and my life." Feel the warm glow of knowing you are enough … life is enough … and knowing … you are likable … you have admirable qualities …. In fact … you notice that you want to show all your friends the good qualities you have inside … qualities you may not have shown them before. Smiling broadly, you say to yourself "I think and speak only positive and truthful statements about myself and others."

It feels good … leaving drama behind … leaving gossip behind … leaving behind old feelings of not enough. Notice the warm sun on your face …. Feel energy pouring through your body …. Notice how much more energy you have when you are happy. As you walk among the brilliant colored flowers … red, pink … purple … yellow … you hear the happy sounds of people in the garden … happy voices ahead on the path. Rounding a corner, you see … people laughing and enjoying each other. You start to pull away … why? What are you thinking about yourself right now? What are you feeling?

Suddenly, the sun warms your face … warms your arms. And you notice … that your heart is full of warmth. Your heart is expanding with warmth … as these people gesture to you to come over. Walking toward them, you resolve to show them who you really are … to let go of any fear … to remember that you are a likeable person with many good qualities.

Approaching the happy group … you feel accepted … wanted … and you know and say … "I enjoy enriching, fulfilling relationships based on mutual respect." You enjoy the positive feelings of being free of drama … free of needing to be noticed … free of competing with others …. Holding your head high … you are happy to notice how good you feel … how much energy you have … how much you have to offer others. Smiling with an outstretched hand to people in the group … your head is high and you feel proud as you think and say to yourself "I am content and happy with myself and my life."

As you continue to speak … you breathe deeply … feeling lighter and lighter … happier and happier … supporting yourself by choosing kind words … feeling stronger and happier every minute.

As you enjoy the party … feeling good … feeling strong … feeling happy … you sit with your new friends and accept them … just the way they are … and you feel alive in ways you never imagined … strong in ways you never imagined …. You say "I control the words I speak. I am full of life and vitality."

Feeling satisfied … you rise from the table … waving goodbye …. You are surprised to see all of your family and friends stand and cheer for you … applauding for you …. Acknowledge that you have taken control of your life … your friends and family admire you. Feel proud … feel deserving of admiration.

 MESMERIZING MORSEL

"We are addicted to our thoughts. We cannot change anything if we cannot change our thinking."

—Santosh Kalwar, author

As you happily walk back through the garden … toward the stairs … you're surprised to notice how light you feel … how free you feel … how enjoyable it is to feel accepted … just the way you are.

Walking along the garden path, you pass some people …. They smile welcomingly at you … and a warm glow of pride spreads through your body …. It feels good to give people something valuable. It is so easy to be kind.

As you approach the stairs … you feel happy and content …. You deserve the pride and freedom you feel. Walking toward the stairs and … taking a deep breath, smelling the scent of flowers … enjoying being free of the need for attention … content with yourself … you feel strong and your life is full of potential. Smiling, you start up the stairs and on the count of five are awake, alert, and happy to be you.

One, coming up.

Two, becoming more awake, more alert, more aware.

Three, feeling fine … eyes start to flutter.

Four, feeling great … toes start to wiggle.

Five, feeling awake, aware, and fully restored to normal consciousness.

Every time you are challenged by the need to create drama, pinch yourself and say "My subconscious mind powerfully supports me. I think and speak only positive and truthful statements about myself and others."

Allowing Weight Loss

 Track 3

Posthypnotic Suggestions

- Each and every day, I am closer to my ideal weight.

- I enjoy my strong, healthy body, full of life and vitality.

- I crave foods brimming with vitality that feed my cells and strengthen my body.

- Only healthy foods attract my attention and excite my taste buds, and I am satisfied and full with what I eat.

- My body easily digests, absorbs, and eliminates my food.

Now that you've descended the stairs and entered the garden … you can use this relaxed, alert state of mind to powerfully support change. At the bottom of the stairs … see the garden inviting you forward … and notice the warm glow of delight spreading through your body … as you recognize where you are … and anticipate enjoyment.

Moving forward onto the garden path … you hear the call of birds as they fly past … and the buzz of bees gathering nectar in the blossoming flowers. You feel the warm sun on your head … your face … your chest. Warm, relaxing energy spreads through your body … helping you feel even more alive … more vital. Notice how strong and happy you feel …. Notice how nice it is to be you.

As you continue meandering among the flowers … no place to go … nowhere you have to be … nothing you have to do … feel the breeze across your skin … and notice the soft grass under your bare feet.

And walking, you remember why you came here today … to support yourself in losing weight …. Take a moment to feel your body … feel it strong and lean …. See yourself active and enjoying a strong, healthy body …. Feeling happy, feeling proud … notice how loose and comfortable your clothes are …. You say to yourself "Each and every day, I am closer to my ideal weight." Feel the warm glow of success fill your heart … as you know your healthy choices enliven your body with vitality.

Approaching a water fountain … you lean forward and look into the reflective pool … proud and happy to see how healthy and lean you look … and you know your strong choices are helping your ideal weight manifest every day, in every way.

Continuing to walk … you breathe deeply … feeling lighter and lighter … happier and happier … making the decision to support your body by choosing healthy foods … that make you stronger and healthier every day.

As you enjoy the garden … you notice you are hungry … and you have a healthy appetite … you are hungry for good foods …. And now you hear a group of people calling you … calling for you to join the party.

Rounding the corner … you see your friends and family … sitting at a table … laughing and enjoying each other's company … surrounded by platters of food …. Even as you smell the delicious vapors … you notice that foods you once loved are unappealing, even somewhat repellent … and say "Only healthy foods attract my attention and excite my taste buds." Looking at all the food on the table … you notice you are drawn only to healthy foods. You know and say "I crave foods brimming with vitality, foods that feed my cells and strengthen my body."

SUBCONSCIOUS SCAFFOLDING

This script for weight loss focuses on cravings and managing what you eat. You can include suggestions and scripts to address speeding up your metabolism, improving your digestion, and losing pounds. Replace existing suggestions, or add a few new ones in.

Just for a moment, remember the many benefits you receive from eating healthy foods. Imagine your life free of excess weight …. See yourself at your ideal weight … feeling good … feeling strong … feeling happy.

Now sitting with your friends, you accept a plate of crisp, healthy food …. As you eat, you feel alive in ways you never imagined … strong in ways you never imagined …. You know and say "I enjoy my strong, healthy body, full of life and vitality."

Having eaten, you feel satisfied … and rise from the table … waving goodbye …. You are surprised when your whole family stands and cheers for you … acknowledging that you have taken control of your life.

As you happily walk back through the garden … toward the stairs … you're surprised to notice how light you feel … how loose your clothes are … how enjoyable it is to be your ideal weight.

Walking along the garden path, you pass some people … who you don't even know …. They smile admiringly at you … and a warm glow of pride spreads through your body …. It feels good to look and be strong and healthy at your ideal weight. You look forward to enjoying having less weight … enjoying physical activities you haven't been able to do until now.

As you see the stairs … you feel happy and content …. You deserve the pride and freedom you feel. As you move toward the stairs … taking a deep breath … smelling the scents of flowers … enjoying being free of cravings and full of control … you feel strong … knowing your life is full of potential. Smiling, you start up the stairs and on the count of five are awake, alert, and happy.

One, coming up.

Two, becoming more awake, more alert, more aware.

Three, feeling fine … eyes start to flutter.

Four, feeling great … toes start to wiggle.

Five, feeling awake, aware, and fully restored to normal consciousness.

Every time you're challenged by tempting foods or overeating, pinch yourself and say "My subconscious mind powerfully supports me. Only healthy foods attract my attention and excite my taste buds, and I am satisfied and full with what I eat."

The Least You Need to Know

- Addictions are trying to fill an unmet need.
- It's easier to quit an addictive behavior if you have a plan and a support team.
- Self-hypnosis scripts can be adapted to fit any habit you want to break.
- Self-hypnosis can be geared toward reducing cravings, reducing withdrawal symptoms, and achieving a new life.
- An excellent posthypnotic suggestion for any addiction is "My subconscious mind powerfully supports me in this change."

11

Freedom from Overpowering Emotions, Fears, and Phobias

Emotions are the rocket fuel that propels your dreams to the stars. If you recall, Chapters 4 and 5 revealed how emotions empower your goals and explained their ability to convey messages from your subconscious mind. As you may already know, emotion can be like an unruly child and undermine your happiness.

The scripts in this chapter help you understand the subconscious messages and how they can enable you to release old emotional patterns, fears, and phobias.

In This Chapter

- Distinguishing helpful emotions from old patterns
- Learning how to use emotional energy
- Using scripts to overcome emotional drain
- Employing scripts to release fears and phobias

The Powerful Impact of Emotions

There isn't a single activity you perform or thought you have that isn't infused with an underlying stream of emotions. Emotions emphasize what is important, warn you of what is dangerous, and give purpose to your life. You might find them annoying, unruly, and difficult to deal with, but emotions are essential to all aspects of your life. How will you know that you're in danger if you never feel fear? What value does success have if it doesn't bring you happiness? Emotions are the measure and reward of all that you do.

While emotions give meaning to your life, like most people, you may find using them to be confusing. You may suppress uncomfortable feelings and, instead of dealing with them, store them in your subconscious, where they become distortions of reality. Now, rather than help you understand and enjoy life, they sabotage your goals and happiness. They build up inside and explode at the worst possible moments.

Because self-hypnosis communicates directly with the subconscious, it can help determine the useful information in your emotions and release old emotional patterns that are holding you back. With hypnosis, your subconscious mind releases old hurts and heals past trauma. Once your emotions are freed from the past, they're available to fuel your dreams.

 WISE COUNSEL

Fears, phobias, and unhealed trauma have deep-seated origins. The scripts here are geared to successfully overcoming the debilitating effects without going deeply into uncovering causes. Regression therapy for that purpose is best done with a professional therapist; after a few sessions, you will have a powerful, personalized self-script.

The Unresolved Past

The difficulty understanding the messages emotions convey is that often emotions don't give present-time information. Instead, they tell you where you were hurt in the past and are still stuck in old trauma. Of course you know that you were hurt when your boyfriend dumped you and took up with your best friend, but do you realize that your choice to become a research archive manager was an attempt to avoid personal interactions and the painful rejection they might bring?

The ghosts of past emotions haunt the present and may keep you from the happiness you deserve. Everyone has fears and phobias and everyone, including you, deserves to be loved and enjoy good, trustable friendships. Healing the pain of your past can liberate you to enjoy the many gifts of today.

In the end, your deepest wounds, once healed, or the phobias that you were most afraid of, once conquered, become your greatest strengths. The mastery you gain in overcoming them becomes the greatest gift you give the world. In healing your trauma and mastering your fear, you learn something valuable. Sharing your strategy and success might even be your life's purpose.

Clearing Muscle Memory

As you know from Chapter 4, your emotional past is carried in patterns of muscle tension. Your body posture, aches, and pains reveal where you store the results of past, hurtful events. Scripts in this chapter include references to common body sensations related to the emotion being cleared. Be sure to personalize this to match your own particular pattern of muscular tension.

In addition, take note of the scripting that establishes new body patterns and adjust the script to describe the posture that conveys the emotion you want to express. Feeling comfortable and relaxed with these suggestions will maximize your subconscious acceptance of them and your ability to incorporate them in your life. Once accepted, they become part of the subconscious signal that establishes your new program.

Personalizing Your Script

The subjects and emotions in this chapter are very personal. To maximize the benefit, personalize the scripts and create your own excellent, posthypnotic suggestions, replacing each section with your personal details. (See Chapter 7 for guidelines to be sure the scripts are congruent with your inner truth.)

If you struggle with emotional patterns not addressed here, see which script matches the closest and rewrite it to your need. For example, panic attacks fit well with the anxiety script, frustration fits with the anger script, and grief fits with the freeing past trauma script. Write the specific emotion you want to focus on into the script; be sure the muscle memory works for you and the goals fit your intentions. Regarding fears and phobias, replace your phobia with the one listed and personalize the script based on you worst scenarios. Always precede each script with key 1, instant relaxation, and your induction script from Chapter 7. Make it fun!

 HYPNOTIC CONNECTION

According to certified hypnotherapist Geoffrey J. N. Knight, one in nine people have a phobia of some sort. This constitutes more than 11 percent of the population.

Releasing Fixed Emotional Patterns

Emotional patterns begin early in life. Even before your own experiences became engrained, you watched how your parents behaved and mimicked them. Consequently, some of what you carry is yours, while much is a projection from others and doesn't belong to you. In either case, you can let go of what no longer serves you.

The function of emotions is to provide information and energy. They rise, deliver their messages, provide energy to do something about the messages, and retreat. If they rise and never go away, they're like a fire alarm that keeps ringing after the fire is out. Your job is to assure your subconscious that you received the message and then turn off the alarm. You don't need to suppress the feeling. This ignores the message or contains the energy, which stores it in muscle tension. By acknowledging the emotion, you can release the pattern.

Relieving Anxiety and Worry

 Track 4

Posthypnotic Suggestions

- I am free of worry and anxiety. I choose trust.

- I am powerfully focused in the present moment.

- Right here, right now, I have everything I need. I am safe.

- I have everything I need to overcome any difficulty.

- The past has no hold over the future I now create. I leave behind mine and everyone else's worry and anxiety. I choose trust.

- My subconscious mind powerfully supports me in releasing all fear-based thinking and actions.

Now that you've descended the stairs and entered the garden ... you can use this relaxed, alert state of mind to powerfully support change. As you step off the last stair and sink into the soft, grassy soil ... notice the deep peace ... total contentment ... that sweeps through you ... breathing deeply, filling your lungs with clear, fresh air ... walking along the garden path ... and saying "I am free of worry and anxiety. I choose trust." Your whole being fills with peace ... and freedom.

As you move into the warmth of the sun ... feeling the warmth spread over your face ... your throat ... your chest ... your back ... warmth moving through your whole body ... you smile, recognizing the garden ... and anticipating enjoyment.

Walking among the flowers, you notice a fresh breeze, a different breeze … and feel it brush across your skin … sending shivers down your spine. Turning your head into the breeze … you notice ahead of you … a brook …. Walking toward the sunlit brook … you see a lovely island in the middle … just big enough for a bench for one …. The bench sits among the ferns … in the midst of brilliant, sparkling water … flowing under the warm sun.

Standing at the water's edge … you jump … landing easily on the small island … breathing deeply, filling your lungs with peace and calm … feeling alive … and happy to be you. Sitting down on the bench … you realize you have a choice. You can choose to indulge anxiety and worry … or you can choose to trust. It's not a difficult choice to make … you enjoy trusting … it feels good to trust … and you know and say "Right here, right now, I have everything I need. I am safe."

Taking a deep breath … suddenly you are surrounded by butterflies. Orange, blue, purple, yellow butterflies … rolling, floating … brushing over your skin as they gently sail along on the breeze. You notice how fragile they are … yet how adeptly they fly … how trustingly they sail on the wind. It feels good … to imagine floating like a butterfly … following the currents of life. It feels good to trust life.

SUBCONSCIOUS SCAFFOLDING

When writing your own script, try to give your internal feelings texture by matching them with elements in the external environment.

Unexpectedly, a butterfly lands on your hand. Focusing on the butterfly … you notice how gentle it is … how fragile it seems … yet it has no fear. You know it is a choice to trust … and you enjoy choosing trust. Yet … you know your worry and anxiety have a message …. You wonder, does the butterfly know the message? Take a minute and listen to the message of your anxiety and worry …. Take a minute to know what they want to convey. Understand your strong desire to keep you … your loved ones … and the whole world safe.

Suddenly you are laughing! How absurd to think … that your worry will ensure safety. The butterfly gently lifts … is picked up and tossed by a strong breeze … is rolled and rocked … buffeted to and fro …. The same breeze lifts your hair … and as you watch … the butterfly balances itself … and sails happily away. You know and say "I have everything I need to overcome any difficulty."

Opening your arms wide … you stand up before the stream …. A multitude of butterflies surround you … and you delight in realizing … you left your worry and anxiety behind. Breathing deeply … you know you're free …. Oxygen and light fill your lungs … you're free …. Exhaling … inhaling … each breath fills you with life …. You feel alive like you've never felt before.

Images of your family … friends … world events … pass through your mind's eye. Everyone is safe … everything moves on without your worry. It is a choice to trust. It feels good to trust …. Your chest expands … your muscles soften … your face relaxes … your eyes are clear …. In fact, you see the moment more clearly than you ever have before. You know and say "The past has no hold over the future I now create. I leave behind mine and everyone else's worry and anxiety. I choose trust."

Just for a moment ... you remember how happy your family is when you don't worry about them .... For just a moment, you remember how good it feels to be free. Now imagine your life free of your limiting thoughts and worry. Smiling, you know and say "My subconscious mind powerfully supports me in releasing all fear-based thinking and actions."

Feeling proud, feeling happy ... you jump back over the brook ...say good-bye to the healing waters ... give thanks to the butterflies ... and walk back through the garden ... heading toward the stairs .... Knowing you can always return ... you reach the stairs ... take a deep breath and ... start up. On the count of five, you are awake, alert, and happy.

One, coming up.

Two, becoming more awake, more alert, more aware.

Three, feeling fine ... eyes start to flutter.

Four, feeling great ... toes start to wiggle.

Five, feeling awake, aware, and fully restored to normal consciousness.

Every time you are challenged by worry and anxiety, smile, relax the muscles in your face, and say "My subconscious mind powerfully supports me in releasing all fear-based thinking and actions. Right here, right now, I have everything I need. I am safe."

Leaving Anger Behind

Posthypnotic Suggestions

- I listen to anger and protect my boundaries with calm, powerful strength.

- I pay attention to my inner anger meter and choose to switch off anger and switch on empowerment.

- I watch obstacles melt before my powerful intent.

- Right here, right now, I am the master of my emotions.

- I have everything I need to overcome any difficulty.

- The past has no hold over the future I now create. I leave behind everyone else's opinions and projections. I am enough.

- My subconscious mind powerfully supports me in releasing all fear-based thinking and angry actions.

- Anger does not control me. I listen to the message and choose my response.

MESMERIZING MORSEL

"Anybody can become angry—that is easy, but to be angry with the right person and to the right degree and at the right time and for the right purpose, and in the right way—that is not within everybody's power and is not easy."

—Aristotle, philosopher

As you step off the last stair and sink into the soft, grassy soil … notice the deep peace … total contentment … that sweeps through you …. Breathing deeply, filling your lungs with clear, fresh air … walking along the garden path … you believe and say "I listen to anger and protect my boundaries with calm, powerful strength."

Your whole being fills with peace … and freedom. As you move into the warmth of the sun … feeling the warmth spread over your face … your throat … your chest … warmth moving through your whole body … you smile, recognizing the garden … and anticipating enjoyment.

Walking among the flowers … feeling peaceful and calm … purple, orange, yellow flowers … you enjoy the relaxing … and enjoyable … calm.

Suddenly, you notice a strong breeze … and hear the crack of thunder. Wind whips across your skin … sending shivers down your spine. The sky darkens. Your heart jumps with excitement … and … turning your head into the wind … you notice that you are standing near the edge … of a deep canyon. Walking toward the edge, into the strong wind … your clothes are whipped across your body … your hair is whipped across your face. You feel alive with excitement … alive in a way you rarely are. Standing on the edge of the canyon … lightning strikes on the other side … wind tosses trees …. You feel powerfully exhilarated and realize … you enjoy the power, and at times … enjoy feeling angry … enjoy unleashing your power … like the storm. At the same time, you know … how much more powerful it is to be the master of your emotions. You know and say "Right here, right now, I am the master of my emotions. I am in control of my anger." It feels good to be in control.

Standing at the canyon's edge … feeling the wind, hearing the thunder … you understand … acting on your anger is a choice. You are not at the mercy of your anger … you choose to be angry … or not. Right now you know and say "Anger does not control me. I listen to the message and choose my response."

Breathing deeply, filling your lungs with life … feeling alive … you experience the masterful power of being in control. Your body grows in stature … you become taller … stronger … yet more relaxed … more in command … more you. Feeling powerful … feeling strong … feeling alive … you realize that no obstacle or injustice can withstand the power of your focused intent. You know and say "I watch obstacles melt before my powerful intent."

As suddenly as it started, the storm passes. The sun emerges from behind dark clouds. The canyon is alight with color … red, pink, gold … bright light shimmers across the canyon wall. You realize you are free …. You can feel anger … gauge its intensity … and choose to respond … you are free. You know and say "I pay attention to my inner anger meter and choose to switch off anger and switch on empowerment."

HYPNOTIC CONNECTION

According to certified hypnotherapist Geoffrey J. N. Knight, anger and anxiety are not the most common emotional complaints; rather, guilt and phobias are far more evident. He has categorized 283 recognized phobias in his medical dictionary.

Your body fills with light … you feel relaxed and powerful … you feel alive in ways you never have before … you are happy to be you. Turning, you begin to walk back through the garden toward the stairs. You know and say "The past has no hold over the future I now create. I leave behind everyone else's opinions and projections. I am enough."

Images of your family … friends … world … events … pass through your mind's eye. Nothing can disturb your peace … nothing can force you to be less powerful than you are. It feels good to release anger …. Your chest expands … your muscles soften … your face relaxes … your eyes are clear. Just for a moment, you remember how happy your family is when you're happy …. Just for a moment, you remember how good it feels to be free. Now, imagine your life free of your angry behavior ….

Smiling, you know and say "My subconscious mind powerfully supports me in releasing all fear-based thinking and actions."

Feeling proud, feeling happy … you give thanks to the thunder … the wind … the canyon … and continue walking back through the garden … heading toward the stairs … giving thanks to the elements … for helping you find your inner power. Knowing you can always return … you reach the stairs … take a deep breath and … start up the stairs. On the count of five, you are awake, alert, and happy. Life is good.

One, coming up.

Two, becoming more awake, more alert, more aware.

Three, feeling fine … eyes start to flutter.

Four, feeling great … toes start to wiggle.

Five, feeling awake, aware, and fully restored to normal consciousness.

Every time you are challenged by anger, stand tall and relaxed and say "Right here, right now, I am the master of my emotions. I choose how I respond."

Freeing the Ghosts of Trauma

Posthypnotic Suggestions

- I am free of past trauma and pain. I choose to heal.

- I am powerfully focused on the present moment.

- Right here, right now, I have everything I need. I am whole.

- I forgive myself and everyone involved as I let go of past hurt.

- The past has no hold over the future I now create. I leave behind everything that doesn't serve my highest good. I choose love.

- My subconscious mind powerfully supports me in releasing all fear-based thinking and actions.

As you step off the last stair and sink into the soft, grassy soil … notice the deep peace … total contentment … that sweeps through you … breathing deeply, filling your lungs with clear, fresh air … walking along the garden path … and saying "I am free of past trauma and pain. I choose to heal." Your whole being fills with peace … freedom … and love.

As you move into the warmth of the sun … feeling the warmth spread over your face … your throat … your chest … warmth moving through your whole body … you smile, recognizing the garden … and anticipating enjoyment.

Walking among the flowers, listening to the birds calling … the bees buzzing … you notice a fresh breeze, a different breeze … and feel it brush across your skin … sending shivers down your spine. Turning your head into the breeze … you notice ahead of you … a small gazebo tucked into a clearing among the flowers …. Walking toward the sunlit structure … you see how lovely and safe it feels … just big enough for you … in the midst of brilliant sparkling flowers … under the warm sun.

 MESMERIZING MORSEL

"What is needed, rather than running away or controlling or suppressing or any other resistance, is understanding fear; that means, watch it, learn about it, come directly into contact with it. We are to learn about fear, not how to escape from it."

—Jiddu Krishnamurti, spiritual leader and teacher

Moving inside … you see a comfortable sofa … with warm, plush blankets … soft, plush pillows. Sinking into the soft, comfortable, safe sofa … you feel supported in ways you never have before. Taking a deep breath … filling your lungs with peace and calm … feeling alive … and happy to be you. Relaxing … you allow the sofa to fully support you … letting go of everything you don't need … into the powerful support of the sofa. You feel safe, supported, loved. Because you are so safe and because it is time … you allow old pictures of past pain to rise in your mind's eye. Old hurt … rejection … abandonment … loss … all the past situations you have carried for so long … now is the time to let them go.

Because you are safe … and because it is time … and because you have a choice … you choose to forgive yourself and others. You are able to be thankful for all you have learned. You are able to let go of the past. In your mind's eye, you see all your past hurt getting into a boat and sailing away. You wave and say "The past has no hold over the future I now create. I leave behind everything that doesn't serve my highest good. I choose love."

As you watch the boat sail away, you feel free in ways you never have before … you feel safe in ways you never have before … you feel strong and loved in ways you never have before … and yet, it feels so natural … so normal to be safe and … to be loved. It feels so natural to be free of past pain. A shaft of sunlight shines into the gazebo, filling you with warmth, filling you with love. Healing energy … engulfs you … moves through you into every cell …. Every part of you feels reborn, revitalized, and healed. You know and say "Right here, right now, I have everything I need. I am whole." It feels good to be healed.

Suddenly you are laughing! How much there is to look forward to! You feel excited to embrace life. Standing in the circle of sunlight … opening your arms wide … you delight in realizing … your pain has sailed away. Breathing deeply … you exult in knowing you're free …. Oxygen and light fill your lungs … you're free …. Exhaling … inhaling … each breath fills you with life …. You feel alive like you've never felt before. You feel joy you've never felt before.

Images of people you love … family … friends … and events you enjoy … pass through your mind's eye. Everyone welcomes you … everything opens to your newfound joy. It is a choice to trust and love. It feels good to trust and love …. Your chest expands … your muscles soften … your face relaxes … your eyes are clear …. You see the moment more clearly than you ever have before. Just for a moment … you imagine your life free of your limiting past.

You know and say "My subconscious mind powerfully supports me in releasing all fear-based thinking and actions."

Feeling proud, feeling happy … you leave the warm safety of the gazebo … taking the healing strength with you … taking joy with you … giving thanks and feeling gratitude …. You walk back through the garden … past the lovely flowers … all seeming to look at you … with love and pride … heading toward the stairs … giving thanks to the elements … to the garden … to the sunlight … for helping you heal. Knowing you can always return … you reach the stairs … take a deep breath and … start up the stairs. On the count of five, you are awake, alert, and happy. Life is good.

One, coming up.

Two, becoming more awake, more alert, more aware.

Three, feeling fine … eyes start to flutter.

Four, feeling great … toes start to wiggle.

Five, feeling awake, aware, and fully restored to normal consciousness.

Every time you are challenged by an old pattern, smile, relax your face, and say "My subconscious mind powerfully supports me in releasing all fear-based thinking and actions. Right here, right now, I have everything I need. I am whole."

Conquering Fears and Phobias

Fears and phobias are natural aversions with unnatural intensity. Although their initial function was undoubtedly meant to keep you safe, the overreaction has far exceeded safety and blossomed into constraint. If you allow fears and phobias to determine what you do and don't do, you are living a life in prison. Many of the phobias you carry were probably handed down from your parents, with dire warnings intended for your benefit.

HYPNOTIC CONNECTION

One of the most complete lists of overcoming phobias CDs created by a successful hypnotherapist can be found at glennharrold.com/hypnosis-guides-mp3-downloads. html.

Do you remember being told to never go swimming until an hour after eating? Or to always wear your good underwear in case you're in an accident? Some of the advice parents give is good, some is a reflection of what their own parents told them, and some is a result of their own fear. In most cases, you probably dumped the advice that made no sense, but in other cases, words of warning became messages of doom that took over your mind and body.

The phobia you suffer from may have an essence of truth, or not; either way, it can be totally debilitating. Fear of spiders, snakes, heights, flying, leaving the house, being in social situations, and so forth can cause so much anxiety that it becomes impossible to function. Overcoming such fears requires taking control and facing them head on. Naturally, self-hypnosis can be an amazing tool for your self-mastery. At the same time, having the support of a therapist is helpful should old traumas surface.

Overcoming your phobia doesn't mean soldiering through fearful situations; it means approaching the fearful situation in small steps and building on success. Maybe start by being in the same room with a spider in a glass jar. You may need to spend a fair amount of time with each small step until success beings to replace fear.

Desensitizing Phobias

Self-hypnosis can be helpful in desensitizing your fear as you tackle your phobia. It allows you to experience the fearful situation from a place of separation. Using the session to successfully meet the situation you are afraid of trains the subconscious mind. Afterward, as you meet your phobia in waking state and work your way through it, you may still feel fear, but alongside it is confidence that helps you move forward. Success is measured by how many steps you've taken, not whether the fear was totally gone. Can you imagine looking at a spider's web without running to hide? Can you imagine sitting on a bench along a cliff walk and not have your feet alive with tingles? Each small step is a masterful success.

As always, change the script to fit your issue and start with the induction in Chapter 7. When replacing your phobia with the ones in the following script, you'll want to recreate your fear. For example, if you are afraid of flying, start your session script seeing yourself at home, leaving for the airport, walking through the lobby, getting on the plane, and flying. Support yourself through every step, meeting and conquering your fear. If you have agoraphobia and are afraid of leaving your house, imagine yourself successfully walking out the door, feeling confident and happy as you address your feelings. The same with social phobias or any fear that holds you back from being all that you can be.

 MESMERIZING MORSEL

"I have learned over the years that when one's mind is made up, this diminishes fear; knowing what must be done does away with fear."

—Rosa Parks, civil rights activist

Overcoming Phobias

Posthypnotic Suggestions

- I am safe, capable, and free of fear.

- Nothing threatens me; I am safe and free of fear.

- Right here, right now, I have everything I need. I am safe.

- I handle encounters with spiders/snakes/bees/dogs with total confidence.

- The past has no hold over the future I now create. I leave behind my fear of spiders/snakes/dogs/bees and everything that doesn't serve my highest good.

- My subconscious mind powerfully supports me in releasing all fear.

As you step off the last stair and sink into the soft, grassy soil ... notice the deep peace ... total contentment ... that sweeps through you ... breathing deeply, filling your lungs with clear, fresh air ... walking along the garden path ... and saying "My subconscious mind powerfully supports me in releasing all fear." Your whole being fills with peace ... freedom ... and love.

As you move into the warmth of the sun ... feeling the warmth spread over your face ... your throat ... your chest ... warmth moving through your whole body ... you smile, recognizing the garden ... and anticipating enjoyment.

Walking among the flowers, listening to the birds calling ... the bees buzzing ... you notice the brightly colored flowers ... as you meander along the path ... red, pink, purple, blue, yellow flowers. Walking and enjoying the gentle breeze across your skin ... the warm sun on your face. Turning ... you notice ahead of you ... a small glass table tucked into the flowers ... under a large umbrella. There is one chair ... a beverage ... and tasty food.

The sun is warm on your face .... The breeze is gentle on your skin. You sit down, feeling hungry, feeling ready to relax ... noticing how lovely and safe it feels ... just enough for you ... in the midst of brilliant sparkling flowers ... under the warm sun.

Sitting and eating ... you suddenly see something move from the corner of your eye. Turning your head ... you see ... a spider/snake/dog/bee. Dread fills your body .... Your muscles tighten ... you want to scream but you can't ... you want to run but you can't ... terror grips your mind .... But suddenly, you remember to use your imagination ... and ... pulling down a glass wall ... you are separated from the thing you're afraid of.

Breathing deep ... breathing fresh, crisp air into your lungs ... letting go of fear ... you know and say "Right here, right now, I have everything I need. I am safe." Taking a deep breath ... filling your lungs with peace and calm ... feeling alive ... and happy to be you. Relaxing ... you allow the chair to fully support you ... letting go of everything you don't need ... into the powerful support of the chair. Because you are so safe and because it is time ... you allow old pictures of past fear to rise in your mind's eye. Old fear ... spiders or snakes ... dogs or bees ... all the past situations you have carried for so long ... now is the time to let them go. Because you are safe ... and because it is time ... and because you have a choice ... you choose to let go of fear.

Looking through the glass at the thing you're afraid of, you see it as if for the first time. You see how small it is ... you see how much more power you have than it does ... you see how afraid it is of you. You understand that it will hurt you only if it is afraid. Looking more closely, you see that it is nothing. It is so small, so insignificant. Taking away the glass wall ... you sit down next to the thing you have been afraid of in the past ... but are not afraid of now. It really is nothing at all. Just another life form. You know and say "The past has no hold over the future I now create. I leave behind everything that doesn't serve my highest good."

Pretty soon, the snake/spider/dog/bee wanders away .... For a brief minute, you feel alone. You are happy to notice how calm you feel ... happy to notice how triumphant you feel ... happy to notice how confident you feel. As you watch the thing move away, you feel free in ways you never have before ... you feel safe in ways you never have before ... you feel strong and loved in ways you never have before ... and yet, it feels so natural ... so normal to be safe and ... to be free of fear. It feels so natural to be free of the past. Every part of you feels *confident, strong, and free. You know and say "Nothing threatens me; I am safe and free of fear." It feels good to be free.*

It feels good to be strong …. Your chest expands … your muscles soften … your face relaxes … your eyes are clear …. You see the moment more clearly than you ever have before. Just for a moment … you imagine your life free of your limiting past.

You know and say "My subconscious mind powerfully supports me in releasing all fear."

Feeling proud, feeling happy … you leave to return home … taking the healing strength with you … taking joy with you … giving thanks and feeling gratitude …. You walk back through the garden … past the lovely flowers … heading toward the stairs … knowing that anyplace, anytime, you can return to this confident state and know that you are free of fear. You can face spiders/snakes/dogs/bees by pinching your thumb and third finger together and saying "Nothing threatens me; I am safe and free of fear." Peace and calm flood your body.

Giving thanks to the elements … to the garden … to the sunlight … knowing you can always return … you reach the stairs … take a deep breath and … start up the stairs. On the count of five, you are awake, alert, and happy. Life is good.

One, coming up.

Two, becoming more awake, more alert, more aware.

Three, feeling fine … eyes start to flutter.

Four, feeling great … toes start to wiggle.

Five, feeling awake, aware, and fully restored to normal consciousness.

Every time you're challenged by the thing you were afraid of, take a deep breath, pinch your thumb and third finger together, and say "Nothing threatens me; I am safe and free of fear." When you do, you will feel peace and calm.

The Least You Need to Know

- Self-hypnosis communicates directly with the subconscious to determine the useful emotional information and release old emotional patterns that are holding you back.
- If emotions such as fear and anxiety rise and never go away, they are like an alarm that you've forgotten to turn off.
- Self-hypnosis can desensitize your fear.
- To write a script to let go of past trauma or phobias, include what your fear is, facing it, overcoming it, and living free of it.

CHAPTER

12

Personal Empowerment

Now that you've taken charge of your life by countering bad habits and overcoming your fears and phobias, you're ready to move forward and craft the life you deserve. To create and enjoy your magnificent life, start with self-appreciation. This chapter focuses on using self-hypnosis to feel good about you. It supports you to act on your goals with confidence.

The scripts in this chapter begin with improving your self-image and confidence while increasing your magnetic qualities. With these features in hand, you're ready to look at scripts for maximizing success and developing your public presence while fearlessly learning and using new skills.

In This Chapter

- Using your sacred space
- Reinforcing your self-esteem and confidence
- Increasing your magnetism
- Getting the most from success
- Improving your public speaking skills
- Learning a new skill

Developing Your Inner Support

As you let go of negative thinking and old, worn-out habits, you're eliminating influences keeping you from happiness. It's not easy work, but with your subconscious mind as your ally, you'll employ a hidden resource in rescripting your life. Moving forward in bold new directions, it's time to use your subconscious to bolster your self-esteem, confidence, and magnetism to attract the conditions you seek.

Accessing these resources is fun and empowering. It can also be intimidating. Adding a simple element to your self-hypnosis program can help. You may have noticed in previous scripts that while you always begin in the calm, peaceful garden at the bottom of the stairs that you came down during the induction, you quickly move to a scene or location that matches and supports the function of the script. By establishing an inner sacred space, you can make that scene one that empowers you.

SUBCONSCIOUS SCAFFOLDING

This would be a good time for you to return to Chapter 8 and do the exercise for creating a sacred space. Whether you did the exercise or not, your internal sacred space already exists—you just need to uncover it.

Creating a personal sanctuary or sacred space in your hypnosis sessions provides a distinct ambience for boosting your inner resources. Once you start using it, you automatically increase the effectiveness of your self-hypnosis. *Sacred* means worthy of respect or dedication; inner sacred space is an internal landscape that helps you feel supported, alive, and energized. It is a tool that enlivens the following scripts or any endeavor you focus on.

When you're ready, the following scripts can bolster your self-esteem, restore confidence, and increase your magnetism. Be sure to distinguish them with personalized posthypnotic suggestions and script elements. If you're not sure how to personalize the script, return to Chapter 7 for the basics.

Bolstering Self-Esteem and Confidence

Posthypnotic Suggestions

- I am proud of my accomplishments and abilities.
- I leave victim thinking behind. I am in charge of what I think about me.
- I am confident I have exactly what is needed when it is needed.

> - I am enough just the way I am. I have value and gifts to offer the world.
>
> - I am confident in all I do.

As you step off the last stair and sink into the soft, grassy soil … you notice the deep peace and total contentment that moves through you. Taking a deep breath … filling your lungs with clear, fresh air … you walk along the garden path. As you walk past lovely flowers of pink, yellow, purple, blue … your whole being fills with peace and freedom …. Moving into the warmth of the sun … feeling the warmth spread over your face … your throat … your chest … warmth moving through your whole body … you smile, recognizing the garden and anticipating enjoyment.

Wandering along the lovely garden path … nowhere to rush to … nowhere you need to be … you look at the beautiful flowers … seeing how they open to the sun … and notice an opening within yourself … to an inner light that fills you. You feel safe … uplifted … and proud. You notice you are standing taller … and your head is held higher …. You sense the sparkle of your eyes … and notice a lift in your step …. You believe … and say "I am proud of my accomplishments and abilities."

Walking among the flowers … feeling peaceful and calm … purple, orange, yellow flowers … you enjoy the relaxing … and enjoyable … calm. Even as you feel proud, you notice an old message, an old voice reminding you of your failures. You feel a little sad for this voice … because you know that it is old and weak …. You understand this voice is dying … and that you're forever free. You're free of old limits based on someone else's fear …. Feeling strong … feeling proud … feeling confident … you know and say "I leave victim thinking behind. I am in charge of what I think about me."

Looking ahead, you feel a surge of excitement as you see the opening to your sacred space …. Wanting to rush ahead … you calm yourself and move intentionally … with thought and appreciation … toward the sanctuary of your inner sacred space …. Stopping at the entrance, you pause in acknowledgment of the gift of this sacred place …. Stepping inside, take a minute to absorb the scene and objects that are special to you.

 HYPNOTIC CONNECTION

If you wonder whether or not you have self-esteem issues, you might find it interesting to take a simple self-esteem test. You can find one at your-self-esteem.com/self-esteem-resources/self-esteem-test.php.

Settling into the seat that is made for you … notice the feeling of acceptance and welcome … notice the upsurge of energy throughout your system. You are charged and ready to go! Feeling calm … and relaxed … yet charged and ready for action … imagine all you want to accomplish …. Know that you have a series of action steps that you're taking to reach your goals. Know that you have everything it takes to succeed … and feel good about yourself. Feel proud knowing that you are talented … kind … and honest. Know and say "I am confident I have the abilities and talents I need." Feel yourself swell with energy … fill with light.

Take a moment to see yourself ... as the best that you are. Know and say "I am enough just the way I am. I have value and gifts to offer the world." Stay in this moment as long as you like. When you're ready, head back through the garden toward the stairs.

Feeling proud ... feeling happy ... you give thanks to the garden ... your sacred space ... and yourself. Continue walking back through the garden ... heading toward the stairs ... knowing you can always return. Reaching the stairs ... you take a deep breath and start up. On the count of five, you are awake, alert, and happy. Life is good.

One, coming up.

Two, becoming more awake, more alert, more aware.

Three, feeling fine ... eyes start to flutter.

Four, feeling great ... toes start to wiggle.

Five, feeling awake, aware, and fully restored to normal consciousness.

As you go forward and meet challenges while you reach for your goals, stand tall and relaxed and say "I am proud of my accomplishments. I am enough just the way I am. I am confident in all I do."

Magnifying Magnetism

Posthypnotic Suggestions

- I am alive with energy and magnetism.

- Everything I want is magnetically attracted to me.

- I perfectly maintain the balance between giving and receiving, sharing energy as and when it is best for everyone.

As you step off the last stair and sink into the soft, grassy soil ... you notice the deep peace and total contentment that flows through you. Taking a deep breath ... filling your lungs with clear, fresh air ... you walk along the garden path. As you walk ... your whole being fills with peace and freedom. Moving into the warmth of the sun ... feeling the warmth spread over your face ... your throat ... your chest ... warmth moving through your whole body ... you smile, recognizing the garden and anticipating enjoyment.

Wandering along the lovely garden path ... nowhere to rush to ... nowhere you need to be ... you look at the beautiful flowers, seeing how they open to the sun ... and notice an opening within yourself ... to an inner light that fills you. You feel safe, uplifted, and alive. You notice you are standing taller ... and expanding .... You feel the sparkle in your eye and notice a lift in your step. You believe and say "I am alive with energy and magnetism."

Walking among the flowers … feeling peaceful and calm … purple, orange, yellow flowers … you enjoy the relaxing … and enjoyable … calm. Looking ahead, you feel a surge of excitement as you see the opening to your sacred space …. Wanting to rush ahead … you calm yourself and move intentionally … with thought and appreciation … toward the sanctuary of your inner sacred space. Stopping at the entrance, you pause and acknowledge the gift of this power spot …. Stepping inside, you take a minute to absorb the scene and objects that are special to you.

 MESMERIZING MORSEL

"The essential element in personal magnetism is a consuming sincerity—an overwhelming faith in the importance of the work one has to do."

—Bruce Barton, author, advertising magnate, and congressman

Settle into the seat that is made just for you … noticing the feeling of acceptance and welcome … noticing the upsurge of energy through your system …. You are charged and ready to go! Feeling calm … and relaxed … yet charged and ready for action … imagine all your old limitations melting before the strength of your inner light.

Feel your personal space expand as your energy grows …. Feel your boundaries expand as you inflate with energy and life force.

Take a moment to see yourself … as a being full of unlimited potential. See yourself as the best that you are … Know and say "Everything I want is magnetically attracted to me."

Imagine yourself walking down the street …. People you know and admire are looking at you. Notice the expression on their faces as they feel your energy … feel your happiness … and acknowledge you. Notice how doors magically open …. People you want to see magically appear … as you magnetically attract everything you want …. Caring about others … wanting to share the magnificent energy that pours through you … you know and say "I perfectly maintain the balance between giving and receiving, sharing energy as and when it is best for everyone."

Stay in this wonderful, energized feeling for as long as you like. When you're ready … stand … give thanks to your sacred space … and head back through the garden toward the stairs. Feeling energized … feeling happy … feeling alive … you give thanks to the garden … to your sacred space … to yourself and to a higher power. Continue walking back through the garden … heading toward the stairs … knowing you can always return.

Reaching the stairs … you take a deep breath and start up. On the count of five, you are awake, alert, and happy. It is good to be you.

One, coming up.

Two, becoming more awake, more alert, more aware.

Three, feeling fine … eyes start to flutter.

Four, feeling great … toes start to wiggle.

Five, feeling awake, aware, and fully restored to normal consciousness.

As you go forward creating your life, stand tall and relaxed and say "I am alive with energy and magnetism."

Mobilizing Inner Resources

Feeling confident and energized makes it easy to envision yourself reaching your goals and living the life you were meant to live. Now, it's time to focus on the vision, mission, and goals you set in Chapter 6 and bathe your objectives in success.

In my experience, one of the biggest factors in being able to attain your dreams is the amount of emotional energy you have to invest. As you come against the challenges you must overcome and face fears of public vulnerability, emotional energy will help you rise to the top. Basically, do what you love, speak about what you believe, and share your passion. Never accept failure as the end of the road; it is only a course correction.

 SUBCONSCIOUS SCAFFOLDING

If your concept of emotions is that they typically hold you back rather than move you forward, you need to connect with activities that bring you joy. You may want to use the scripts in Chapter 20 for increasing joy and/or finding your path and purpose.

Use the upcoming scripts with the goals you developed in Chapter 6 and enjoy the power of having your subconscious mind help you move forward. If some posthypnotic suggestions speak more than others, reuse them throughout the script to replace the ones you like less. And always remember, you can use these posthypnotic affirmations anywhere, anytime. Keep the ones that matter to you in a list in your wallet for easy access.

Maximizing Success

Posthypnotic Suggestions

- My subconscious mind powerfully supports the fulfillment of my dreams. I have everything I need to succeed.

- I remain focused on my goals and confident of my success.

- Anything I truly want, I can achieve.

- Success flows toward me as doors magically open and opportunities become available just in the moment I need them.

- I am motivated to live to my fullest potential.

As you step off the last stair and sink into the soft, grassy soil ... you notice the deep peace and total contentment that sweeps through you. Taking a deep breath, filling your lungs with clear, fresh air, you walk along the garden path. As you walk ... your whole being fills with peace and freedom. Moving into the warmth of the sun ... feeling the warmth spread over your face ... your throat ... your chest ... warmth moving through your whole body ... you smile, recognizing the garden and anticipating enjoyment.

Wandering along the lovely garden path ... nowhere to rush to ... nowhere you need to be ... feeling relaxed and happy ... you look at the beautiful flowers, see how they open to the sun ... and notice an opening within yourself ... an opening of an inner light that fills you. You feel safe, uplifted, and alive. You notice you are standing taller ... and feeling confident. You feel the sparkle in your eye and the lift in your step. You believe and say "I remain focused on my goals and confident of my success."

Walking among the flowers ... feeling peaceful and calm ... you notice the lovely colors ... purple, orange, yellow flowers .... You enjoy the relaxing and enjoyable calm. Looking ahead, you feel a surge of excitement as you see the opening to your sacred space. Wanting to rush ahead ... you calm yourself and move intentionally ... with thought and appreciation ... toward the sanctuary of your inner sacred space. Stopping at the entrance, you pause and acknowledge the gift of this sacred place. Stepping inside, you take a minute to absorb the scene and objects that are special to you.

Settle into the seat that is made just for you ... noticing the feeling of acceptance and welcome ... noticing the upsurge of energy through your system. You are charged and ready to go! Feeling calm ... and relaxed ... yet charged and ready for action ... imagine all your old fears melting before the strength of your inner light. Sitting in your sacred space, filled with energy, a vision of your greatest desire spreads before you.

Taking a few minutes, you let the dream you are pursuing fill your mind's eye. You notice how easily this future moves toward you, how effortlessly it is arriving. You know and say "Success flows toward me as doors magically open and opportunities become available just in the moment I need them."

Looking at the beautiful dream, you move beyond wanting it to living it. Take a few minutes and feel what it's like to be successful. Imagine what you are wearing, what your body language looks like, and how you feel. You know and say "My subconscious mind powerfully supports the fulfillment of my dreams. I have everything I need to succeed."

 MESMERIZING MORSEL

"If you can dream it, you can do it."

—Walt Disney, business magnate and animator

Feel your personal space expand as your energy grows. Feel your boundaries expand as you inflate with energy and life force.

Take a moment to see yourself ... as a being full of unlimited potential. See yourself as the best that you are. Know and say "Anything I truly want, I can achieve."

Imagine yourself walking down the street ... people you know and like are looking at you and giving you a high-five. Notice the happiness on their faces as they acknowledge your success. In succeeding, you have proven to everyone that they can achieve their dreams as well. Dedicate time to sharing your new knowledge with others. Feel your happiness ... and acknowledge yourself. As you fully accept and feel the fulfillment of your dreams, you know you can achieve them perfectly. You know and say "I remain focused on my goals and confident of my success."

Stay in this wonderful, energized feeling for as long as you like. When you're ready, stand ... give thanks to your sacred space ... and head back through the garden toward the stairs. Feeling energized, feeling happy ... feeling alive ... you give thanks to the garden ... to your sacred space ... to yourself and to a higher power. Continue walking back through the garden ... heading toward the stairs ... knowing you can always return.

Reaching the stairs ... you take a deep breath and start up. On the count of five, you are awake, alert, and happy. It is good to be you.

One, coming up.

Two, becoming more awake, more alert, more aware.

Three, feeling fine ... eyes start to flutter.

Four, feeling great ... toes start to wiggle.

Five, feeling awake, aware, and fully restored to normal consciousness.

As you move forward, meeting challenges while you reach for your dreams, stand tall and relaxed and say "I remain focused on my goals and confident of my success."

Becoming a Captivating Public Speaker

Posthypnotic Suggestions

- I am perfectly calm and at ease as I enjoy speaking to large groups of people.

- I convey the excitement and enjoyment I feel as I speak about what I love.

- Everything I do and say works to the good delivery of my message.

- I am clear, concise, and engaging as I share my passion.

- I articulate perfectly what I want to say.

- My subconscious powerfully supports me as a successful public speaker.

As you step off the last stair and sink into the soft, grassy soil … you notice the deep peace and total contentment that sweeps through you. Taking a deep breath, filling your lungs with clear, fresh air, you walk along the garden path. As you walk … your whole being fills with peace … yet you are powerfully excited. Moving into the warmth of the sun, feeling the warmth spreading over your face … your throat … your chest … warmth moving through your whole body … you smile, recognizing the garden and anticipating enjoyment.

Moving purposefully along the garden path … carrying materials for a presentation … you see ahead the public venue where people are gathering. Your heart begins to beat a little faster as you approach and can hear individual conversations; everyone is excitedly waiting to hear the presentation … excitedly waiting to hear you. At first, you feel nervous knowing everyone is here to listen to you …. Your palms sweat … your legs shake … your muscles tense and your mind seems blank … then you remember that you enjoy speaking about your passion … and perfect calm spreads through you. You relax and … know and say "I am perfectly calm and at ease as I enjoy speaking to large groups of people."

SUBCONSCIOUS SCAFFOLDING

Some time-tested tips for successful public speaking are: know your topic, know your audience, practice your speech beforehand so you can visualize your success, speak clearly and loudly, make eye contact and be aware of body language, and accept your audience's desire for your success.

As you step onto the stage and approach the podium … a hush overcomes the crowd. You feel a lurch in your stomach and think you might be ill … then you look over the heads of the crowd and notice the beautiful flowers … purple, pink, and yellow …. Notice how they're opening to the sun … and notice an opening within yourself … an opening of an inner light that fills you. You feel safe, uplifted, and alive. You notice you are standing taller … and feeling confident. You feel the sparkle in your eye and the lift in your step as you approach the podium. Standing before the podium, preparing to speak, you believe and say "I convey the excitement and enjoyment I feel as I speak about what I love."

You begin to speak and everyone remains quiet, listening with rapt attention. They laugh when you tell a joke … and nod when you make important points. You feel they are in the palm of your hand and then … unexpectedly, you lose what you are saying. For a moment, you panic … then you remember … the audience needs a pause to take in the information. You turn your loss of words to a meaningful pause and know and say to yourself "Everything I do and say works to the good delivery of my message. I am clear, concise, and engaging as I share my passion."

The audience looks appreciative as you continue to speak. You know and say to yourself "I articulate perfectly what I want to convey." You enjoy speaking to the crowd and enjoy the appreciation they have for you. It is nice to have your passion appreciated by others.

When the presentation is over … you are surprised by how loudly everyone claps … surprised by how proud and happy you feel. You are relaxed, calm, and accepting of the praise … for doing such a fine job.

Taking a few minutes, you let the experience of being a powerful public speaker sink in to your body, mind, and emotions. What does your body feel like? What are you thinking? Notice how easy and effortless it is to speak publically. You know and say "My subconscious powerfully supports me as a successful public speaker." You know that new speaking engagements now flow toward you as doors magically open and new opportunities become available.

Stay in this wonderful, energized feeling for as long as you like. When you're ready, stand … give thanks to your audience … the garden and your subconscious mind. Head back through the garden toward the stairs. Feeling energized, feeling happy … feeling alive. Continue walking back through the garden … heading toward the stairs … knowing you can always return.

Reaching the stairs … you take a deep breath and start up. On the count of five, you are awake, alert, and happy. Life is good.

One, coming up.

Two, becoming more awake, more alert, more aware.

Three, feeling fine … eyes start to flutter.

Four, feeling great … toes start to wiggle.

Five, feeling awake, aware, and fully restored to normal consciousness.

Now, as you pursue and accept speaking engagements, stand tall and relaxed and say "My subconscious powerfully supports me as a successful public speaker."

Mastering a New Skill

Posthypnotic Suggestions

- I master new skills easily, as if I have already learned them and need only to remember.

- I direct the energy of any frustration I feel into perseverance and accomplishment.

- My subconscious mind powerfully supports me in effortlessly remembering and using the skills I develop.

As you step off the last stair and sink into the soft, grassy soil … you notice the deep peace and total contentment that sweeps through you. Taking a deep breath, filling your lungs with clear, fresh air, you walk along the garden path. As you walk … your whole being fills with peace and freedom. Moving into the warmth of the sun, feeling the warmth spreading over your face … your throat … your chest … warmth moving through your whole body … you smile, recognizing the garden and anticipating enjoyment.

HYPNOTIC CONNECTION

Research published in 2009 in the online *Journal of Happiness Studies* revealed that working hard to improve a skill often creates intense stress during the process, but for those who persevere, produces greater overall daily happiness when accomplished.

Looking ahead, you feel a surge of excitement as you see the opening to your sacred space. Wanting to rush ahead … you calm yourself and move intentionally through the garden, noticing the beautiful flowers … hearing the birds. When you arrive at the sanctuary of your inner sacred space, you stop at the entrance, pause, and acknowledge the gift of this sacred place. Stepping inside, you take a minute to absorb the scene and objects that are special to you.

Settling into the seat that is made just for you … you notice someone standing in the corner waiting for you. At first, you are startled … then you realize that this is the master you engaged to help you … with the new skill you are learning. Sitting before you, the master opens a mirror. Looking in, you see yourself learning your new skill. You see yourself effortlessly using the skill in many different situations. Pause for a minute and remember why you are learning this skill and where you intend to use it. Imagine yourself using this skill in the specific situation you will encounter. As you watch, notice that you effortlessly remember what to do and how to do it. You know and say "I master new skills easily, as if I have already learned them and need only to remember."

Suddenly, the master snaps the mirror case closed and then reopens it. You look inside and this time see … another scene …. You see yourself frustrated and wanting to quit. You remember this feeling, remember your face scrunched and your neck and shoulders tight and constricted. You remember feeling like exploding with frustration. Now, looking in the mirror, you see frustration is only energy. You notice the energy of frustration can easily be directed. It can easily increase your resolve. It can easily inspire you to perfect your skills even further. Watch the energy of frustration motivate you toward your goals you know and say "I direct the energy of any frustration I feel into perseverance and accomplishment."

Snapping the mirror case closed and then reopening it, the master shows you a new scene. You see yourself in many different situations, using your skill effectively and masterfully in each one. You see yourself teaching this skill to others … noticing the relaxed, open expression on your face and in your body. You see the easy motions and competent execution of this skill. You notice something that once seemed hard is now easy. Projecting yourself into this future, you know and say "My subconscious mind powerfully supports me in effortlessly remembering and using the skills I develop."

The master snaps shut the mirror case and bows to you. You notice that the master is your subconscious mind …. You notice that now … you are the master. You feel acceptance … and a welcome upsurge of energy through your system. You are charged and ready to go! Feel calm … and relaxed … yet charged and ready for action …. Suddenly you imagine yourself walking down the street …. People you know and like are looking at you and giving you a high-five. Notice the happiness on their faces as they acknowledge your success. In succeeding, you have proven to everyone that they can learn new skills, too.

 MESMERIZING MORSEL

"I am always doing that which I cannot do, in order that I may learn how to do it."

—Pablo Picasso, artist

Stay in this wonderful, energized feeling for as long as you like. When you're ready, stand ... give thanks to your sacred space ... and head back through the garden toward the stairs. Feeling energized, feeling happy ... feeling alive ... you give thanks to the garden ... to your sacred space ... to yourself and to a higher power. Continue walking back through the garden ... heading toward the stairs ... knowing you can always return.

Reaching the stairs ... you take a deep breath and start up. On the count of five, you are awake, alert, and happy. Life is good.

One, coming up.

Two, becoming more awake, more alert, more aware.

Three, feeling fine ... eyes start to flutter.

Four, feeling great ... toes start to wiggle.

Five, feeling awake, aware, and fully restored to normal consciousness.

As you go forward, learning new skills that will serve your higher goals, you stand tall and relaxed and say "My subconscious mind powerfully supports me in effortlessly learning, remembering, and using the skills I develop."

The Least You Need to Know

- Feeling good about yourself is essential to creating the life you want.
- Inner sacred space empowers your inner resources.
- You can use the posthypnotic suggestions to support your vision anywhere, anytime.
- You can redirect the energy of frustration into perseverance.

Vibrant Health Through Self-Hypnosis

The mind has great influence over your health, as research in mind-body medicine reveals. Once considered alternative medicine, now that science understands the biochemical basis for how the mind interacts with the body, mind-body medicine is considered complementary. Reflecting that approach, integrative departments exist in most medical facilities.

You won't be surprised to learn that self-hypnosis is one of the most studied and beneficial of modalities in mind-body medicine. In this part, you learn to use the power of your subconscious mind to promote your vibrant health and pain-free living.

Mind-Body Medicine

In the age of science and technology, you may have lost sight of a basic truth: the most important factor in your health is you. Your thoughts, attitudes, beliefs, and emotions impact your health every bit as much as your genetic risk factors. Research into mind-body medicine reveals that your lifestyle choices, how you handle stress, and how you focus your thoughts and emotions play important roles in your health.

While all medical conditions benefit from a positive state of mind, certain conditions lend themselves to a mind-body approach to health more easily than others. Immune-system and stress-related conditions are very responsive to and good candidates for improvement using self-hypnosis. Self-hypnosis marshals your thoughts and emotions and turns them into powerful forces for your healing. The scripts in this chapter support a balanced immune system and address health impacts from stress.

In This Chapter

- Discovering the power of mind-body medicine
- Knowing the impact of your mind and emotions on immunity
- Employing hypnosis scripts for immune support
- Understanding the impact of stress and emotions on your health
- Using hypnosis scripts for stress-related health issues

Using Mind-Body Medicine

Have you ever noticed that when you're sick, you feel better when the sun comes out or when you're happy? You may be languishing in bed feeling bad, and then people come to say hello and suddenly you feel better. That's the basis of mind-body medicine: your health is affected by your environment and the people around you, plus your emotions, thoughts, and beliefs.

The branch of science that researches how the mind affects the body is called *psychoneuroimmunology (PNI)*. It began in 1964 when psychiatrist George Solomon noticed that the symptoms of rheumatoid arthritis worsened when people with the disease were depressed. If you have arthritis, or any chronic disease, you have probably noticed that this is true.

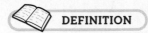 **DEFINITION**

Psychoneuroimmunology (PNI) is the field of medicine focused on the influence of emotional stress on the nervous and immune systems, especially in relation to disease.

Your immune system fights against viruses, bacteria, and other microbes. It monitors cell activity and kills cancer cells. A strong immune system is vital for creating good physical health. Weakness is only one type of immune dysfunction. In addition, your immune system can get confused and treat harmless substances as attacking agents, causing allergies. Or your immune system can mistakenly decide that your own tissue is an invading microbe and attack it, causing autoimmune disorders.

While there are many causes of immune diseases, PNI reveals that your thoughts and emotions play a big role. An overactive immune system that is allergic to every flower and dust ball can be triggered by overactive emotions. An immune system attacking its own body may be aggravated by feelings of self-denigration or inner self-conflict. While emotions are not the cause of these problems, they certainly can be aggravating factors. No matter what, your chances of creating optimal health are improved when your body, mind, and spirit are working together in harmony.

The following two scripts strengthen and direct the immune system. Use them at the first sign of illness or imbalance and personalize them to the body region and type of illness you're fighting. Find a quiet place and read the scripts several times throughout the day. Before beginning the script, be sure to use the induction in Chapter 7 or your instant relaxation skill. Also, remember to use instant relaxation with one or two of the subconscious suggestions whenever you need a boost.

Strengthening Immunity

 Track 5

Posthypnotic Suggestions

- I am strong, safe, and protected.

- My immune system defends me perfectly.

- My immune cells form an unbeatable army, which stands guard over my health.

- My body knows exactly what to do. Each immune cell responds effortlessly to every threat.

- My subconscious mind powerfully supports my immune system, overcoming every threat. I am strong, healthy, and full of vitality.

Now that you've descended the stairs and entered the garden ... you can use this relaxed, alert state of mind to powerfully support change. Knowing you are deeply ... totally ... relaxed ... you may notice the soft ... comfortable armchair ... that is positioned on the edge of the garden. Walk among the lovely flowers ... hearing the calls of the birds ... feeling the soft breeze across your skin ... feeling the warmth of the sun on your face ... your shoulders ... your back ... softening your muscles as you become even more relaxed ... more alert and more aware.

You may notice your heart leaps at the idea of escaping into this soft, comfortable chair ... sinking into its warm support ... totally held in safety and comfort. Sitting down ... you descend into the cozy, soft cushions ... and are aware that you can relax even more.

 WISE COUNSEL

The positive side of PNI is the realization that you have more control over your health than you thought. The negative side is the unfounded tendency to blame yourself when you become ill. You're really not in control of every illness, only your attitude toward it.

In fact, every time you enter a trance ... you discover you can let go of one more tension ... one more distraction. See your tension dissolve ... as you melt into the chair ... and notice the soft ... comfortable glow in your body. You may notice how completely supported you feel ... how every part of you is cradled in support ... how you feel able to let go even more.

As you sit in the chair in the garden … listening to the sounds … feeling the breeze … you notice how strong and full of energy you feel. In fact, you feel your energy expand inside of you … as you fill with a warm glow. Suddenly, you recall a health issue you have … and remember how badly it makes you feel … how weak and out of control you feel …. At first, upon remembering this, you start to panic … feeling invaded and under attack …. And then you remember … you are fine …. Your immune system is strong, balanced, wise, and triumphant. You know and say "I am strong, safe, and protected. My immune system perfectly defends me."

You see each one of your immune cells … alert … on guard … proud to fulfill its job … happy to be strong and proficient. You see each cell filled with light … moving quickly at the first sign of threat … disabling bacteria and other microbes … moving quickly to get rid of disease and eliminate illness. As you see your immune cells working so efficiently … so vigilantly … you feel proud, safe, and secure. You know and say "My immune cells form an unbeatable army, which stands guard over my health."

It is exciting to see how your immune cells know exactly what to do …. It feels safe to know that no matter what … your immune cells are guided by the wisdom of your body. Feeling safe and protected … you know and say "My body knows exactly what to do. Each immune cell responds effortlessly to every threat."

Now … you notice … the profound enjoyment you have in life as your immune system fights disease and protects you from invasion. You feel your body glow with health … as all the unhappy feelings you have experienced … are washed away … floating away … as you hear the musical … soothing sounds … of the garden. The sun warms you … filling your heart …. Your heart is expanding … allowing your whole being to glow with health … and gratitude. Gratitude grows, filling your whole body … and with gratitude comes the determination to heal. You clasp your hands and know and say "My subconscious mind powerfully supports my immune system, overcoming every threat. I am strong, healthy, and full of vitality."

 MESMERIZING MORSEL

"A sad soul can kill you quicker than a germ."

—John Steinbeck, author

Take a few minutes to enjoy the garden … the armchair … and to visualize your new life … based on solutions and gratitude.

When you're ready … no need to get up …. Bringing your comfortable support with you … bringing your feelings of gratitude with you, count from one to five. On the count of five, you will be fully awake, fully aware, fully restored.

One, coming up.

Two, becoming more awake, more alert, more aware.

Three, feeling fine … eyes start to flutter.

Four, feeling great … toes start to wiggle.

Five, feeling awake, aware, and fully restored to normal consciousness.

As you continue your day, know that every time you encounter an immune challenge, you can clasp your hands and know and say "My immune system has all the information it needs. It produces a balanced, effective defense against invasion and protects me from disease."

Immune Intelligence: Alleviating Allergies and Halting Autoimmunity

Posthypnotic Suggestions

- My environment supports me. My immune system safely accepts the presence of nonthreatening substances.

- I unconditionally accept myself; my immune system accepts and protects the cells of my body.

- My immune system has all the information it needs. It produces a balanced, effective defense against invasion and protects me from disease.

- My immune system has all the information it needs. It is wise and makes good decisions.

Now that you've reached the bottom of the steps and are deeply … totally … relaxed … you walk among the lovely flowers … hearing the calling of the birds … feeling the soft breeze across your skin … feeling the warmth of the sun along your face … your shoulders … your back … softening your muscles as you become even more relaxed … more alert and aware.

In fact, every time you enter a trance … you discover you can let go of one more tension … one more distraction. See your tension dissolve … as you notice how completely supported you feel … how you feel able to let go even more.

As you walk through the garden … listening to the sounds … feeling the breeze … you notice how strong and full of energy you feel. In fact, you feel your energy expand inside … as you fill with a warm glow. Suddenly, you see a flower you are allergic to. Before you even smell it … your nose starts to drip … your eyes start to itch … you feel you want to sneeze. In fact … you begin to feel under attack … invaded … and you start to panic … and you feel very sad because you love the flowers … love the garden …. And just as you feel very sad and invaded and under attack … you stop … and remember: you are fine … your immune system is strong, wise, and triumphant. It knows what is safe and what is harmful. Suddenly, you remember … the environment supports you. With a huge sigh of relief … you realize your body knows just what to do. You know and say "My environment supports me. My immune system safely accepts the presence of nonthreatening substances."

HYPNOTIC CONNECTION

Researchers now understand that certain allergies, such as hay fever, eczema, and asthma, are regulated by hormones and brain chemicals released into the bloodstream in response to stress. So while you may not have control over whether or not stressful events occur, you can control how you respond.

Feeling safe ... relaxed ... and very calm ... you walk through the garden ... enjoying all the different flowers ... knowing your body supports you in enjoying all aspects of life. You see each of your immune cells ... alert ... on guard ... and wise. Each cell knows exactly what to do ... knows exactly how to recognize the other cells in your body ... and how to know what cell is a foreign invader. You know and say "I unconditionally accept myself; my immune system accepts and protects the cells of my body."

It is exciting to see how your immune cells know exactly what to do .... It feels safe to know that no matter what ... your immune cells are guided by the wisdom of your body. Feeling safe and protected ... you know and say "My immune system has all the information it needs. It is wise and makes good decisions."

Now ... you notice ... the profound enjoyment you have in life as your immune system fights disease and protects you from invasion. You feel your body glow with health ... as all the unhappy feelings you have experienced ... are washed away ... floating away ... as you hear the musical ... soothing sounds ... of the garden. The sun warms you ... filling your heart ... expanding your heart ... allowing your whole being to glow with health ... and gratitude. Gratitude fills your whole body ... with gratitude comes determination to heal. You know and say "I unconditionally accept myself; my immune system accepts and protects the cells of my body."

Take a few minutes to enjoy the garden ... and to visualize your new life. When you're ready ... taking your comfortable support with you ... bringing your feelings of gratitude with you ... count from one to five. On the count of five, you will be fully awake, fully aware, fully restored.

One, coming up.

Two, becoming more awake, more alert, more aware.

Three, feeling fine ... eyes start to flutter.

Four, feeling great ... toes start to wiggle.

Five, feeling awake, aware, and fully restored to normal consciousness.

Every time you encounter substances that used to trigger allergies, or every time your body fights against itself, you know and say "My immune system has all the information it needs. It is wise and makes good decisions."

Stress and Its Link to Your Health

Over the past several decades, research has revealed that nearly 80 percent of all disease is related to chronic stress. If you've experienced prolonged stress, you can probably understand, yet you might also know that stress has another side. Stress is the driving force behind growth and development. Can you strengthen your muscles without the regular physical stress of exercise? Will you push yourself to learn something you find difficult if you don't have to? The positive side of stress is that it can enhance mental function, help you identify priorities, increase determination, and create bonding in communities and families.

 MESMERIZING MORSEL

"I realized that if my thoughts immediately affect my body, I should be careful about what I think. Now if I get angry, I ask myself why I feel that way. If I can find the source of my anger, I can turn that negative energy into something positive."

—Yoko Ono, artist and singer

The reality is that stress is an essential part of life and without it, your health and well-being suffers. The more one studies, the clearer it becomes that prolonged stress is only part of the health issue; how you handle stress is the rest. So what is the difference between stress that harms your health and stress that enhances it? If you've read earlier chapters, you already know the answer: your thoughts, attitudes, and beliefs, which are linked to your perceptions.

According to positive psychologist Shawn Achor, author of *Before Happiness: The Five Hidden Keys to Achieving Success, Spreading Happiness, and Sustaining Positive Change*, the most important factor is your perception. Achor's research indicates that if you perceive stress as harmful to you, it is; and if you perceive stress as having life-enhancing properties, it does. In other words, how you react to stress is determined by your perception; if you can view it as a challenge that will ultimately strengthen you, the harmful effects of stress are significantly lessened.

Dealing with Emotional Stress

Thoughts and emotions are key to health because they produce physical effects. In general, the term *chronic stress* means extended psychological, mental, and emotional strain. If you're like most people, you've had plenty of opportunity to experience chronic stress's detrimental effects.

Emotions such as anger and fear are part of your fight-or-flight survival response, intended to elevate your stress hormones so that you can respond to danger. In small doses, they help strengthen you. In prolonged doses, they create excessive responses that put a strain on your physical system, especially your adrenal glands and immune functions.

Prolonged emotional stress is known to increase your risk of heart disease, diabetes, and irritable bowel. In addition, emotional stress damages relationships with partners, children, friends, and co-workers, not to mention the disruption that occurs to your self-care practices. In short, there is no part of your life that is unaffected by emotional tension. Fortunately, self-hypnosis is an exceptional tool to help change your patterned response to stress.

The Benefits of Health Scripts

In response to mind-body research and patient demand, hospitals and clinics around the globe are incorporating guided imagery, meditation, hands-on healing, self-hypnosis, and other alternative healing modalities into patient care. Self-hypnosis is an exceptional tool because it gives the patient vital control. With self-hypnosis, you have the ability to improve your health and even the outcomes of medical procedures, and it is a skill you can tap into anytime, anywhere.

 WISE COUNSEL

Remember that while self-hypnosis can support your health and well-being, it's not a replacement for medical care. If you're on medications for high blood pressure or insomnia, do not stop taking them without your doctor's supervision.

The scripts in this section ease the general effects of stress and address two of the most common stress-related health issues: high blood pressure and insomnia. Personalize the scripts to match your situation and utilize the posthypnotic suggestions that best meet your needs. As always, find a relaxing, safe place to practice and start with the induction in Chapter 7.

Reducing Stress

Posthypnotic Suggestions

- I respond to stress with calm and relaxed self-assurance.

- My body and mind are free of stress; I am relaxed, calm, and clear. I am stronger from this experience.

- Stress is a life-enhancing challenge; my mind is sharp and clear, my muscles are relaxed, and I am free of tension.

- Every day, in every way, my subconscious mind supports me. I am stress free.

Now that you've reached the bottom of the steps and are deeply … totally … relaxed … you may notice the beauty of the garden …. See the lovely flowers … pink, purple, blue, and yellow … and notice the warm sun on your head … face … body. You feel your body softening, your muscles releasing tension …. Notice the calm, comfortable glow in your body. As you walk easily, gracefully through the garden, allow any distracting thoughts that come into you mind … to go right out the other side. See your thoughts as birds soaring away on the horizon. You may notice how completely supported you feel … how every part of you is cradled in support … how you feel able to let go even more.

In this relaxed, alert state, you reminisce over the stressful day … or week … or event … you just experienced. In this state, you notice the stressful feelings … your tight muscles, furrowed brow, and anxious eyes … and see clearly how your reaction held you back. In this relaxed state, you see … stress really doesn't matter … because you know … and say to yourself … "I respond to stress with calm and relaxed self-assurance." You watch as your stressful feelings … soar away into the sky.

Suddenly, you remember an upcoming situation … a situation you are not looking forward to … one that makes your muscles tight with strain, your stomach ache with tension. Remembering that you are in control …. See yourself in this situation with a calm mind … relaxed body …. Taking a deep breath, you know and say "My body and mind are free of stress; I am relaxed, calm, and clear. I am stronger from this experience." Now take a moment to visualize yourself successfully meeting this challenge. [Long Pause]

Watch as stress washes away … disappears into the beautiful sky as you know and say … "Stress is a life-enhancing challenge; my mind is sharp and clear, my muscles are relaxed, and I am free of tension."

SUBCONSCIOUS SCAFFOLDING

One stress-busting strategy recommended by psychologists is to remove yourself from the stressful situation, even for a brief period. What better way to take a break than five minutes of instant relaxation followed by a stress-clearing mini-session?

Notice the profound enjoyment you have in life. All the stressful feelings you experienced … are washed away … floating away in the water fountain … as you hear the musical … soothing sounds … of the beautiful flow … washing your old feelings away. The sun warms you … filling your heart … expanding your heart … allowing your heart to glow … with gratitude. Gratitude fills your whole body … with gratitude comes the determination to succeed. You know and say out loud as you take a deep breath and release all tension "Every day, in every way, my subconscious mind supports me. I am stress free."

Take a few minutes to enjoy the garden … and to visualize yourself reacting to stress with ease and grace …. Feel grateful for your ability to rise above the turmoil.

When you're ready … bringing your comfortable support … your calm assuredness … your feelings of gratitude with you, count from one to five. On the count of five, you will be fully awake, fully aware, fully restored.

One, coming up.

Two, becoming more awake, more alert, more aware.

Three, feeling fine … eyes start to flutter.

Four, feeling great … toes start to wiggle.

Five, feeling awake, aware, and fully restored to normal consciousness.

Going forward, know that every time you encounter stress, with nothing more than a deep breath you can shift your reality to accept the presence of stress as life enhancing. Know and say "My body and mind are free of stress; I am relaxed, calm, and clear. I am stronger from this experience."

Lowering Blood Pressure

Posthypnotic Suggestions

- With three deep breaths, my blood pressure drops as I feel calm and tension free.

- Every breath I take lowers my blood pressure. My muscles relax, my emotions calm, and my mind focuses.

Now that you've reached the bottom of the steps and are deeply … totally … relaxed … you may notice the soft … comfortable armchair … that is positioned on the edge of the garden. You may notice your heart leaps at the idea of escaping into this soft, comfortable chair … sinking into its warm support … being totally … held in comfort. As you settle into the cozy … soft cushions … you are aware that you can relax even more. In fact, every time you enter a trance … you discover you can let go of one more tension … one more distraction.

See your tension dissolve … as you melt into the chair … and notice the soft … comfortable glow in your body. Feel the sun on your head, warming your head … face and body. Allow distracting thoughts that come into your mind … to go out right out the other side. See your thoughts as birds, soaring away on the horizon. You may notice how completely supported you feel … how every part of you is cradled in support … how you feel able to let go even more.

 MESMERIZING MORSEL

"The power of love to change bodies is legendary, built into folklore, common sense, and everyday experience. Love moves the flesh, it pushes matter around …. Throughout history, 'tender loving care' has uniformly been recognized as a valuable element in healing."

—Larry Dossey, author

Gazing contentedly around … you might enjoy noticing … the abundant blossoming … of beautiful flowers … attended to by busy bees … droning in the background … droning in your mind … taking you further into relaxation. Next to you is a fountain, and you watch the water sliding down and slipping away.

In this relaxed, alert state, you realize that your body is listening to your thoughts … your body is responding to your emotions. Suddenly, you remember something important that you haven't done … something that makes you jump with concern …. You realize your blood pressure is rising …. You start to feel afraid and then you realize … and see clearly … how this reaction is holding you back. In a relaxed state, you see that you are in control of your reactions …. You are in control of how your thoughts affect you …. You realize you can support your body. You know … and say "With three deep breaths, my blood pressure drops as I feel calm and tension free." You watch as your body responds …. You relax and your blood pressure drops to normal levels. Watch as your blood pressure drops like the mercury in a thermometer.

Now, notice the profound enjoyment you have in life. All the unhappy feelings you have experienced … the fears you hold … are washed away … floating away in the water fountain … as you hear the musical … soothing sounds … of the beautiful flow … washing your old feelings away and lowering your blood pressure. The sun warms you … filling your heart … expanding your heart … allowing your heart to glow … with gratitude. Gratitude fills your whole body … with gratitude comes your determination to succeed. You know and say out loud "Every breath I take lowers my blood pressure. My muscles relax, my emotions calm, and my mind focuses."

Suddenly, as you watch … all the problems that cause your blood pressure to rise … have no effect … and your blood pressure lowers before the power of your subconscious mind. Your blood pressure lowers as you know you are powerfully supported … only relaxed gratitude remains.

Take a few minutes to enjoy the garden … the armchair … and to visualize your new, health-filled life.

When you're ready … no need to get up … taking your comfortable support with you … bringing your feelings of gratitude with you, count from one to five. On the count of five, you will be fully awake, fully aware, fully restored.

One, coming up.

Two, becoming more awake, more alert, more aware.

Three, feeling fine … eyes start to flutter.

Four, feeling great … toes start to wiggle.

Five, feeling awake, aware, and fully restored to normal consciousness.

As you continue your day, you know that every time you feel your blood pressure rise, just by breathing with awareness, your blood pressure lowers. You know and say "Every breath I take lowers my blood pressure. My muscles relax, my emotions calm, and my mind focuses."

Falling Asleep with Ease

Posthypnotic Suggestions

- As easily as thoughts flow into my mind, they flow out the other side, creating a gentle rise and fall that rocks me into easy sleep.

- Whenever my head touches the pillow, my body relaxes, my mind calms, and I fall asleep with ease.

SUBCONSCIOUS SCAFFOLDING

Sleep hygiene is an important element in curing insomnia. This means performing all non-sleep-related activities outside of the bedroom—for example, no TV or computer in bed. Also, eliminate ambient light and make self-hypnosis for insomnia part of your nighttime routine.

Now that you've reached the bottom of the steps and are deeply … totally … relaxed … you may notice the soft … comfortable armchair … that is positioned on the edge of the garden. You may notice your heart leap at the idea of escaping into this soft, comfortable chair … sinking into its warm support … being totally … held in comfort. As you settle into the cozy … soft cushions … you are aware that you can relax even more. In fact, every time you enter a trance … you discover you can let go of one more tension … one more distraction. See your tension dissolve … as you melt into the chair … and notice the soft … comfortable glow in your body. Allow distracting thoughts that come into you mind … to go out right out the other side. See your thoughts as birds, soaring away on the horizon. You may notice how completely supported you feel … how every part of you is cradled in support … how you feel able to let go even more.

Next to you is a fountain, and you watch the water sliding down and slipping away. In this relaxed state, you know and say "As easily as thoughts flow into my mind, they flow out the other side, creating a gentle rise and fall that rocks me into easy sleep."

You notice the profound relaxation you feel as soon as your head touches your pillow. Your thoughts are washed away … floating away in the water fountain … as you hear the musical … soothing sounds … of the beautiful flow … washing your thoughts away. The sun warms you … filling your heart … softening your muscles, quieting your mind. You know and say to yourself "Whenever my head touches the pillow, my body relaxes, my mind calms, and I fall easily asleep."

Allow yourself to know … that whenever you decide to go to sleep … just by using your posthypnotic suggestions, you fall asleep easily … as you enjoy the garden … the armchair … when your head touches the pillow.

When you're ready ... no need to get up ... just go to sleep. But if you need to get up ... when it's time to wake up ... and only when it's time to wake up ... count from one to five. On the count of five, you will be fully awake, fully aware, fully restored.

One, coming up.

Two, becoming more awake, more alert, more aware.

Three, feeling fine ... eyes start to flutter.

Four, feeling great ... toes start to wiggle.

Five, feeling awake, aware, and fully restored to normal consciousness.

Whenever you lie down to go to sleep, feel the garden and sink into the armchair, feeling supported and relaxed. Know and say to yourself "Whenever my heads touches the pillow, my body relaxes, my mind calms, and I fall asleep with ease."

The Least You Need to Know

- In mind-body medicine, your health is affected by your environment, the people around you, your relationships, your emotions, your thoughts, and your beliefs.
- Mind-body medicine focuses on the interaction between the mind and the body; it uses the power of your thoughts and emotions to positively influence your physical health.
- Stress-related health conditions and immune-system imbalances are key areas of focus, as both are highly responsive to changes in thoughts and emotions.
- Research shows that if you perceive stress as harmful to you, it is; if you perceive stress as having life-enhancing properties, it does.
- Prolonged emotional stress is known to increase your risk of heart disease, diabetes, and irritable bowel, to name a few stress-related diseases.
- Self-hypnosis helps you reduce stress and improve all aspects of your health.

Self-Hypnosis and Medical Treatments

Surgery and other medical interventions are routine events for doctors. In fact, doctors often feel so comfortable with these commonplace procedures they forget how much anxiety patients experience. When you're the patient, however, there's nothing commonplace or comfortable about most medical procedures. They can be stressful, painful, financially draining, and scary.

Would you be interested in a technique that puts you in control to increase positive medical outcomes? Self-hypnosis is used to reduce anxiety and pain while improving the body's response to medical interventions, creating more successful outcomes. In short, using self-hypnosis makes an unpleasant procedure manageable.

Currently, self-hypnosis is used more frequently and in more diverse settings than ever before. So the next time you're facing a painful dental procedure, a claustrophobic MRI test, surgery, or any other challenging medical procedure, consider the scripts in this chapter to support you in obtaining exceptional outcomes.

In This Chapter

- Discovering the benefits of self-hypnosis for a positive medical outcomes
- Writing self-hypnosis scripts for surgery, dental interventions, and medical procedures
- Using self-hypnosis to overcome anxiety, reduce pain, and improve healing time

Surgery Preparation and Recovery

Anticipating surgery—no matter how necessary or how improved your life will be as a result—raises concerns and worries. The first worry, naturally, focuses on coming through the surgery safely. After that, you may be concerned about how successful the surgery will be, how much pain you'll be in, and how long it will take before you can return to your normal activities.

HYPNOTIC CONNECTION

Psychologist Guy H. Montgomery, PhD, at Mount Sinai School of Medicine tested the effectiveness of a 15-minute presurgery hypnosis session in a 2007 article published in the *Journal of the National Cancer Institute*. His team found that patients who received hypnosis reported less postsurgical pain, nausea, fatigue, and discomfort. They also required fewer analgesics and sedatives during surgery.

While the success of the surgery depends largely on the skill of your doctor, how your body responds to the intervention and how well your healing mechanisms kick in depends in large part on you. This is where self-hypnosis can give you an edge. The effectiveness of medical self-hypnosis to improve outcomes is well researched; it can help you, your doctor, and your body to establish the most successful results possible.

A quick search of published, peer-reviewed research posted on pubmed.com reveals several hundred studies on positive uses of medical hypnosis. Preoperative use of self-hypnosis is one of the many areas showing pronounced benefit. Self-hypnosis is shown to significantly and consistently reduce the pain, unpleasantness, and discomfort of surgery.

The following are some of many possible benefits:

- Relaxes patients, reduces anxiety, and increases positive expectations
- Decreases stress and shock experienced by the body during surgery
- Can decrease bleeding during surgery
- Improves body response so that time needed for the surgery is reduced
- Decreases amount of anesthesia and sedation needed during surgery
- Reduces side effects of nausea and fatigue
- Implements quicker return of normal body functions, such as appetite, thirst, urination, and defecation
- Reduces pain
- Reduces the amount of pain medication used after surgery

- Speeds recovery time
- Improves healing outcomes

Hypnosis works for many people, and it can work for you. You take control of the part of your experience that no one else can take charge of so you are supported in every way possible.

Self-Hypnosis for Surgery

To prepare for the best possible surgical experience, self-hypnosis for surgery begins well before you go to the hospital. Ideally, you'll want to start your self-hypnosis program the day you book your surgery. Begin with a weekly session using the following script to introduce your subconscious mind to a new way of approaching surgery. In the week before, you might want to use your hypnosis script every day, helping to engrain the program deeply in your subconscious. However, if your surgery is tomorrow and you just learned about self-hypnosis, it's not too late! Start right now by simply reading the script. Envision the elements of the script and imagine yourself in it. Begin as soon as you can; even reading the script only once on the day of surgery can produce positive benefits.

It's normal and natural, as you think about and prepare for surgery, to feel anxious and concerned. When you do, use key 1, instant relaxation, along with one of the posthypnotic affirmations to help you feel calm, relaxed, and in command as the day approaches or at any time: on your way to the hospital, during surgical prep, as you're going under the anesthesia, and as you're coming awake.

 HYPNOTIC CONNECTION

There are many excellent prerecorded CDs for surgery preparation and recovery. I recommend the Ericksonian hypnosis CDs from the Milton H. Erickson Institute at miltonherickson.com.

Be sure the script and posthypnotic suggestions you use reflect your concerns and inner beliefs. There may be images or thoughts in the script that you might not believe or can't use. No problem; just remove and replace them with ideas you believe. There are unlimited posthypnotic suggestions—more than those shown in the script. Choose the ones you like best or use your own and insert them into the script. Remember to always begin your session with the induction in Chapter 7.

You may even find it beneficial to read the script aloud and create a recording, reading it to yourself in second person, like the example script is written, or speaking in the first person if that feels more empowering. If you're comfortable, you can talk with your doctor and medical team about using your tape during the actual surgery. I know a man who took a recorder and headphones into surgery, setting himself up in his own personal world. You might also ask the anesthesiologist to turn on a recorder for you and play the script in the room during surgery.

Whether you've been using the script for a while or only started the day of your surgery, whether you're using a recording or not, take a copy of the script with you to the hospital and read it while you wait. You will be powerfully supporting your body's ability to respond to your surgery.

Successful Surgery with a Speedy Recovery

Posthypnotic Suggestions

- Having surgery is a choice to heal. I am filled with healing energy. I am ready for the best possible outcome on my healing journey.

- I now release all fear. I am calm, confident, and ready for a healthy body, mind, and soul.

- My body knows exactly what to do. My body responds effortlessly to the surgical interventions with perfect blood pressure, lowered pain response, and an excellent outcome.

- No matter what happens, I am safe and protected by a strong spiritual force.

- Every time I hear my breath … in and out … I know I am fine.

- My body, mind, and soul cooperate with my medical team as we work together to create healing.

- I am ready for a positive surgical experience.

- My subconscious mind powerfully supports my healing; my body knows exactly what to do for the best possible outcome.

- I am relaxed, free of anxiety, and ready to heal.

As you step off the last stair … feeling relaxed … calm … and aware … you step into the garden … and are delighted to remember what a pleasure it is to relax. Hearing the birds, seeing the flowers, feeling the warm sun on your head … face … shoulders … and back, spreading relaxation through every part of your body … you enjoy the breeze on your face … and, recognizing the garden, you are excited to anticipate feeling great.

Walking along the garden path … enjoying the brightly colored flowers … you know you are on your way to surgery … and start to feel nervous … start to feel anxious … and then you remember that your body is filled with healing energy. You know that you are ready for surgery …. You are ready to heal …. You know that having surgery is a powerful choice to heal. You know and say "Surgery is my choice to heal. I am filled with healing energy. I am ready for the best possible outcome to my healing journey."

As you walk through the garden … you notice the blue … purple … pink … and yellow flowers …. And ahead, you see a comfortable armchair … your armchair … and you feel calm and relaxed … walking toward the armchair … looking forward to sinking into the comfortable … safe support … of the totally relaxing armchair … that is sitting next to a gentle, rhythmic water fountain.

You settle into the chair … knowing you are having surgery … yet unconcerned because you know … your body is fully cooperating with this surgery … and you know your body knows exactly what to do. Your body knows how much blood pressure is needed, how fast your heart needs to beat … how much medicine you need …. Your body knows exactly how to heal … and has taken on your desire to work with the medical team. You know and say "My body knows exactly what to do. My body responds effortlessly to the surgical interventions with perfect blood pressure, lowered pain response, and an excellent outcome."

As you relax … you hear the sounds of the fountain, the rhythmic movement of the water … and feel totally calm. You are so calm … so relaxed, that quite naturally … quite normally … you invite your spiritual guides to be present with you throughout your surgery. You feel this presence alongside you now … and you enjoy and take comfort in it. You feel calm, relaxed, and peaceful. Your heart is full. You know and say "No matter what happens, I am safe and protected by a strong spiritual force."

 MESMERIZING MORSEL

"The natural healing force within each one of us is the greatest force in getting well."

—Hippocrates, ancient Greek physician

You relax … feeling confident and calm … letting go of fears … letting go of anxieties … drifting deeper and deeper into relaxation … oblivious to anything except the comfort and support of the armchair … and the sounds of the garden. In fact … all the sounds around you disappear … except for the sound of these words … and the birds … and the water fountain … and your breath … in and out … letting you know that everything is fine. And every time … you hear your breath, now … and during surgery, you know … everything is going just fine.

Your body has everything it needs. Your body knows exactly how to work with your medical team …. It responds with the utmost efficiency and healing. Listening to the fountain, hearing the water flowing, hearing the buzz of the bees in the garden, hearing your breath … you feel safe and protected and know you are fine. Listening to your breath … you relax even more … knowing your body is working to produce the best possible outcome, the best possible healing response.

Now, let your mind drift … and as if watching a movie … see your medical team … and your family … getting ready for the procedure … that will bring you better health. Thank everyone for supporting you … and know that everyone is doing all they can to give you the best results possible.

Take a few minutes to see this scene. [Long Pause]

You know that during the surgery … hearing your breath … in and out … you know you are fine … know you are in the best possible hands … know you have the best possible support … and that your body is working perfectly with your medical team. In fact … you know that during your surgery … the anaesthesia is easily absorbed … and so effective you need very little … but just enough … to feel no pain at all. Your body is cooperating so well … very little medicine of any kind is needed … because your body responds so well.

As a result … you are feeling radiantly confident … talking to your body … encouraging your cells …. You know that each part of you is working to make this a successful procedure. Everyone is focused on helping you feel better … and you already do. You are already starting to heal. You know and say "My body, mind, and soul cooperate fully with my medical team as we work together to create healing."

Even now, you know that … the skill of the surgeon and the medical team are so perfect … the surgery is so effortless … your body responds perfectly … that your surgery is over very quickly. It takes no time at all … because all your cells work together … work with the medical team … for a perfect outcome.

Hearing your breath … in and out … you know that everything is fine. You are calm and relaxed … hearing the sounds of the water fountain … the birds … the bees in the garden … and your breath. Your entire body is already healing …. You are doing an excellent job …. Your blood pressure is perfect, your blood flow is perfect, your whole body is working together for the best possible outcome.

So much so … that when the surgery is over … when you are fully conscious … you notice how relaxed and comfortable you feel. As you recover … so effortlessly … you stop and take a minute to feel your body … to thank your body … to thank the spiritual presence that stayed with you … to thank your medical team … and to thank yourself for being positive and choosing to heal.

 HYPNOTIC CONNECTION

According to the website of alternative health guru Deepak Chopra (chopra.com), many scientific studies have found that people who consciously focus on gratitude experience greater emotional well-being and physical health than those who don't. So be sure to end your self-hypnosis sessions with gratitude.

After surgery, you are amazed at how well you feel. You are surprised at how normal you feel …. You easily and effortlessly drink water … easily and effortlessly eat. All your systems work fine. You feel wonderful …. You are already healing quickly and easily. All of your cells are in agreement and your body knows exactly what to do.

Even as you count upward from one to five, coming fully awake … fully aware … you are proud of your choice to heal.

One, coming up.

Two, becoming more awake, more alert, more aware.

Three, feeling fine … eyes start to flutter.

Four, feeling great … toes start to wiggle.

Five, feeling awake, aware, and fully restored to normal consciousness.

As your surgery approaches, anytime you feel anxious, first take a minute to see if your anxiety is trying to tell you something important, like you forgot to attend to a detail or something else you need to take care of. You can then use instant relaxation and know and say "I am ready for a positive surgical experience. My subconscious mind powerfully supports my healing. My body knows exactly what to do for the best possible outcome. I am relaxed, free of anxiety, and ready to heal."

Getting Through Medical Procedures

What? Did you say you can't wait to go in for an MRI? Are you deliriously happy to have a root canal? Not likely! In fact, if you're like many people, you may have an absolute phobia about medical procedures and have put off important tests and treatments long past safety. Actually, as challenging as many procedures are, they're made substantially worse by the degree of your resistance. Resistance tightens your muscles, elevates your blood pressure, and increases your pain sensitivity.

Fortunately, there's a way out. You may not be able to change your need for an MRI, an uncomfortable gynecological exam, or a difficult dental procedure; however, you can change your reaction and lessen your discomfort. You can undergo the procedure while in charge of yourself, lowering your sensitivity to pain and improving your outcomes. As with surgery, your body listens to the messages that you provide.

Because you're choosing to have the procedure and choosing to heal, choose also to make it as pain free and comfortable as possible. The next two scripts take you into your power spot developed in Chapter 8 as you vacation in the dentist's chair or take a relaxing break during medical procedures. Adjust the script and suggestions to best fit you and, as always, begin with the induction in Chapter 7.

It is great if you can use the hypnotic script several times before undergoing your procedure. When you arrive at the medical facility, visualize yourself confident, calm, and relaxed. Use instant relaxation along with the posthypnotic suggestions to relieve anxiety and reduce pain. Bring the script with you and read it to yourself, visualizing your inner sanctuary and enjoying a time-out during your procedure.

Vacationing in the Dentist's Chair

Posthypnotic Suggestions

- I release all fears now. I am calm, confident, and ready for a healthy body, mind, and soul.

- Every sound of the dentist's drill and equipment deeply relaxes me … deeply calms me … and takes me farther into my inner sanctuary.

- I let go of anxiety and feel happy pursuing dental appointments and choosing healthy teeth. I know that healthy teeth are important to a healthy body.

As you step off the last stair … feeling relaxed and calm … deeply relaxed … deeply calm … you walk into the garden … feeling the sun warm on your face … your shoulders … your chest … melting your muscles … allowing you to relax even further. You listen to the birds … the buzzing bees … feeling the wind across your face. As you walk … you look ahead and see your favorite armchair … your very comfortable armchair … on the top of a hill overlooking a gently rolling valley. Feeling excited … anticipating something wonderful … you walk toward the armchair … looking forward to relaxing even further … feeling calm and relaxed.

 HYPNOTIC CONNECTION

If you're interested in pursuing more audio tools, try healing mogul Andrew Weil's CD set titled *Heal Yourself with Medical Hypnosis.* Weil acknowledges that hypnosis is a legitimate tool for easing pain and anxiety while maximizing the effect of medical treatments.

As you approach your favorite armchair … you see it is now a dentist's chair … a comfortable dental chair … that looks like a comfortable recliner. At first you feel nervous, then you remember that you are relaxed and comfortable … releasing all fear of dental procedures … releasing all old experiences. Knowing that you want healthy teeth … want a good smile … and want to keep all your teeth … pain free … into your old age. Knowing that you are in control … knowing your body knows exactly how to respond … you walk toward the dental chair with confidence. You let go of all fear … all anxiety.

Settling into the chair … you look over the beautiful valley, full of brightly colored flowers and trees … and listen to the birds … hear the bees and know and say "I release all fear now. I am calm, confident, and ready for a healthy body, mind, and soul."

Deep calm overcomes you …. Deep relaxation softens every muscle. You are calm … and totally cooperative. Suddenly, you understand … your body can take care of everything … and you can retreat to your inner power spot … retreat to your internal sanctuary … and enjoy using this time to create something wonderful.

Now, sitting in the chair … opening your mouth wide for the dentist … you know your body can respond to every need … and you are free to go to your inner sanctuary … to retreat to a place where there is no pain … where you can release all fear. You know and say "Every sound of the dentist's drill and other equipment deeply relaxes me … deeply calms me … and takes me farther into my inner sanctuary."

Now, from within your inner power spot … you enjoy working on a creative project … or imagining a happy time. You may even imagine the entire dental experience if you desire … with ease and comfort …. See yourself making the appointment with confidence and ease … arriving at the dentist, anticipating healthy teeth … sitting in the chair feeling calm and relaxed … leaving the dentist's office with a happy smile and jaunty gait. You take a minute to envision this whole sequence. Every sound takes you deeper into a relaxed, happy calm. You know your body knows exactly what to do and you can take time out. You can relax in your power spot and enjoy taking a vacation.

It is good to be healthy. Know and say "I let go of anxiety and feel happy pursuing dental appointments and obtaining healthy teeth. I know that healthy teeth are important to a healthy body."

Even as you count upward from one to five, coming fully awake … fully aware … you are proud of your choice to heal.

One, coming up.

Two, becoming more awake, more alert, more aware.

Three, feeling fine … eyes start to flutter.

Four, feeling great … toes start to wiggle.

Five, feeling awake, aware, and fully restored to normal consciousness.

Now, as your dental visit approaches, you can always instill relaxed confidence by using instant relaxation and knowing and saying "I release all fear now. I am calm, confident, and ready for a healthy body, mind, and soul."

Tolerating MRIs and Medical Procedures

Posthypnotic Suggestions

- I release all fear now. I am calm, confident, and ready for a healthy body, mind, and soul.

- Every sound of the medical equipment deeply relaxes me ... deeply calms me ... and takes me farther into my inner sanctuary.

- I let go of anxiety and feel happy pursuing health.

 SUBCONSCIOUS SCAFFOLDING

Be sure to personalize this script with imagery and suggestions that match the procedure you will be undergoing. Take your biggest fear and create an image of what would make you feel safe. For example, if you're claustrophobic in the machine used to do an MRI scan, create space around yourself.

As you step off the last stair ... feeling relaxed and calm ... deeply relaxed ... deeply calm ... you walk into the garden ... feeling the sun ... warming your face ... your shoulders ... your chest ... melting your muscles ... allowing you to relax even further. You listen to the birds ... the buzzing bees .... feeling the wind across your face ... letting go of every concern ... letting go of everything except how completely relaxed you feel. As you walk ... you look ahead and see your favorite armchair ... your very comfortable armchair ... on the top of a hill overlooking a gently rolling valley. Feeling excited ... anticipating something wonderful ... you walk toward the armchair ... looking forward to relaxing even further ... feeling calm and relaxed.

As you approach your favorite armchair ... you see it is now a medical exam table ... a very comfortable exam table ... that looks like a reclining armchair. At first you feel nervous, then you remember that you are relaxed and comfortable ... releasing all fear of this procedure ... releasing all old experiences. Knowing that you want to be healthy ... want your body to be strong and vital ... and want to keep all your health ... into your old age.

Praise yourself for choosing to have this procedure ... for choosing health. Applaud your body's ability to cooperate fully with your medical team. Knowing that you are in control ... knowing your body knows exactly how to respond, you approach the exam table with confidence ... letting go of all fear ... all anxiety ... feeling deeply relaxed ... and calm. You approach the exam table with confidence, ease, and pride.

Settling onto the table ... you look over the beautiful valley, full of brightly colored flowers and trees ... and listen to the birds ... hear the bees and know and say "I release all fear now. I am calm, confident, and ready for a healthy body, mind, and soul."

Deep calm overcomes you ... deep relaxation softens every muscle. You are calm ... and totally cooperative. Suddenly you understand ... your body can take care of everything ... and you can retreat to your inner power spot ... retreat to your internal sanctuary ... and enjoy using this time to create something wonderful.

Now, comfortably positioned on the exam table ... allowing complete cooperation with the medical team ... you know your body can respond to every need ... and you are free to go to your inner sanctuary ... to retreat to a place where there is no pain ... where you can release all fear. You know and say "Every sound of the medical equipment deeply relaxes me ... deeply calms me ... and takes me farther into my inner sanctuary."

Now, from within your inner power spot ... imagine the entire experience ... making the appointment with confidence and ease ... arriving at the medical facility anticipating health ... going through the procedure ... knowing ... you have all the space you need. No matter how small or tight the machine and equipment are ... you have enough space all around you ... all the space you need ... feeling your skin ... feeling the air on your skin ... lying on the exam table feeling calm and relaxed ... you have everything you need. Every sound takes you deeper into a relaxed, happy calm. It is good to be healthy.

Now, from within your inner power spot ... you can enjoy working on a creative project ... or imagining a happy time. If you want, you can even imagine the entire medical experience ... with ease and comfort ... seeing yourself making the appointment with confidence and ease ... arriving at the facility anticipating health ... lying on the exam table feeling calm and relaxed ... leaving the dentist's office with a happy smile and jaunty gait. Take a minute to vision this whole sequence. Every sound takes you deeper into a relaxed, happy calm. You know your body knows exactly what to do and you can take time out. You can relax in your power spot and enjoy going on an adventure.

It is good to be healthy. Know and say "I let go of anxiety and feel happy pursuing health."

Now imagine it is over and you are leaving the medical facility ... you have a happy smile and jaunty gait. You feel proud and happy and free. You know you have supported your health.

Even as you count upward from one to five, coming fully awake ... fully aware ... you are proud of your choice to heal.

 WISE COUNSEL

Emotions always carry a message. Using hypnosis to submerge uncomfortable emotions won't work. Eventually, you will need to explore where the emotion comes from and what it is communicating.

One, coming up.

Two, becoming more awake, more alert, more aware.

Three, feeling fine ... eyes start to flutter.

Four, feeling great ... toes start to wiggle.

Five, feeling awake, aware, and fully restored to normal consciousness.

Now, as your medical procedure approaches, you can always instill relaxed confidence by using instant relaxation and knowing and saying "I release all fear now. I am calm, confident, and ready for a healthy body, mind, and soul."

The Least You Need to Know

- Patients who receive hypnosis report less postsurgical pain, nausea, fatigue, and discomfort, plus they require fewer analgesics and sedatives during surgery.
- Self-hypnosis puts you in control of parts of your experience that no one else can take charge of.
- Your body knows exactly what to do to heal, and with support from your subconscious, you can improve your healing results.
- You can use the self-hypnosis scripts to be free of anxiety and fear in surgery, dental procedures, MRIs, and any other medical procedure.

Healing with Your Subconscious Mind

Healing the cause of pain and illness is a concern for many people, and there are a considerable number of health-promoting modalities to use, with self-hypnosis at the fore-front. One of the many benefits of self-hypnosis is that it increases the effectiveness of any treatment you're using, as it supports your body's healing mechanisms. Self-hypnosis decreases pain and other symptoms while improving your body's healing ability.

Health is the most important factor in your happiness, and you deserve to give yourself your own best effort. Your sub-conscious mind is a powerful healing force that you can activate on your behalf anytime, anywhere. While self-hypnosis does not replace medical treatment, it does support the best outcome in your treatment plan, as you'll see in this chapter.

In This Chapter

- Understanding the message of acute and chronic pain
- Using the power of focused attention to reduce pain
- Finding the message in your pain
- Discovering the hidden gift in your illness
- Using self-hypnosis to improve health, reduce fatigue, and speed healing

Controlling Pain

Would you be surprised to learn that pain affects more people than diabetes, heart disease, and cancer combined? The most common area for pain is the lower back, followed by headaches, neck pain, and face pain. In fact, pain is so persistent that an estimated $635 billion is spent each year for medical treatment and lost productivity. If you have pain, what's more interesting than statistics is what you can do to become pain free.

Happily, your perception and experience of pain can be influenced by your subconscious mind. In some cases, using the power of your attention to ease pain can produce immediate and profound results. In other cases, you may need to interact with your pain and understand its function and message. It may be difficult to accept pain has purpose, but it does; it alters your behavior in order to avoid danger.

HYPNOTIC CONNECTION

The power of the mind to impact the body is well known in medicine. It's called the *placebo effect*. Research into new medicines attempts to factor out the placebo effect in drug trials by having a control group in every study. The control group does not receive the medication being tested, but takes an indistinguishable sugar pill. People in the study don't know whether they're receiving the sugar pill placebo or the actual drug. A surprising number of people receiving the placebo have significant improvements in symptoms simply because they believe the drug is working. Imagine harnessing the power of the mind to help your body feel better!

The function of acute pain is obvious—it's a warning and the message is easy to understand: "*Stop,* that burner is hot—remove your hand immediately!" Acute pain is an alert that damage to your body is occurring. Pain continues during healing to remind you that you're injured. You won't accidently grab something with your burned hand when throbbing pain alerts you to its vulnerable state.

Chronic pain is different from acute pain. Healing processes appear stalled because chronic pain lasts long after an injury is healed. Often, chronic pain can't be traced to an original source; other times, it might arise from an unhealed injury, fibromyalgia, overwork, metabolic imbalance, or a degenerative disease, such as arthritis. There seems no function or message to chronic pain, but what if there were? Chronic pain might be alerting you to a larger danger, trying to adjust your behavior in regard to larger imbalances, such as poor lifestyle choices, hidden medical problems, or unresolved emotional trauma reflected in your body. Understanding the message may be the key to eliminating the pain.

It you have pain from migraines, back trouble, IBS, fibromyalgia, chemotherapy treatment, or from any other source, the scripts that follow can help. They allow you to take control and reduce your perception of pain. The most challenging aspect to using these scripts is making the decision to do it and being committed to following through. Don't cave at the first upsurge of pain—stay with the techniques and commit to giving your body every chance to succeed.

Personalize the scripts and posthypnotic suggestions and be sure to start with the induction in Chapter 7 or use instant relaxation before you begin.

Focusing and Following Pain Reduction

 Track 6

Posthypnotic Suggestions

- Pain does not control me; my subconscious mind powerfully supports me in eliminating pain.

- Every day, in every way, I am better and better. I live with more grace, more ease, and more freedom from pain.

- I turn off pain sensors and choose to feel comfortable sensations.

Now that you've descended the stairs and entered the garden ... you can use this relaxed, alert state of mind to powerfully support change. As you step off the last step, imagine sinking into the soft, grassy soil ... and notice the deep peace and total contentment that sweeps through you. Taking a deep breath ... filling your lungs with clear, fresh air ... you walk along the garden path. As you walk past lovely flowers of pink, yellow, purple, blue ... your whole being fills with peace and freedom.

Moving into the warmth of the sun, feeling the warmth spread over your face ... your throat ... your shoulders ... warmth moving through your whole body ... allowing your muscles to relax even further. You know and say "Pain does not control me. My subconscious mind powerfully supports me in eliminating pain."

 SUBCONSCIOUS SCAFFOLDING

The focusing and following pain reduction script is a classic self-hypnosis approach to pain that is excellent for acute and chronic issues. Use the entire script the first time, and then modify it for fast pain relief by using key 1, instant relaxation, before focusing on and following your pain as described in the script. You will be amazed at how effective just two minutes of this technique can be!

Wandering along the lovely garden path … nowhere to rush to … nowhere you need to be … you look at the beautiful flowers, noticing how they open to the sun … and becoming aware of an opening within yourself … to an inner light that fills you. Looking ahead, you feel a surge of relief as you see your personal sacred space … your inner power spot. Stopping at the entrance, you pause in acknowledgment … and stepping inside … take a minute to absorb the ambience … to honor the objects and the setting that are special to you.

Settling into the seat that is made just for you … getting comfortable … relaxing even further … allowing your body to fill with energy … you turn your attention to what is bothering you … turn your full attention to the pain in your body. You know that your attention is a powerful, pain-breaking tool … you know that when you resist pain, it becomes even more influential … dictating what you can and can't do … deciding your life. Using your attention … you are taking control of your life … taking control away from pain.

Focus your full attention on your area of pain. Send your attention like a laser beam directly into your pain. Find the very center of it … and focus all of your awareness on that spot … penetrating like a laser to the very deepest part of it. Now relax all of the muscles that surround your pain …. Soften the tissue that your pain lives within. Instead of surrounding your pain with tension … isolate it in a sea of relaxation. Let it float … within a sea of no resistance …. Allow your pain to float outside of gravity. With nothing to hold on to … notice how small your pain becomes … even disappearing … or perhaps moving to a new location.

Follow the pain to wherever it moves … and send your laserlike attention fully into the center of the new pain. Relax the muscles …. Relax the tissue … that surrounds you. Allow the pain to float freely … no attachments … within the center of relaxation. You feel safe, uplifted, and proud. You believe and say "Every day, in every way, I am better and better. I live with more grace, more ease, and more freedom from pain."

Noticing that your pain has changed…. shift your perspective … and take your attention to a part of your body that has no pain … that is always pain free. Maybe it's your nose … your earlobe … or the side of your toe. No matter how small this place is … take your full attention to this spot. Feel its healthy vitality … feel the absolute freedom from painful sensation … and let this feeling grow. Breathe into this area … and with your breath … let the feeling in this area get as big as it can …. Let this feeling get so big … that it is all you notice.

Suddenly you realize … when you feel pain … you can focus on the pain and turn off the pain sensors …. And you can focus on comfortable areas … can choose to feel comfortable sensations … or nothing at all. You know and say "I turn off pain sensors and choose to feel comfortable sensations."

Feeling proud, feeling happy … feeling in control … give thanks to the garden … give thanks to your sacred space … and step outside … walking back through the garden … heading toward the stairs … knowing you can always return. Reaching the stairs … you take a deep breath and start up. On the count of five, you are awake, alert, happy, and pain free.

 MESMERIZING MORSEL

"Pain comes in many forms; all of which are painful, all of which are controllable."

—Cathal O'Brian, hypnotherapist and author

One, coming up.

Two, becoming more awake, more alert, more aware.

Three, feeling fine … eyes start to flutter.

Four, feeling great … toes start to wiggle.

Five, feeling awake, aware, and fully restored to normal consciousness.

As you go forward, every time you feel pain, focus your awareness and follow it as you know and say "I turn off pain sensors and choose to feel comfortable sensations." Allow pain-free areas to grow larger and larger.

Conversing with Pain

Posthypnotic Suggestions

- Pain does not control me. My subconscious mind powerfully supports me in understanding the message of my pain.

- I listen to and heed the signals from my body, acting on them before the signals turn into pain.

- I choose to focus on and feel comfortable sensations.

- I choose to listen to my pain and understand what I need to learn and grow.

As you step off the last step and sink into the soft, grassy soil … you notice the deep peace and total contentment that sweeps through you. Taking a deep breath … filling your lungs with clear, fresh air … you walk along the garden path. As you walk past lovely flowers of pink, yellow, purple, blue … your whole being fills with peace and freedom.

Moving into the warmth of the sun, feeling the warmth spread over your face … your throat … your chest … warmth moving through your whole body … your muscles relax even further and you smile … recognizing the garden and anticipating relief. You know and say "Pain does not control me. My subconscious mind powerfully supports me in understanding the message of my pain."

Wandering along the lovely garden path … nowhere to rush to … nowhere you need to be … you look at the beautiful flowers, seeing how they open to the sun … and notice an opening within yourself … to an inner light that fills you. Looking ahead, you feel a surge of relief as you see the opening to your personal sacred space … your inner power spot. Stopping at the entrance, you pause in acknowledgment … and stepping inside … take a minute to absorb the ambience … to enjoy the objects that are special to you.

Settling into the seat that is made for just for you … getting comfortable … relaxing even further … feeling the energy of your power spot filling your body … you turn your attention to what is bothering you …. You turn your full attention to the pain in your body. You know that your attention is a powerful tool of awareness … and when you resist pain … the pain becomes even more influential … dictating what you can and can't do … deciding your life.

Suddenly, you have a new thought. You realize … that the pain doesn't enjoy hurting you. The pain doesn't enjoy its job. You know that the pain is telling you something … that it has a message from your body … and also … you know that your pain needs something from you … in order to leave. You know and say "I listen to and heed the signals from my body, acting on them before the signals turn into pain."

SUBCONSCIOUS SCAFFOLDING

Versions of the conversing with pain script are part of most body awareness pain techniques. It is incredibly revealing and can be used with any type of pain; however, it has greatest application with chronic or recurring pain.

Now … you find you really want to know … and understand … your pain. So focusing your full attention on your pain … you begin to explore it with the language of imagery. Seeing your pain as separate from you … letting images flow freely into your mind … allowing answers to arrive quickly without thought … arriving as images … or words … or simply a sense of knowing. You ask:

Does your pain have a shape? Take a moment to define the shape. [Long Pause]

Does it have a color? Take a moment to see the color. [Long Pause] What is the texture of your pain? Take a few seconds to feel the texture. [Long Pause]

Does your pain have motion? Take a few seconds to observe the motion. [Long Pause]

And if your pain were alive … what type of life form would it be? Take a moment to observe the life form.

Now that your pain is separate from you and alive, ask it:

What is its function? Take a moment to listen. [Long Pause]

What message does it have for you? [Long Pause]

What does it need from you? [Long Pause]

Now ask your pain … what you can shift to make it happier and reduce your discomfort. Does it want to be larger, smaller, a different color, a different shape?

Knowing what your pain needs … make the changes … use your attention … go into the center of the pain … and change it … to what it wants to be. Make the color exactly what your pain wants … change the texture … shift the shape. And if you don't know … if you're unsure … just make changes … and notice when your pain feels less intense … and more comfortable.

As you make changes ... as you connect with and understand your pain ... as you meet your pain with compassion ... ask it what else you can do to ease its burden. Take a few moments and listen. [Long Pause] If you need to, write it down.

Now ... noticing that your pain has changed ... thank it for talking with you ... and appreciate yourself ... for taking this first step in listening to your body.

It might be nice ... before leaving your power spot ... to focus your attention on a part of your body that has no pain ... that always feels pain free. Maybe it's your nose ... your earlobe ... or the side of your toe. No matter how small this place is ... take your full attention to this spot. Feel the healthy vitality ... feel the absolute freedom from sensation ... and let this grow. Let this feeling absorb more and more of your attention ... let this feeling get so big that it is all you can notice. Let your body enjoy the wonderful sensations of comfort.

Suddenly you realize ... your body wants to be pain free ... and using your attention ... you can help ... you can choose to focus on comfort ... choose to feel comfortable sensations ... or to feel nothing at all. You know and say "I choose to focus on and feel comfortable sensations."

 WISE COUNSEL

Pain can be an indicator of serious physical problems. While self-hypnosis is an excellent adjunct treatment, be sure you have adequately checked out the physical causes of your pain.

Feeling proud, feeling happy ... feeling in control ... you give thanks to the garden ... your sacred space ... and you step outside ... giving thanks ... walking back through the garden ... heading toward the stairs ... knowing you can always return. Reaching the stairs ... you take a deep breath and start up. On the count of five, you are awake, alert, happy, and pain free. Life is good.

One, coming up.

Two, becoming more awake, more alert, more aware.

Three, feeling fine ... eyes start to flutter.

Four, feeling great ... toes start to wiggle.

Five, feeling awake, aware, and fully restored to normal consciousness.

As you go forward, every time you feel pain, you know and say "I choose to listen to my pain and understand what I need in order to learn and grow."

Overcoming Illness and Injury

Your body has powerful healing mechanisms that counter illness and heal injuries. Chapter 13 revealed the power of the mind to strengthen your immune system, and the strengthening immunity script in Chapter 13 is a great place to start your self-hypnosis healing program.

Like pain, injury and illness can be acute or chronic. Sometimes chronic and/or potentially terminal illnesses and injuries provide a unique opportunity for growth and learning. Many people with cancer reveal that in coming to terms with the disease, they experienced profound shifts in perspective. Often, the change in perspective allowed healing of relationships and old emotional wounds. Chronic illnesses, such as irritable bowel syndrome (IBS), fibromyalgia, and chronic fatigue, are also often helped through an understanding of underlying emotional and mental factors.

 HYPNOTIC CONNECTION

While you might not say that illnesses happen for a reason, you can say that you choose to use the power of an illness for growth. If this is an interesting concept, you might want to check out Louise Hay's book, *You Can Heal Your Life*.

The first healing script, finding the opportunity within illness, can be used to dialogue with the subconscious mind to hear the message within your illness or injury. It can be used to understand cancer, degenerative diseases, and any chronic illness. The second script, re-energizing to overcome fatigue, helps overcome exhaustion, a common complaint with all debilitating illnesses and especially chronic fatigue syndrome. The third script, super healing injuries and illness, helps boost your healing response and is great for acute and chronic illnesses and injuries. As always, personalize your scripts and always begin with the induction in Chapter 7.

Finding the Opportunity Within Illness

Posthypnotic Suggestions

- My illness does not define me. My subconscious mind powerfully supports my value, path, and purpose.

- I enjoy every moment of life. I give and receive love.

- I listen to and heed the signals from my body and powerfully support my immune system in doing exactly what needs to be done in order to heal.

- I am alive within waves of joy and choose to focus my thoughts and attention on life.

As you step off the last stair and sink into the soft, grassy soil … you notice the deep peace and total contentment that sweeps through you. Taking a deep breath … filling your lungs with clear, fresh air … you walk along the garden path … feeling vital and alive. As you walk past lovely flowers of pink, yellow, purple, blue … your whole being fills with peace and freedom.

Moving into the warmth of the sun, feeling the warmth spread over your face … your throat … your chest … warmth moving through your whole body … your muscles relax even further and you smile … recognizing the garden and anticipating enjoyment. You realize how nice it is to be accepted as you are …. You realize how hard it is that people now see you as a disease … as a certain type of patient … or a set of symptoms. It is nice to be here … to be seen as yourself. You know and say "My illness does not define me. My subconscious mind powerfully supports my value, path, and purpose."

Wandering along the lovely garden path … no need to rush … nowhere you need to be … listening to the calling of birds … the sound of the breeze through the trees … feeling the breeze on your skin … you look at the beautiful flowers, seeing how they open to the sun … and notice an opening within yourself … to an inner light that fills you. You know and say "I enjoy every moment of life. I give and receive love."

Looking ahead, you feel a surge of joy as you see the opening to your personal sacred space … your inner power spot. Stopping at the entrance, you pause in acknowledgment … and stepping inside … take a minute to absorb the ambience … to enjoy the objects that are special to you.

Settling into the seat that is made for just for you … getting comfortable … relaxing even further … you turn your attention to what is bothering you … turn your full attention to the illness in your body.

SUBCONSCIOUS SCAFFOLDING

This script of finding the opportunity within illness is incredibly revealing and can be used with any type of illness, injury, and chronic pain. It can be adapted for cancer or any degenerative disease.

Suddenly you see your illness, injury, or pain in a new light …. You understand that it isn't sent to punish you … realize … that your body is supporting you as best it can. Even as angry as you are … as grief filled as you are … as much as you don't want this condition … you know that it represents an opportunity to learn something new … to change something in your life … something that you never could have understood before. You realize that by learning what you can … you are strengthening your immune system … helping it do exactly what is needed for healing.

You know and say "I listen to and heed the signals from my body and powerfully support my immune system in doing exactly what needs to be done to heal."

Now … you find that you are really curious … really want to know … and understand … what this condition can teach. Focusing your full attention on your symptoms … you begin to explore your condition with the language of imagery.

Sitting in your special chair in your power spot … you pull up another chair … bringing it opposite you. It's a very comfortable chair and you invite your illness, injury, or pain to sit in it … to sit and have a conversation with you. Imagine it now … your condition sitting in this chair …. What does it look like? Is it old or young? Big or small? Does it seem comfortable sitting in the chair?

Because you're very angry at having this condition … because you feel a lot of grief over the many things … and people … it has separated you from, you start the conversation by telling it exactly how you feel. Take a moment and tell the image in the chair opposite you everything … what you've given up … how it interferes with enjoying your life … how it has taken over every decision … how it hurts your relationships …. Take a moment and tell it everything about how you feel. [Long Pause]

Are you finished? Tell it a little bit more. And when you're done … look again …. Is there anything lying underneath what you've already said? And is there anything deeper than that?

Now that everything has been said … now that there is nothing more … nothing you need to say … seeing your illness, injury, or pain as separate from you … letting images flow freely into your mind … allowing answers to arrive quickly without thought … arriving as images … or words … or simply a sense of knowing … sit back and listen.

What does your illness have to say? What does it need you to know? Take as long as you need and write things down if you want.

Now … noticing that your time is coming to an end … thank your illness for talking with you … and appreciate yourself … for taking this first step in using your illness to grow and learn.

It might be nice … before leaving your power spot … to focus your attention on a part of your life that brings you joy. Take your full attention to the people … places … animals … activities that bring you joy. Feel the energy of joy spreading through your body … vitalizing every cell. Feel the power of gratitude lifting your heart higher …. Feel healthy vitality … absolute freedom … and let this feeling grow. Let this feeling absorb more and more of your attention …. Let this feeling get so big that it is all you can notice. Let your body enjoy the wonderful sensations of joy, gratitude, love, and comfort.

Suddenly you realize … that your body wants to enjoy being alive … and using your attention … you can help. You can choose to focus on life … choose to be in this moment. You know and say "I am alive within waves of joy and choose to focus my thoughts and attention on life."

 MESMERIZING MORSEL

"Find a place inside where there's joy, and the joy will burn out the pain."

—Joseph Campbell, philosopher and author

Feeling proud, feeling happy … feeling in control … you give thanks to the garden … your sacred space … and you step outside … walking back through the garden … heading toward the stairs … knowing you can always return. Reaching the stairs … you take a deep breath and start up. On the count of five, you are awake, alert, happy, and pain free. Life is good.

One, coming up.

Two, becoming more awake, more alert, more aware.

Three, feeling fine … eyes start to flutter.

Four, feeling great … toes start to wiggle.

Five, feeling awake, aware, and fully restored to normal consciousness.

As you go forward, whenever you feel you are lost in your illness, you know and say "I am alive within waves of joy and choose to focus my thoughts and attention on life."

Re-Energizing to Overcome Fatigue

Posthypnotic Suggestions

- I am alive with energy, radiating vitality and life force.

- My every cell is rejuvenated with vitality and alive with life force.

- I am alive with energy. I have enough energy to do everything I want to do.

- I perfectly maintain the balance between giving and receiving, sharing energy as and when it is best for everyone.

As you step off the last stair and sink into the soft, grassy soil … you notice the deep peace and total contentment that sweeps through you. Taking a deep breath, filling your lungs with clear, fresh air, you walk along the garden path. As you walk … your whole being fills with peace and freedom. Moving into the warmth of the sun, feeling the warmth spread over your face … your throat … your chest … warmth moving through your whole body … you smile, recognizing the garden and anticipating enjoyment.

Wandering along the lovely garden path … nowhere to rush to … nowhere you need to be … you look at the beautiful flowers, seeing how they open to the sun … and notice an opening within yourself … to an inner light that fills you. You feel safe, uplifted, and alive. You notice you are standing taller … and expanding. You feel the sparkle in your eye and notice a lift in your step. You believe and say "I am alive with energy, radiating vitality and life force."

WISE COUNSEL

Fatigue is a primary symptom in many serious medical conditions. Be sure your medical issues are being addressed as you support your energy levels with self-hypnosis.

Walking among the flowers … breathing in … breathing out … with each breath, your body is filled with life force. Inhale vitality … energy … light. Exhale tension … fatigue … despair. In your mind's eye, see your breath reaching every cell …. See every cell expanding with energy … filling with light … shimmering with luminosity.

Feel your personal space expand … as your energy grows. Feel your boundaries expand … as you fill with energy and life force.

Take a moment to see yourself … as a being full of unlimited potential. See yourself as the best that you are. Know and say "My every cell is rejuvenated with vitality and alive with life force."

Imagine yourself with enough energy to walk down the street … your gait bouncing … head held high … having enough energy to greet people you know and like. Notice the expression on their faces as they feel your energy … feel your happiness … and are pleased for you. Notice how good it feels to have enough energy to do all the things you love to do … to have enough energy to complete your work … enough energy to enjoy your life. Caring about others … wanting to share your energy … you know and say "I perfectly maintain the balance between giving and receiving, sharing energy as and when it is best for everyone."

Taking this wonderful, energized feeling with you … head back through the garden … toward the stairs. Feeling energized, feeling happy … feeling alive … give thanks to the garden … to yourself and to a higher power. Continue walking back through the garden … heading toward the stairs … knowing you can always return.

Reaching the stairs … you take a deep breath and start up. On the count of five, you are awake, alert, and happy. Life is good.

One, coming up.

Two, becoming more awake, more alert, more aware.

Three, feeling fine … eyes start to flutter.

Four, feeling great … toes start to wiggle.

Five, feeling awake, aware, and fully restored to normal consciousness.

As you go forward creating your life, stand tall and relaxed and say "I am alive with energy. I have enough energy to do everything I want to do."

Super Healing Injuries and Illness

Posthypnotic Suggestions

- My body restores and regenerates damaged tissue, replacing compromised cells with healthy cells.

- My body knows exactly what to do and has everything it needs to heal quickly, effectively, and completely.

- My subconscious mind powerfully supports my body in healing every injury and illness quickly and completely.

- Nothing stands in the way of my powerful and complete healing.

Now that you've reached the bottom of the steps and are deeply … totally … relaxed … you walk among the lovely flowers … hearing the calling of the birds … feeling the soft breeze across your skin … feeling the warmth of the sun along your face … your shoulders … your back … softening your muscles as you become even more relaxed … more alert and aware.

In fact, every time you enter a trance … you discover you can let go of one more tension … one more distraction. See and feel your tension dissolve … as you notice how completely supported you feel … how you are able to let go even more.

As you walk through the garden … listening to the sounds … feeling the breeze … you notice how strong and full of energy you are. In fact, you feel your energy expand … as you fill with a warm glow.

Ahead, you see the entrance to your sacred power spot. Your energy quickens … as you realize … this is the perfect place to heal. Moving inside, you take a moment to absorb the ambience … enjoy the sacred objects … and appreciate the opportunity to heal.

Feeling safe … relaxed … and very calm … suddenly you are excited to explore your healing power. Sitting in the comfortable chair designed especially for you … you recline and relax. Allowing your body to fill with the power of this spot … knowing your attention is a powerful tool for healing … you close your eyes … and bring your attention into your injury or illness.

Focusing your attention … using it like a powerful laser … you sweep the laser beam across the area of your injury or illness … penetrating every cell … using the laser light to repair damaged tissue … increase nutrients … eliminating waste. You know and say "My body restores and regenerates damaged tissue, replacing compromised cells with healthy cells."

Using your attention like a healing laser … you stimulate your immune cells … trusting your body to do exactly what is needed … exactly when it's needed. You know and say "My body knows exactly what to do and has everything it needs to heal quickly, effectively, and completely."

It is exciting to see how your immune cells know exactly what to do …. It feels safe to know that no matter what … your immune cells are guided by the wisdom of your body. Feeling safe and protected … you know and say "My subconscious mind powerfully supports my body in healing every injury and illness quickly and completely."

Now … you notice … the profound enjoyment you feel in having a healthy body. You feel your body glow with health …. As your injured cells are restored … you feel the strength of your muscles, your bones, your lungs, your heart, your digestion … and your whole body. Strength flows through you and you take a deep breath, knowing and saying "Nothing stands in the way of my powerful and complete healing."

Take a few minutes to enjoy the garden … to visualize your strong, healthy body. When you're ready … taking your comfortable support with you … bringing your feelings of gratitude with you … count from one to five. On the count of five, you will be fully awake, fully aware, fully restored.

One, coming up.

Two, becoming more awake, more alert, more aware.

Three, feeling fine … eyes start to flutter.

Four, feeling great … toes start to wiggle.

Five, feeling awake, aware, and fully restored to normal consciousness.

Now, every time you feel discouraged by the restrictions placed on your life by your illness or injury, take a deep breath and know and say "Nothing stands in the way of my powerful and compete healing."

The Least You Need to Know

- Pain affects more people than diabetes, heart disease, and cancer combined.
- The purpose of pain is to alter your behavior to avoid damaging actions.
- Chronic pain might be adjusting for larger imbalances, such as lifestyle choices that don't support you, hidden medical problems, or unresolved emotional trauma reflected in your body.
- Focusing your attention can reduce pain and speed healing.

Enjoying Positive Aging

As you get older, it's nice to know you've already proven yourself and can relax to enjoy being you. There are many benefits of aging, yet it's easy to succumb to all the negative aging messages from society and fall prey to beliefs of limitation. Fortunately, there are specific steps you can take to enjoy the benefits of a long life.

The scripts in this chapter help you feel good about your older body and overcome some of the difficult signs and symptoms of changing hormones. If you're suffering from painful joints or other health issues, be sure to also use the scripts in Chapter 15. Declining memory and intellectual function often concern elders, so scripts in this chapter will stimulate your mind. However, if you're struggling to learn new skills, you might also use the mastering a new skill script in Chapter 12.

In This Chapter

- Discovering the most important element to long life
- Learning self-hypnosis for positive aging
- Using self-hypnosis to overcome symptoms of menopause and male aging
- Supporting your memory
- Ways to stimulate memory and mental function

The Secret of Long Life

It's natural to want to live a long life and even more natural to want to age with health and vitality. How long you'll live and how well depends on your genes, diet, exercise, exposure to danger, and, to some degree, sheer luck! It's obvious that you have control over some factors and not over others. You might find it interesting that the most important element in promoting long life is something over which you have 100 percent control: a positive attitude!

The Albert Einstein College of Medicine's Institute for Aging Research conducted a Longevity Project, studying 243 people between the ages of 100 and 107 years (known as *centenarians*) to look for the key element to living a long life. The study found that the single most important component to living a long life isn't diet, exercise, or the avoidance of stress; the most important factor is how well a person handles stress.

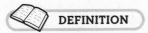 **DEFINITION**

Centenarians are people who have lived for 100 or more years.

You know from earlier chapters that how you manage stress relates to your view of reality. No surprise, the Longevity Project seems to confirm that opinion. The centenarians in the study all had two things in common: a positive attitude for life and good emotional expression! They laughed a lot and were easygoing, optimistic, and extroverted. In addition, instead of bottling up emotions and pretending everything was fine when it wasn't, they also expressed their painful feelings to others, too.

You might be wondering if the people in the study had easy lives and the answer is no. Quite the opposite—in fact, many were child survivors of Nazi concentration camps. However, they chose not to be prisoners to their trauma. Their experience taught them that life is precious and should be lived to the fullest, so they learned to feel their pain, express it, and then move on to enjoy life.

You can use these important lessons at any age to improve the quality of your life. Signs and symptoms of aging ease as resistance to life is lessened. Makes sense, right? The following scripts help to enlist a positive attitude toward aging and improve the function of all your organs and body systems. Be sure to use the full induction in Chapter 7 before starting the script. And don't forget—have fun!

Developing an Inner Smile for Positive Aging

Posthypnotic Suggestions

- Every day, in every way, I am better and better. I take time to enjoy life and give enjoyment to others.

- Age does not control me. Age is only a number …. My subconscious mind powerfully supports me in living a youthful life filled with new adventure and appreciation.

As you step off the last stair and sink into the soft, grassy soil … you notice the deep peace and total contentment that sweeps through you. Taking a deep breath … filling your lungs with clear, fresh air … you walk along the garden path, allowing your whole being to fill with peace and freedom.

 MESMERIZING MORSEL

"Each morning we are born again. What we do with today is what matters most."

—Jack Kornfield, Insight Meditation teacher and psychotherapist

With every step through the garden … hearing the calling of birds … feeling the breeze … you notice how much better you feel, how much more freedom is in every movement. With every step … your back is straighter … you are taller … and you walk freer … proud to have lived so many years … proud to have learned so much. You know you haven't done everything right … and you also know that it's okay … you've learned and grown … and with every step, you accept yourself more. You know and say "Every day, in every way, I am better and better. I take time to enjoy life and give enjoyment to others."

Moving into the warmth of the sun, feeling the warmth spreading over your face … your throat … your chest … warmth moving through your whole body … your muscles relax even further and you smile … recognizing the garden and anticipating enjoyment. You know and say "Age does not control me. Age is only a number …. My subconscious mind powerfully supports me in living a youthful life filled with new adventure and appreciation."

Wandering along the lovely garden path … nowhere to rush to … nowhere you need to be … you look at the beautiful flowers, seeing how they open to the sun … and noticing an opening within yourself … to an inner light that fills you. Looking ahead, you feel a surge of enjoyment as you approach your personal sacred space … your inner power spot. Stopping at the entrance, you pause in acknowledgment … and stepping inside … taking a moment to absorb the ambience … to honor the objects that are special to you.

Settling into the seat that is made just for you ... getting comfortable ... relaxing even further ... allowing your body to fill with energy ... you focus your full attention on your body. You know that your attention is a powerful tool. As you sit ... relaxed ... enjoying life ... you think of someone you love ... a person you enjoy seeing ... and you allow a smile to light your face. You let the joy and love you feel ... flood out of your face and flow to this other person ... knowing it makes this person's life better to be appreciated ... knowing it encourages this person to like themselves a little bit more. Suddenly you wonder "How often do I smile at myself? How often do I give myself this same encouragement?" And you realize ... not often enough.

SUBCONSCIOUS SCAFFOLDING

Traditional Chinese Medicine (TCM) says that when you smile, your organs secrete sweet substances; when you scowl, your organs secrete sour substances. This is another way to say that your mental attitude impacts your body. The remedy to internal sourness is to spend time every day smiling at each of your internal organs. This script takes that philosophy to heart.

Taking a deep breath ... relaxing even more ... you focus the glowing smile on your face ... internally ... using your attention softly .... Turn your attention to the inside of your body .... Turn your attention to your organs ... and beam a radiant smile at each organ. Starting with the heart ... smile at your heart .... Let the heart swell with enjoyment at being appreciated. Then smile at your lungs ... your stomach ... your spleen ... taking several minutes at each organ to fully send and receive the inner smile .... At your liver and gall bladder ... your intestines ... your kidneys and bladder. Smile at all of your glands ... at your bones ... at your muscles. Allow the glowing acceptance of your smile to spread throughout your entire body ... resting on areas that hurt ... and smiling comfort ... resting at organs that don't function well ... and smiling reassurance ... resting on areas that are weak and smiling encouragement.

Feeling proud, feeling happy ... feeling in control ... you give thanks to the garden ... to your sacred space ... as you step outside ... walking back through the garden ... heading toward the stairs ... knowing you can always return. Reaching the stairs ... you take a deep breath and, giving thanks ... start up. On the count of five, you are awake, alert, happy, and pain free. Life is good.

One, coming up.

Two, becoming more awake, more alert, more aware.

Three, feeling fine ... eyes start to flutter.

Four, feeling great ... toes start to wiggle.

Five, feeling awake, aware, and fully restored to normal consciousness.

As you go forward, every time you feel annoyed with your body, annoyed with being old, you smile at yourself and know and say "Age does not control me. Age is only a number .... My subconscious mind powerfully supports me in living a youthful life filled with new adventure and appreciation."

Overcoming Signs and Symptoms of Menopause

Posthypnotic Suggestions

- Every day, in every way, I am better and better. I release any negative judgments I've unconsciously accepted about aging and menopause.

- My body ages with grace, ease, and freedom.

- I love and accept my body in all stages of life.

- My subconscious mind powerfully intercepts and eliminates uncomfortable symptoms of menopause.

As you step off the last stair and sink into the soft, grassy soil … you notice the deep peace and total contentment that sweeps through you. Taking a deep breath … filling your lungs with clear, fresh air … you walk along the garden path, allowing your whole being to fill with peace and freedom.

With every step through the garden … hearing the calling of birds … feeling the breeze … you notice how much better you feel, how much more freedom is in your every movement. With every step … your back is straighter … you are taller … and you enjoy knowing how much is ahead of you … how many things you have yet to accomplish … how many people you have yet to meet. With every step, you accept yourself more. Suddenly, you realize how many negative messages you have accepted about menopause. You realize how many beliefs you've taken on that simply aren't true. With a breath of expansion, you know and say "Every day, in every way, I am better and better. I release any negative judgments I've unconsciously accepted about aging and menopause."

 MESMERIZING MORSEL

"Transformation is my favorite game and in my experience, anger and frustration are the result of you not being authentic somewhere in your life or with someone in your life. Being fake about anything creates a block inside of you. Life can't work for you if you don't show up as you."

—Jason Mraz, singer/songwriter

In fact … moving into the warmth of the sun, feeling the warmth spread over your face … your throat … your chest … warmth moving through your whole body … you realize that aging is an opportunity to be free of other people's limiting thoughts …. You realize … this is your chance to be fully who you are. You know and say "I love and accept my body in all stages of life."

Now, letting go of old limiting beliefs … you know that your subconscious mind powerfully supports you in releasing signs and symptoms of menopause and aging. You know you can do it … because your subconscious mind is a powerful tool. You know that every time you feel a hot flash or begin to sweat … the hot flash easily dissipates and the sweating stops. Every time you feel overwhelmed … you easily gain emotional control. You know that you sleep soundly … lose weight easily … stay fit with pleasure … and continue to enjoy great sex. In fact, every time your body produces a symptom, you know you are being asked to let go of an old belief. Relaxing even further … you smile … knowing how powerful your subconscious mind is … you know and say, "My subconscious mind powerfully intercepts and eliminates uncomfortable symptoms of menopause."

Feeling proud, feeling happy … feeling in control … you walk back through the garden … heading toward the stairs … knowing you can always return. Reaching the stairs … giving thanks … you start up. On the count of five, you are awake, alert, happy, and pain free. Life is good.

One, coming up.

Two, becoming more awake, more alert, more aware.

Three, feeling fine … eyes start to flutter.

Four, feeling great … toes start to wiggle.

Five, feeling awake, aware, and fully restored to normal consciousness.

As you go forward, every time you feel an annoying symptom of menopause, knowing you are being asked to let go of an old belief, you smile and know and say "My subconscious mind powerfully intercepts and eliminates uncomfortable symptoms of menopause."

Overcoming Signs and Symptoms of Male Aging

Posthypnotic Suggestions

- Every day, in every way, I am better and better. I release any negative judgments I've unconsciously accepted about male aging.

- My body ages with strength, virility, and ease.

- My subconscious mind powerfully intercepts and eliminates uncomfortable symptoms of male aging.

As you step off the last stair and sink into the soft, grassy soil … you notice the deep peace and total contentment that sweeps through you. Taking a deep breath … filling your lungs with clear, fresh air … you walk along the garden path, allowing your whole being to fill with peace and freedom.

WISE COUNSEL

Decreasing sexual function can be embarrassing for many men. However, don't let that keep you from proper medical advice. Often, simple nutritional changes and/or hormone support can boost your vitality to where you want to be.

As you walk through the garden … hearing the call of birds … feeling the breeze … you notice how much better you feel, how much more freedom is in every movement. With every step … your back is straighter … you are taller … and you enjoy knowing how much is ahead of you. You enjoy knowing how many things you have yet to explore … how many people you have yet to meet … and you also know … that it is perfectly fine to relax. It comes as a surprise to you … that it is a relief to know you have nothing to prove … nothing you have to do … you are enough.

Suddenly, you realize how many negative messages you've picked up about male aging. You realize how many beliefs you've accepted that simply aren't true. You know and say "Every day, in every way, I am better and better. I release any negative judgments I've unconsciously accepted about male aging."

Now, letting go of old limiting beliefs … you know that your subconscious mind powerfully supports you in releasing signs and symptoms of male aging. You know you can do it … because your subconscious mind is a powerful tool. You know that every time you feel signs you associate with male aging … they are easily replaced with strength, virility, and ease. You know that you sleep soundly … lose weight easily … keep all your hair … stay fit with pleasure … and continue to enjoy great sex. You know and say "My body ages with strength, virility, and ease."

In fact, every time your body produces a symptom, you know you are being asked to let go of an old belief. Relaxing even further … you smile … knowing how powerful your subconscious mind is …. You know and say "My subconscious mind powerfully intercepts and eliminates uncomfortable symptoms of male aging."

Feeling proud, feeling happy … feeling in control … you give thanks to the garden … and your subconscious mind as you walk back … heading toward the stairs … knowing you can always return. Reaching the stairs … giving thanks … you start up. On the count of five, you are awake, alert, happy, and pain free. Life is good.

 MESMERIZING MORSEL

"I truly believe that age—if you're healthy—age is just a number."

—Hugh Hefner, businessman and adult magazine publisher

One, coming up.

Two, becoming more awake, more alert, more aware.

Three, feeling fine … eyes start to flutter.

Four, feeling great … toes start to wiggle.

Five, feeling awake, aware, and fully restored to normal consciousness.

As you go forward, every time you feel an annoying symptom of male aging—knowing you are being asked to let go of an old belief—you smile and know and say "My subconscious mind powerfully intercepts and eliminates uncomfortable symptoms of male aging. My body ages with strength, virility, and ease."

Improving Mental Function

One of the most aggravating problems for all people and especially for those who are aging is faulty memory. Forgetting words, dates, and names is frustrating and embarrassing. Forgetting where you parked the car or what road you're driving on is terrifying. While some people notice a loss of memory as they age, others notice difficulty changing from one thought to another, finding that switching gears is harder than when they were younger. If these changes correspond to natural aging, they undermine your confidence and destabilize your ability to live independently.

Fortunately, there are things you can do to retain a good memory. Repetitive thoughts use the same neural pathways in your brain and, over time, thinking new thoughts and developing new pathways become more difficult to do. If you stop the cycle of repetitive thoughts and spend time every day learning new skills, your chances grow of keeping your brain young and agile.

Challenge yourself to learn new things, engage in new activities, and stretch your mental abilities. You may want to avoid all that computer technology that makes your eyes spin, but if you continue to develop new skills and stay connected to new technology, you have a better chance of retaining good memory and keeping your intellect sharp.

 HYPNOTIC CONNECTION

According to online *Psychology Today,* in 1956, psychologists thought our short-term memory capacity was somewhere between five and nine items in a list. Today's experts say the true capacity of short-term memory is closer to four items in a list. In addition, experts say the brains of older people are sifting through more information than those of younger brains. So if you can't remember all 19 items on your grocery list or only instantly recall one name out of the hundreds of people you've met, maybe you're being too hard on yourself!

Remember, everything you've ever experienced lives somewhere in the subconscious mind. The trick is to keep the pathways of memory open. Self-hypnosis works with the subconscious mind to boost your recall and sharpen your intellect. Remember to use the induction in Chapter 7 before you start.

Enhancing Memory

Posthypnotic Suggestions

- I easily remember names, dates, places, events, and details with perfect clarity.

- My mind functions perfectly, with flawless memory.

- I trust my memory to recall everything I need, exactly when I need it.

- Every day, in every way, my memory improves.

As you step off the last stair and sink into the soft, grassy soil … you notice the deep peace and total contentment that sweeps through you. Taking a deep breath … filling your lungs with clear, fresh air … you walk along the garden path, allowing your whole being to fill with confidence and freedom.

As you walk through the garden … hearing the call of birds … feeling the breeze … you notice how clear your mind is, how sharp your memory is. You enjoy knowing that everything that has ever happened exists in your subconscious mind. You enjoy knowing that your brain has total recall … and you also know … that the more you relax … the clearer your mind is … and the better your memory. In fact, every time you need to remember something … you know that all you have to do is relax. You know and say "I easily remember names, dates, places, events, and details with perfect clarity."

It comes as a surprise to you … to understand that it is okay to remember everything. Suddenly, you realize how many negative messages you have picked up and accepted about poor memory. You realize these beliefs are simply not true. You know and say "My mind functions perfectly, with flawless memory."

Now, letting go of old limiting beliefs … you know that your subconscious mind powerfully supports you in maintaining perfect recall. You know you can do it … because your subconscious mind is a powerful tool. Taking a minute, you imagine seeing friends … being at work … solving problems … and doing everything with perfect memory. You know and say "I trust my memory to recall everything I need, exactly when I need it."

In fact, every time you have trouble remembering something you know, you are being asked to let go of an old belief. Relaxing even further … you smile … knowing how powerful your subconscious mind is … you know and say, "Every day, in every way, my memory improves."

Feeling proud, feeling happy … feeling in control … you give thanks to your subconscious mind as you walk toward the stairs … knowing you can always return. Reaching the stairs … giving thanks … you start up. On the count of five, you are awake, alert, happy, and pain free. Life is good.

One, coming up.

Two, becoming more awake, more alert, more aware.

Three, feeling fine … eyes start to flutter.

Four, feeling great … toes start to wiggle.

Five, feeling awake, aware, and fully restored to normal consciousness.

 MESMERIZING MORSEL

"Nothing fixes a thing so intensely in the memory as the wish to forget it."

—Michel de Montaigne, French philosopher and writer

As you go forward, every time you experience difficulty remembering something, you know you are being asked to let go of old beliefs. Relaxing, you know and say "I trust my memory to recall everything I need, exactly when I need it."

Sharpening Intellectual Skill

Posthypnotic Suggestions

- I easily perform complex mental functions.

- My mind is sharp, clear, and focused.

- My subconscious mind powerfully supports me so that I learn and use new technology easily.

- I understand and follow complicated instructions effortlessly.

As you step off the last stair and sink into the soft, grassy soil … you notice the deep peace and total contentment that sweeps through you. Taking a deep breath … filling your lungs with clear, fresh air … you walk along the garden path, allowing your whole being to relax into confident ease.

As you walk through the garden … hearing the call of birds … feeling the breeze … you notice how clear your mind is, how sharp and focused your thoughts are. You enjoy knowing that your brain is capable of increasing your intellectual ability. You enjoy knowing that, the more you relax … the clearer your mind is … and the better you perform intellectual functions. Taking a moment … you remember all the mental functions you perform every day … and see yourself easily accomplishing each task with clarity. In fact, you know that every time you need to perform a mental task … all you have to do is relax and know and say "I easily perform complex mental functions."

It comes as a surprise to you ... to suddenly realize how many negative messages you have picked up and accepted about your diminishing mental function. You realize these messages are simply not true. You know and say "My mind is sharp, clear, and focused."

You even realize that you can learn new skills with ease. Your mind is sharp, clear, and focused ... and you are able to effortlessly learn new abilities. Remembering how confused you often feel with new technology ... you take a moment to see yourself easily mastering the skills of new technology. Letting go of old limiting beliefs that held you back ... you know that your subconscious mind powerfully supports you in maintaining sharp intellectual skill. You know you can master new technology ... because your subconscious mind is a powerful tool. You know and say, "My subconscious mind powerfully supports me so that I learn and use new technology easily."

In fact, every time you have trouble mastering a task ... or understanding an instruction ... you know you are being asked to let go of an old belief. Relaxing even further ... you smile ... knowing how powerful your subconscious mind is .... You know and say "I understand and follow complicated instructions effortlessly."

 WISE COUNSEL

Mental confusion can be a sign of easily corrected physical conditions, such as dehydration or poor nutrition. Be sure to support your mental function with advice from health-care professionals.

Feeling proud, feeling happy ... feeling in control ... you give thanks to your subconscious mind as you walk toward the stairs ... knowing you can always return. Reaching the stairs ... giving thanks ... you start up. On the count of five, you are awake, alert, happy, and pain free. Life is good.

One, coming up.

Two, becoming more awake, more alert, more aware.

Three, feeling fine ... eyes start to flutter.

Four, feeling great ... toes start to wiggle.

Five, feeling awake, aware, and fully restored to normal consciousness.

As you go forward, every time you experience difficulty performing an intellectual function, you relax and know and say, "My mind is sharp, clear, and focused. I easily perform complex mental functions."

The Least You Need to Know

- The most important factor to longevity is how well a person handles stress.
- The ability to handle stress well depends on a positive attitude and an ability to express emotions.
- Your subconscious mind can positively impact your unconscious aging beliefs.
- If you continue to develop new skills and stay connected to new technology, you have a better chance of retaining your memory and keeping your intellect sharp.
- Everything you've ever experienced lives somewhere in the subconscious mind.
- Self-hypnosis works with the subconscious mind to boost your recall and sharpen your intellect.

Unleashing Your Highest Potential

Now that you've addressed your self-limiting beliefs and are using self-hypnosis to sharpen your skills and move ahead with your goals, it's exciting to focus on other areas of life. Is your relationship all that you want it to be? Is your creative energy flowing freely? Are you moving toward a compelling future?

Part 5 brings all the aspects of this book together as you explore your love life, creative expression, past lives, intuitive perceptions, and spiritual connection. Here you put self-hypnosis to work to enhance your inner life as you connect more fully with what's essential within you.

Radiant Love

The desire to love and be loved is one of the key motivations in life. Relationships of all kinds—partner, parent, child, or friend—form the center of life and create the foundation for health and happiness. No matter how much you enjoy spending time alone, or how much you prefer to remain single, connection with people is essential to your well-being.

The scripts in this chapter are geared toward love relationships. However, several can be modified to strengthen friend and family connections as well. A relationship with another is enhanced by a strong relationship with your inner self. So before using the scripts in this chapter, you may want to revisit Chapter 12 to boost your self-esteem, confidence, and magnetism.

In This Chapter

- Overcoming fear of intimacy
- Finding and keeping a mate
- Improving affection and connection
- Restoring your sex drive

Connection: The Elixir of Love

The desire for loving companionship often creates such a strong yearning that it overrides all other goals and desires. Relationships are important. The sharing of yourself with another opens and strengthens you. In addition, relationships teach you about yourself, revealing your strengths as well as your deep, inner fears. Perhaps most importantly, they show you to what degree you value yourself; being able to balance your needs with those of another, have boundaries and still be open, and be independent while still sharing your soul challenges the strongest self-esteem and the best of connections. Relationships offer a profound arena for personal growth.

Hand in hand with deep yearning for a relationship, deep fears may also be present. Past hurts and false beliefs can create fear of intimacy and/or aversion to relationships. You may hide your less-than-perfect aspects of yourself for fear of being judged and rejected. A true partner doesn't wish to criticize your wounds, but rather wants to support your healing. If you want the experience of uplift from a strong, loving relationship, you must risk being seen as who you are.

 SUBCONSCIOUS SCAFFOLDING

> Relationships can cause deep-rooted insecurities to surface. Understanding that your fears and your partner's fears trigger each other can help you both to overcome them to develop greater intimacy. For example, your fear of rejection may get triggered alongside your partner's fear of losing freedom. Owning your fear and communicating with your partner is essential to creating intimacy. Help yourself heal by using the script for freeing the ghosts of trauma in Chapter 11.

The following scripts deal with pursuing, obtaining, and sustaining a good relationship. Addressed are issues of overcoming the fear of intimacy, finding your perfect partner, and maintaining love and connection in an established relationship. As you read, put your partner's name in the appropriate places and modify the script to make it personal to you. Remember to start with the induction in Chapter 7 and know that simply reading the scripts in a relaxed state while imagining the scenes and engaging them emotionally is all you need do to replace false, subconscious beliefs with ones that represent your true desires.

Overcoming Your Fear of Relationships

Posthypnotic Suggestions

- I purposefully eliminate my belief that dysfunctional relationships are normal and release my false ideas about partnerships.

- I completely love, accept, and respect myself. I trust myself completely.

- I am able to safely enjoy deep intimacy with another.

- My subconscious mind powerfully supports my desire for a partner and intercepts and eliminates false ideas about relationships.

As you step off the last stair and sink into the soft, grassy soil … you notice the deep peace and total contentment that sweeps through you. Taking a deep breath … filling your lungs with clear, fresh air … you walk along the garden path … allowing your whole being to fill with peace and freedom.

With every step through the garden … hearing the calling of birds … feeling the breeze … you notice how alive you feel … how much freedom you enjoy. You notice how with every step along the beautiful sunlit path … your body feels more open … your heart feels more full … and your whole being is radiantly you. As you walk along the path … enjoying the flowers, the butterflies, the birds … you enjoy knowing how much you have to share with others. Realizing how many people there are in the world … knowing how many people you have yet to meet … you know there is someone who is just right for you.

Yet you notice … that this thought brings an uncomfortable feeling … and you begin to remember past relationships that didn't work out … past times that you were hurt. You remember all the people you've known who were in relationships. You think of your parents … your grandparents … your aunts, uncles … friends. You think of television personalities and power couples. As you think of these relationships, you realize … you have accepted many dysfunctional behaviors … many behaviors that don't express respect and love. You realize you have avoided relationships because of this. Yet you know you have been brainwashed …. You know relationships don't have to be like this. You know and say "I purposefully eliminate my belief that dysfunctional relationships are normal and release my false ideas about partnerships."

You continue to walk along the path … feeling more free … more alive … and lighter than you have in a very long time. You think about all the beliefs you have that keep you from relationships … such as your fear that you might lose yourself … have less freedom … be restricted … controlled … judged and hurt. You think of the lack of respect … rejection … and cruelty … you have seen or experienced in relationships. You know that relationships don't have to be this way. You know true relationships are based on respect … caring … and love. You also understand that you must love and respect yourself. You know and say "I completely love, accept, and respect myself. I trust myself completely."

MESMERIZING MORSEL

"Intimacy is not a happy medium. It is a way of being in which the tension between distance and closeness is dissolved and a new horizon appears. Intimacy is beyond fear."

—Henri Nouwen, priest and author

With every step through the garden … you accept yourself more.

In fact … moving into the warmth of the sun, feeling the warmth spread over your face … your throat … your chest … warmth moving through your whole body … you realize that loving yourself allows you the joy of being intimate and close with another person … and you realize … this is your chance to be fully who you are. It is safe to be with someone … and you are safe to be with. You know and say "I am able to safely enjoy deep intimacy with another."

Now, letting go of old limiting beliefs … you know that your subconscious mind powerfully supports you in releasing all the fears you hold about relationships, all the restrictions you have placed on yourself. You know you are loveable and trustworthy and that you can love and trust others. You know you can be more yourself with another person … more independent even than you are right now. Relaxing even further … you smile … knowing how powerful your subconscious mind is …. You know and say "My subconscious mind powerfully supports my desire for a partner and intercepts and eliminates false ideas about relationships."

Feeling proud, feeling happy … feeling in control … you walk back through the garden … heading toward the stairs … knowing you can always return to the garden. Reaching the stairs … giving thanks … you start up. On the count of five, you are awake, alert, and radiantly happy. Life is good.

One, coming up.

Two, becoming more awake, more alert, more aware.

Three, feeling fine … eyes start to flutter.

Four, feeling great … toes start to wiggle.

Five, feeling awake, aware, and fully restored to normal consciousness.

As you go forward, every time you meet someone you are interested in, you smile and know and say "I completely love, accept, and respect myself. I trust myself completely. I am able to safely enjoy deep intimacy with another."

Attracting Your Perfect Partner

Posthypnotic Suggestions

- I radiate positive magnetism, drawing my perfect partner to me.

- I fully accept the person who is a perfect partner for me.

- The person I will be a perfect partner for is magnetically attracted to me.

- I listen to the communications from my subconscious mind and trust myself to know whom I should explore with more and whom I should turn down.

- I am open to new people, saying yes to opportunities to do things I enjoy.

As you step off the last stair and sink into the soft, grassy soil ... you notice the deep peace and total contentment that sweeps through you. Taking a deep breath, filling your lungs with clear, fresh air, you walk along the garden path. As you walk ... your whole being fills with peace and freedom. Moving into the warmth of the sun, feeling the warmth spread over your face ... your throat ... your chest ... warmth moving through your whole body ... you smile, recognizing the garden and anticipating enjoyment.

 HYPNOTIC CONNECTION

According to Michael Losier, host on Oprah Radio XM, in order to find someone who matches your vibrations, you have to do three things: decide what you want, give it attention, and allow it to happen.

As you walk along the path ... enjoying the flowers, the butterflies, the birds ... you enjoy knowing how much you have to share with another. Realizing how many people there are in the world ... knowing how many people you have yet to meet ... you know there is someone who is just right for you.

Yet as you stroll along ... you realize that you hold a deep ... secret fear .... You realize you are afraid you will not meet your perfect partner. You're afraid your perfect partner will walk right by you and never even know you're there. You know this isn't how it's supposed to be ... yet you're afraid you will never meet your perfect mate.

Wandering along the lovely garden path ... you look at the beautiful flowers, seeing how they open to the sun ... and notice an opening within yourself ... to an inner light that fills you. You feel sexy, uplifted, and alive. You notice you are standing taller ... and expanding. You feel the sparkle in your eye and notice a lift in your step. You believe and say "I radiate positive magnetism, drawing my perfect partner to me."

It feels good to know you might soon meet your perfect mate … someone who accepts you as you are … who is loving … interesting … kind and magnetic. You take a moment to imagine all the traits you want to attract … and eliminate from your magnetic field all the traits you are finished with attracting. It feels good to know you can choose the type of person you attract.

You notice anticipation makes you open more to others … so that you are more interested in those around you. Of course, you know that your perfect mate won't be perfect … there are always issues … and you know good relationships are built on mutual acceptance. Wanting to be open … and wanting to see your perfect partner honestly, you know and say "I fully accept the person who is a perfect partner for me."

Walking among the flowers … feeling peaceful and calm … you feel your magnetism continuing to grow … and notice the personal space around you continuing to expand. You imagine yourself walking down the street, meeting people who take notice as you pass. You see yourself receiving attention from people who want to be your companion and partner. Take a moment to see yourself … as someone who makes a perfect partner for someone else. See yourself as the best that you are. Know and say "The person I will make a perfect partner for is magnetically attracted to me."

Imagine yourself attracting someone you want to get to know. See yourself walking and talking with this person …. Notice how he or she looks … how he or she talks … walks … laughs and enjoys so many things you enjoy. You think this might be your perfect partner … then you're not sure. What if this person is not the right one? What if you miss the right one because you are absorbed here? But then you relax … and smile … knowing that you can trust your subconscious mind to know when to move forward, or not. You know that if you listen to the communications from your subconscious mind, you will know exactly what to do. You know and say "I listen to the communications from my subconscious mind and trust myself to know who I should explore with more and who I should turn down."

SUBCONSCIOUS SCAFFOLDING

Messages from the subconscious arrive as emotions, images, intuitions, and sensations. If you've forgotten how to receive the messages from the subconscious, revisit Chapter 5 and key 3, communication with the subconscious mind.

You stay in this wonderful, energized feeling … enjoying the knowledge that the right person is coming toward you … today … tomorrow … sometime very soon. You realize you have to be open to meeting new people … and the best way to do that is to go places you enjoy … and engage in activities that make you happy. You know and say "I am open to new people, saying yes to opportunities to do things I enjoy."

When you're ready … you head back through the garden toward the stairs. Feeling energized, feeling happy … feeling alive … you give thanks to the garden … to yourself and to your perfect partner. Continue walking back toward the stairs … knowing you can always return … taking a deep breath and starting up the stairs. On the count of five, you are awake, alert, and happy. Life is good.

One, coming up.

Two, becoming more awake, more alert, more aware.

Three, feeling fine … eyes start to flutter.

Four, feeling great … toes start to wiggle.

Five, feeling awake, aware, and fully restored to normal consciousness.

As you go forward to meet your perfect partner, stand tall, radiate magnetism, and know and say "The person I will be a perfect partner for is magnetically attracted to me."

Keeping Your Relationship Alive

Posthypnotic Suggestions

- I connect from the deepest part of myself to the deepest part of my partner with respect and love.

- I am alive with love for my partner. I fully accept my partner's needs, as well as my own.

- I fall back in love with my partner.

- My partner and I are magnetically attractive and attracted to each other.

As you step off the last stair and sink into the soft, grassy soil … you notice the deep peace and total contentment that sweeps through you. Taking a deep breath, filling your lungs with clear, fresh air, you walk along the garden path. As you walk … your whole being fills with peace and freedom. Moving into the warmth of the sun, feeling the warmth spread over your face … your throat … your chest … warmth moving through your whole body … you smile, recognizing the garden and anticipating enjoyment.

As you stroll along the ferns, trees, and flowers, you realize that you have a deep … hidden sadness …. You realize you are sad about the distance you have with your partner. You remember the ways that you and your partner no longer take care of each other's feelings … no longer share your thoughts and dreams … no longer feel special in each other's company. You realize you are taking each other for granted and you wonder … do you even still love each other?

Wandering along the lovely garden path … through the ferns, the trees, and the brightly colored flowers … allowing sadness to be fully present … not suppressing what you feel … or trying to make everything right … you accept that you and your partner have forgotten how to be perfect partners. You remember how you were with each other when you first met … how excited you felt to see each other … how you dressed with pride and took care of how you looked … how you shared each other's interests … and talked about ideas.

Thinking of these things while walking along the garden path ... feeling more and more relaxed ... more and more clear ... nowhere to rush to ... nowhere you need to be ... you notice the beautiful flowers, seeing how they open to the sun ... and feel an opening within yourself ... to an inner light that fills you. You feel sexy, uplifted, and alive. You feel softness in your heart ... a sparkle in your eye, and notice a desire to reconnect with your partner. You know you have not accepted your partner for who they are ... have wanted more than is reasonable from him or her ... and that your partner has done the same. You know and say "I connect from the deepest part of myself to the deepest part of my partner with respect and love."

 HYPNOTIC CONNECTION

According to Dr. John Gottman in his book *The Seven Principles for Making Marriage Work,* there are four behaviors during a conflict that are antagonistic to a relationship: contempt, stonewalling (giving the cold shoulder or silent treatment), defensiveness, and criticism. Couples who handle conflict gently, with positive regard and support for each other, seem to last longer. These couples nurture their care and admiration; seek to understand each other; and most importantly, when fighting, turn toward each other instead of away.

It feels good to remember what brought you together ... good to know the core of love is unbroken. You know you both must work at resolving differences. You also know that you have what it takes. Seeing the light within your mate ... you remember what is so special about this person. Take a moment to remember all the things you love about your partner. You know and say "I am alive with love for my partner. I fully accept my partner's needs, as well as my own."

Walking among the flowers ... feeling peaceful and calm ... purple, orange, yellow flowers ... you enjoy the relaxing ... and enjoyable ... calm. You notice that your sadness is no longer present. You feel your magnetism growing ... noticing the personal space around you as it expands. You imagine yourself walking down the street ... seeing your partner walking toward you. You see your partner as others do ... and suddenly you see how special you both are ... and how special you are together. You notice that you truly want to reconnect. You catch your partner's eye and smile .... You see surprise cross your partner's face ... and then caution ... and then a the smile that lights his or her face ... and you feel the magnetic attraction alive between you as you fall in love with each all over again. You know and say "My partner and I are magnetically attractive and attracted to each other."

You stay in this wonderful, energized feeling of love for your partner as you walk back toward the stairs. You know it's okay to let go of old, limiting beliefs about your partner ... okay to forgive the hurt you caused each other. Knowing the love in your relationship is still alive ... you feel energized, happy ... and alive. You give thanks to the garden ... to yourself and to your perfect partner. Taking a deep breath, you begin walking up the stairs. On the count of five, you are awake, alert, and happy. Life is good.

One, coming up.

Two, becoming more awake, more alert, more aware.

Three, feeling fine … eyes start to flutter.

Four, feeling great … toes start to wiggle.

Five, feeling awake, aware, and fully restored to normal consciousness.

As you go forward to meet your partner, stand tall, look into your partner's eyes, and radiate magnetic love as you know and say "I connect from the deepest part of myself to the deepest part of my partner with respect and love."

Sex Divine

Sex is more than a wonderful connection with your mate; sex is important to your health and well-being, is a vital element in expressing love and affection to your partner, and quite frankly, is enjoyable. Along with eating, sleeping, and breathing, sex is a vital impulse. However, it can also be a super-charged subject. Although sex appeal may have been the first thing that attracted you to your partner, it may now be the cause of relational strife. Regardless of your age, who you are, or what you do, sex either brings you closer to your partner or pushes you farther away.

There are lots of reasons sex is an issue. Maybe you and your partner have different sexual needs or desires. Maybe you have lost body tone and no longer feel sexy, or the connection you feel with your partner has waned and it's difficult to feel aroused. Maybe what you need is affection, and your partner responds sexually. Interestingly, however, the main reason people cite for avoiding intimacy is simply a lack of time!

You may wonder how important sex is in a relationship. The real question is, how important is sexual connection to you? Whatever your answer, everyone needs pleasurable touch. It is essential to health, as has been demonstrated in the decline of health in touch-deprived infants. Touch nourishes the brain, and studies reveal that without touch, even adults undergo gradual damage to brain tissue. People deprived of touch often suffer anger, depression, anxiety, and failed relationships, and are more likely to rely on drugs and alcohol to stimulate the pleasure areas of the brain.

 HYPNOTIC CONNECTION

> Touch deprivation is known to cause failure to thrive in infants that can even lead to death. Research conducted by Tiffany Field, head of the Touch Research Institute at the University of Miami School of Medicine, demonstrates that premature infants who were massaged for 15 minutes three times a day gained weight 47 percent faster and showed signs of more rapid nervous system development than others who were left alone in their incubators as standard practice dictated.

So forget about not having time or feeling a little down—sex and affection are important parts of your relationship. You may think you need to look a certain way or be in a certain mood to feel sexy, but the truth is, your biggest sex organ is your brain. It's your thoughts that promote feeling sexual and the images you allow in your head that produce arousal. Ask yourself, what influences your thoughts and images? Different people will have different responses, but for many, the biggest aphrodisiac is connection. Beyond that, your thoughts and images are influenced by—that's right—your subconscious mind!

The first script in this section builds connection and affectionate behavior between you and your partner. The second promotes arousal and sexual function. Be sure to personalize the scripts and anywhere your partner is mentioned; feel free to be specific and add your partner's name. As always, begin with the induction in Chapter 7.

Increasing Connection and Affection

Posthypnotic Suggestions

- I connect with the deepest part of my partner and express my love and affection with ease.

- Being affectionate is an easy and natural expression of my love for my partner.

- I receive affection easily and comfortably, knowing nothing is expected beyond the enjoyment of the moment.

- Connection with my partner is important to me, and I enjoy expressing and receiving affection.

As you step off the last stair and sink into the soft, grassy soil ... you notice the deep peace and total contentment that sweeps through you. Taking a deep breath, filling your lungs with clear, fresh air, you walk along the garden path. As you walk ... your whole being fills with peace and freedom. Moving into the warmth of the sun, feeling the warmth spread over your face ... your throat ... your chest ... warmth moving through your whole body ... you smile ... enjoying your body ... enjoying the feeling of the wind brushing across your skin and the warmth spreading along your body.

Your body is a sensual instrument and touch feels good. You remember snuggling with your partner ... enjoying the connection ... feeling in sync with your partner through touch. You realize how important affectionate touch is and are determined to bring more connection, more affection into your partnership. You know and say "I connect with the deepest part of my partner and express my love and affection with ease."

In the past, being affectionate may have felt difficult. You may have accepted false messages about touch in your childhood. Now, you know that being affectionate is an expression of your true nature. Dropping into deep feelings of caring, you know and say "Being affectionate is an easy and natural expression of my love for my partner."

As you stroll among the ferns, trees, and flowers, you realize that in the past, affection confused you. You didn't know that affection is its own enjoyment …. You thought it always had to end in sex … and although it may … it also may not. And that's okay …. It's good to enjoy affection for its own pleasure.

Thinking of these things while walking along the garden path … feeling more and more relaxed … more and more clear … nowhere to rush to … nowhere you need to be … you notice the beautiful flowers, seeing how they open to the sun … and feel an opening within yourself … to an inner light that fills you. You feel sensual, uplifted, and alive. You feel softness in your heart …. There's a sparkle in your eye and you notice a desire to reconnect with your partner. You know and say "I receive affection easily and comfortably, knowing nothing is expected beyond the enjoyment of the moment."

 SUBCONSCIOUS SCAFFOLDING

Imagine all the ways you enjoy sharing affection and add specific examples to this script to make it more engaging for your subconscious mind.

It feels good to know you can connect with your partner through affection. Thinking about your partner … you see the light within him or her and remember the many special things about this person … remember how special this person makes you feel. Imagining your partner, you know and say "Connection with my partner is important to me, and I enjoy expressing and receiving affection."

Walking among the flowers … feeling peaceful and calm … purple, orange, yellow flowers … you enjoy the relaxing … and enjoyable … calm. You stay in this wonderful, open feeling of affection … as you walk toward the stairs … knowing the love and affection in your relationship is alive …. You feel energized and happy … giving thanks to the garden … to yourself and to your perfect partner. Taking a deep breath, begin climbing the stairs. On the count of five, you are awake, alert, and happy. Life is good.

One, coming up.

Two, becoming more awake, more alert, more aware.

Three, feeling fine … eyes start to flutter.

Four, feeling great … toes start to wiggle.

Five, feeling awake, aware, and fully restored to normal consciousness.

As you go forward, every time you want to connect with your partner with affection, you know and say "I connect with the deepest part of my partner and express my love and affection with ease."

Sizzling Sex: Rediscovering Your Sex Drive

Posthypnotic Suggestions

- My subconscious mind powerfully stimulates my body to feel alive, sensual, and aroused.

- I feel sexy and radiate magnetic sex appeal.

- It is easy and natural to surrender to my intensely sexual feelings.

- Love ignites sexual passion.

As you step off the last stair and sink into the soft, grassy soil … you notice the deep contentment and happiness that sweeps through you. Taking a deep breath … filling your lungs with clear, fresh air … you walk along the garden path. As you walk … your whole being fills with excitement and anticipation.

Moving into the warmth of the sun, feeling the warmth spread over your face … your throat … your chest … warmth moving through your whole body … you smile, feeling your body alive, sensual, and aroused. At first, you wonder if this is okay … and then you know that you are safe. Feeling sensual and being aroused is natural and easy to achieve. You may have had trouble feeling sexual and aroused in the past, but now you know … it is a natural and enjoyable feeling.

You know that what you think controls your sexual urges … and you relax … allowing stimulating images to flood your mind … and stimulating feelings to stream through your body. You begin to resist these feelings … but then you remember … you're safe and it's okay to relax … to move with your sexual feelings … and enjoy them. You know and say "My subconscious mind powerfully stimulates my body to feel alive, sensual, and aroused."

Walking along the path … moving deeper into the soft, welcoming garden … you feel magnetic … and know you are drawing your mate toward you with the sheer force of your sex appeal. You know you don't need to be shy … it's natural to feel sexy …. You know your mate appreciates your sexual energy … and it is safe to be sexual. In the past, you might not have felt attractive … but now you know attraction is about having true feelings of connection. Enjoying your magnetic sex appeal … enjoying being aroused … feeling safe … you know and say "I feel sexy and radiate magnetic sex appeal."

 MESMERIZING MORSEL

"Sex, alone, is a mighty urge to action, but its forces are like a cyclone—they are often uncontrollable. When the emotion of love begins to mix itself with the emotion of sex, the result is calmness of purpose, poise, accuracy of judgment, and balance."

—Napoleon Hill, motivational speaker and author

As you walk along through the ferns, trees, and flowers, you realize that you have an internally increasing desire ... a need to express your sexual feelings to your partner ... to show your love through sexual intimacy. It feels good to know you remember what brought the two of you together ... good to know how attracted you feel to your partner. You remember what is so special about this person ... and remembering causes you to feel even sexier ... even more aroused. You know and say "It is easy and natural to surrender to my intensely sexual feelings."

You stay in this wonderful, energized feeling ... as you walk back through the garden toward the stairs ... knowing that love ignites sexual passion .... You feel energized, happy ... and alive. You give thanks to the garden ... to yourself and to your perfect partner. Taking a deep breath, begin walking up the stairs. On the count of five, you are awake, alert, and happy. Life is good.

One, coming up.

Two, becoming more awake, more alert, more aware.

Three, feeling fine ... eyes start to flutter.

Four, feeling great ... toes start to wiggle.

Five, feeling awake, aware, and fully restored to normal consciousness.

As you move forward to meet your partner, feeling sensual and aroused—radiating sexual magnetism—you know and say, "Love ignites sexual passion. It is easy and natural to surrender to my intensely sexual feelings."

The Least You Need to Know

- Self-hypnosis helps develop intimacy and overcome deep-rooted insecurities.
- Couples whose unions last nurture their care and admiration for each other, an activity that can be supported using self-hypnosis.
- Giving and receiving affectionate touch is essential to well-being.
- Sizzling sex can be restored to your relationship.

Prosperity and Abundance

Money impacts your sense of well-being in countless ways. It directly relates to your security, freedom, and often your self-worth. While the paper and coin that create money have no inherent worth, money represents an agreed-on system of valuing what you produce and what you want to obtain. Not surprisingly, your thoughts, attitudes, and beliefs about money determine your ability to earn it, save it, and spend it wisely.

Naturally, how you think about money is influenced by your subconscious programming. Consequently, using self-hypnosis to engage the subconscious in attracting abundance can produce truly remarkable results. This chapter shifts poverty thinking to prosperity thinking. The scripts assist you in aligning your mission and vision statements to achieve goals that bring greater financial reward and security for you.

In This Chapter

- Changing your abundance vantage point
- Reframing limiting beliefs
- Creating a vision of abundance
- Amassing your fortune

Manifesting Financial Wealth

In order to change your finances, you need to alter the mindset that created the choices that brought you where you are at present. What do you really believe about money? What negative thoughts repeat in your mind when you think about money troubles? What you think creates circumstances by drawing certain experiences toward you, often called the *law of attraction*.

HYPNOTIC CONNECTION

The law of attraction was brought into popular use at the turn of the nineteenth century as part of the New Thought Movement. Despite the archaic language, the older books that were part of this movement are still the best ever written on the subject. They include favorites such as *As a Man Thinketh* (1902) by James Allen, *The Game of Life and How to Play It* (1925) by Florence Scovel Shinn, and *Think and Grow Rich* (1937) by Napoleon Hill (still one of the best-selling books of all time).

To explore your negative beliefs, fill in the blank for the following sentences. Don't think about your answers and don't settle for just one. Keep answering until you have gotten to the bottom of your thoughts, attitudes, and beliefs.

- Money is _____.

- My past behavior around money has been _____.

- To have more money, I am willing to _____.

- More money will change my life by _____.

To create change, you have to shift the limiting attitudes, thoughts, and beliefs that you inherited from your parents and culture, along with the ones you picked up through your own experience. Chapter 1 called this shift in perspective changing your view of reality. It requires you looking from a different vantage point.

The vantage point you see the world from now has prescribed limits about how much money you're allowed to have and still fit in with your friends and family. You have beliefs about who gets to have money and what they have to do to get it. You have opinions of what people who have money are really like and fears about what you personally do or don't deserve. So deciding you want more money entails bucking a lot of engrained and limiting beliefs that you've held for a very long time.

The most important belief you need to adopt in creating financial success is that the change you want is possible. Do you believe abundance is possible? Do you believe it's possible for you? If you're noticing the twinge of doubt, that's where old, negative programming needs to be replaced with a program that supports your highest good.

Old, Limiting Beliefs

How well you're able to attract financial abundance is a pretty good indication of how free you are of negative programming. Just to be clear, if you're struggling to make ends meet, it doesn't mean you're a bad person, aren't spiritual, or are being punished for doing something wrong. It does mean that one way or another, your old programming is tripping you up.

 SUBCONSCIOUS SCAFFOLDING

Did you do the exercise in Chapter 1, noting all the negative thoughts you had in a day? If you did, pull that list out now and take a look. How many of your negative thoughts relate to a lack of money and not being able to obtain abundance? Your thoughts are a clear indication of where you need to focus change.

Take a minute to write down as many of the negative thoughts and beliefs you have about money that you can think of, and then reframe each belief to represent a different vantage point. The following table lists a few of the most common limiting beliefs, along with an alternate perspective.

Shifting Limiting Beliefs

Limiting Belief	Shift in Perspective
Wanting money is selfish.	Money is a vehicle for self-sufficiency and generosity.
There are only so many pieces of the pie; money is a limited resource.	Money is a river of energy in continual flow. Step into the stream.
Having money isn't spiritual.	Money is energy; how you use it makes it spiritual or not.
Some people aren't meant to have money.	You have everything inside that you need to increase your wealth.
The system is rigged for the rich; there's no point in fighting it.	Your intention is the strongest force in your life; you can create and attract financial opportunity.

continues

Shifting Limiting Beliefs   (continued)

Limiting Belief	Shift in Perspective
Money is the root of all evil.	Money is a neutral energy; value it as a resource for doing good, not as a determination of your worth.
Money really isn't important; it's only money anyway.	Money is a resource that does great good; treat it with respect.
Receiving money is an obligation.	Money is energy that moves freely from person to person, creating mutual wealth.
Having money changes people.	Money is energy; what you do with it is up to you.
Having more money than other people is unfair. It feels bad to have something other people need.	Modeling poverty doesn't help anyone. Modeling abundance not only leads the way, it gives you an ability to directly create opportunity for others.

Your beliefs didn't arrive in your mind from nowhere. You accept them because they were taught to you or you've had experiences that make them seem true. Changing them brings up all kinds of emotions. You might feel like a traitor going against things you were taught, or pretentious for wanting things beyond what your friends have. As you work with your negative programming, pay attention to your feelings and address them in light of your shifting perspective. You can then personalize the following scripts by adding your limiting beliefs and the reframes you created.

 MESMERIZING MORSEL

"Don't wait until everything is just right. It will never be perfect. There will always be challenges, obstacles and less than perfect conditions. So what. Get started now. With each step you take, you will grow stronger and stronger, more and more skilled, more and more self-confident and more and more successful."

—Mark Victor Hansen, motivational speaker and author

Principles of Attraction

Changing your vantage point is half the job of prosperity thinking. The other half is creating a compelling vision that inspires you to go to the effort of generating abundance. This is called *forming an intention.* What you focus your attention on is what you create. If you focus on what you don't have, you'll continue to not have it. On the other hand, if you develop an intention of what you do want, one that fully engages your mind and emotions, you draw it toward you. You know you are on the path as synchronicity opens doors and brings you opportunity.

Here are the steps to creating abundance:

- Decide on what needs to change in your life.

- Identify and reframe your limiting beliefs.

- Form an intention that aligns with your vision statement.

- Imagine what abundance will be like; make it engaging and fulfilling.

- Create small goals and action steps that move you toward your intention and align with your mission statement.

- Stay observant to opportunities, people, and events that come toward you to help fulfill your goals.

- Focus every day on your intention. Using self-hypnosis scripts is a great tool.

To be a powerful motivator, your intention needs to reflect your vision, which defines your purpose in life. It then needs to work within your mission statement, the path you're taking to fulfill your vision. If your intention doesn't align with your vision and mission statements, your subconscious mind is working to fulfill competing programs, which produces confusion and chaos. If this sounds like you, check in with your alignment; does your vision and mission truly reflect who you are, and are they reflected in your financial objectives?

Once you have clarity, set your goals and action plans and create your self-hypnosis scripts. The scripts in this chapter can be modified with your goals, or you can create new ones using Chapter 7 for tips. Be sure to look for opportunity and enact your action plans since abundance needs your cooperation to come into your life.

SUBCONSCIOUS SCAFFOLDING

If you haven't already created a vision statement about what you want in life and a mission statement with your goals and action steps, now is a good time to do so. You might want to return to Chapter 6 and align your financial intention with your greater vision.

Prosperity Scripts

In physics, energy is a force that performs work. The more energy gathered, the greater the force and the bigger the project that can be undertaken. This is a good model for thinking about money. You want to attract it, gather it until there is enough to do something with it, and then use it to fulfill a passion or goal. If being rich is your only goal, you may be using money as a measure for self-worth. Would you consider that what you do with your money may be more important than how much you have?

There are two sides to creating abundance; one side brings money to you, while the other gathers it until there is enough to be useful. Imagine trying to fill a water trough using a bucket that is full of holes. You can fill the bucket from the fastest-flowing waterfall, yet there will be little left in it by the time you get to the trough. Look at your spending habits as a bucket with holes. How many of the holes can you easily and effortlessly eliminate without losing any quality of life?

Being able to save money is every bit as important as having a plan to earn it. Some people think spending everything they make is necessary to attract more flow. They need to prove that they've let go of their limiting beliefs in poverty. The question isn't whether there will be more money coming in. Of course there will! The question is how much longer it will take to amass what you need for your goals if you're not gathering and saving as you go.

The following scripts help you bring money in, save it, and use it wisely. As always, use the induction in Chapter 7 before you begin and personalize the scripts with your goals and beliefs.

Attracting Abundance

Posthypnotic Suggestions

- Right here, right now, I am fine. I am sincerely grateful for all that I have.

- Money is a river of energy in continual flow. I am part of the stream, and there is always enough.

- I have everything I need inside myself to create financial abundance.

- What I do has value and I receive abundant compensation. When I receive money, I add value to other people's lives.

- I joyfully accept an overflow of wealth in my life.

- Every day, in every way, my subconscious mind powerfully attracts abundance. Prosperity is a done deal.

As you step off the last stair and sink into the soft, grassy soil … you notice the deep peace and total contentment that sweep through you. Taking a deep breath … filling your lungs with clear, fresh air … you walk along the garden path, allowing your whole being to fill with peace and freedom. As you walk, you notice all the truly wonderful things that exist in your life … notice and appreciate all that you have. Your heart expands and fills with gratitude. You know and say "Right here, right now, I am fine. I am sincerely grateful for all that I have."

MESMERIZING MORSEL

"Develop an attitude of gratitude, and give thanks for everything that happens to you, knowing that every step forward is a step toward achieving something bigger and better than your current situation."

—Brian Tracy, motivational speaker and author

A huge weight feels lifted from your shoulders as you realize there really is such a thing as enough ... because for a while ... it seemed that as soon as one financial need was met ... another rose to take its place. It began to feel as though you could never get ahead ... as though the deck was stacked against you. Now, with every step you take through the garden ... hearing the calling of birds ... feeling the breeze ... you notice how much better you feel, how much more freedom you have. You know you have what it takes to create abundance .... You know that there is such a thing as enough. You know and say "Money is a river of energy in continual flow. I am part of the stream, and there is always enough."

With every step ... your back is straighter ... you are taller ... and you enjoy knowing how much is ahead of you ... how many opportunities await you. You think about your plans and goals ... think about the dreams that you want to fulfill ... about things you have yet to accomplish. With a breath of expansion, you know that the only limits are the ones you place on yourself .... You know you can do anything you put your mind and heart into. You know and say "I have everything I need inside myself to create financial abundance."

With every step, you accept yourself more. Suddenly, you realize how many negative messages you've believed about money that simply aren't true. In fact ... moving into the warmth of the sun, feeling the warmth spread over your face ... your throat ... your chest ... warmth moving through your whole body ... you realize that this is your opportunity to be free of limiting thoughts ... your chance to be fully who you are. You know and say "What I do has value, and I receive abundant compensation. When I receive money, I add value to other people's lives."

Now, letting go of old limiting beliefs ... you know that your subconscious mind powerfully supports you in creating abundance. You know you can do it ... because your subconscious mind is a powerful magnet. Sitting down in the sun ... you imagine yourself sitting in a strong waterfall of money ... see your life filled with a surplus supply of money ... feel the happiness and joy of having all that you need and more ... experience the freedom of being able to pursue your dreams. You see yourself living in the house that is perfect for you and your family ... doing the work you were meant to do and earning wages that provide for you and more. You see yourself enjoying the life you were meant to live. Imagine all the ways your hard work and good fortune bring value to other people. Take a few minutes to fully engage the image of your new life, seeing, feeling, and experiencing abundance. [Long Pause] You know and say "I joyfully accept an overflow of wealth in my life."

It feels good to allow yourself to enjoy money ... powerful to know you can positively change other people's lives. You gladly release the burden of guilt that has held you back ... and with relief ... relaxing even further ... you smile ... knowing how powerful your subconscious mind is ... you know and say "Every day, in every way, my subconscious mind powerfully attracts abundance. Prosperity is a done deal."

Feeling proud, feeling happy … feeling grateful … you walk back through the garden … heading toward the stairs … knowing you can always return. Reaching the stairs … giving thanks … you start up. On the count of five, you are awake, alert, and happy. It is good to be you.

> **SUBCONSCIOUS SCAFFOLDING**
>
> You might want to use two self-hypnosis scripts as part of your action plan for abundance—one to reprogram negative thinking as in Chapter 11, and one to attract abundance.

One, coming up.

Two, becoming more awake, more alert, more aware.

Three, feeling fine … eyes start to flutter.

Four, feeling great … toes start to wiggle.

Five, feeling awake, aware, and fully restored to normal consciousness.

As you go forward, every time you think a negative thought about money, you know you are being asked to let go of an old belief. You smile and know and say "Every day, in every way, my subconscious mind powerfully attracts abundance. Prosperity is a done deal."

Creatively Saving to Build a Fortune

Posthypnotic Suggestions

- I am sincerely grateful for all that I have.

- I enjoy accumulating wealth as I effortlessly gather and save money.

- I enjoy creatively finding ways to reuse, recycle, and conserve.

- I take control of my spending habits, letting go of extravagant behavior and enjoying life more fully.

- I respect the money I earn and choose wisely where I spend it.

- Every day, in every way, my subconscious mind powerfully attracts abundance and prompts me to gather and save it.

As you step off the last stair and sink into the soft, grassy soil … you notice the deep peace and total contentment that sweeps through you. Taking a deep breath … filling your lungs with clear, fresh air … you walk along the garden path, allowing your whole being to fill with peace and freedom. As you walk, you notice all the truly wonderful things that exist in your life … notice and appreciate all that you have. Your heart expands and fills with gratitude. You know and say "I am sincerely grateful for all that I have."

A huge weight lifts from your shoulders as you realize you have control over how you spend money. For a while, you were feeling that you would never reach your goals … never have enough money saved to pursue your dream. Sometimes it felt as though you had to sacrifice too much … and you wondered if you should just give up. Because you enjoy spending money … you thought it would be difficult to save. But now, with every step you take through the garden … hearing the calling of birds … feeling the breeze … you notice how much more freedom you have. You know you can choose wisely … choose when and where you spend money. You realize it is fun to be creative … enjoyable to watch your bank balance grow. You know and say "I enjoy accumulating wealth as I effortlessly gather and save money."

 MESMERIZING MORSEL

"A bargain ain't a bargain unless it's something you need."

—Sidney Carroll, screenwriter

With every step … your back is straighter … you are taller … and you enjoy knowing how easy it is to save money … knowing that soon you will have enough to pursue your dreams. You think about your plans and goals … think about your dreams … and know it is actually fun to be creative. You know and say "I enjoy creatively finding ways to reuse, recycle, and conserve."

With every step, you accept yourself more and realize you don't have to spend money on things you don't really need … or sometimes think you want. You realize you can take control … choose wisely what you want … and don't want. You know and say "I take control of my spending habits, letting go of extravagant behavior and enjoying life more fully."

Now, you realize that when you respect yourself and your hard work … you want to make wise choices and use your money to promote your dreams. You know and say "I respect the money I earn and choose wisely where I spend it."

Taking a moment, letting go of old, limiting beliefs … you know that your subconscious mind powerfully supports you in creating abundance. You know you can do it … because your subconscious mind is powerful. Sitting down in the sun … leaning against a strong oak tree … you imagine your life filled with surplus money … that you have wisely gathered and saved … money you can use to fuel your dreams. You see yourself enjoying the life you were meant to live. You imagine all the ways your abundance brings value to other people. Take a few minutes to fully engage the image of your new life. See, feel, and enjoy it. [Long Pause]

When you're ready ... relaxing even further ... you smile ... knowing how powerful your subconscious mind is .... You know and say "Every day, in every way, my subconscious mind powerfully attracts abundance and prompts me to gather and save it."

Feeling proud, feeling happy ... feeling grateful ... you walk back through the garden ... heading toward the stairs ... knowing you can always return. Reaching the stairs ... giving thanks ... you start up. On the count of five, you are awake, alert, and happy. It is good to be you.

One, coming up.

Two, becoming more awake, more alert, more aware.

Three, feeling fine ... eyes start to flutter.

Four, feeling great ... toes start to wiggle.

Five, feeling awake, aware, and fully restored to normal consciousness.

As you go forward, every time you are tempted to spend more money than you really want to, you know you are being asked to let go of an old belief. You smile and know and say "I enjoy accumulating wealth as I effortlessly gather and save money."

The Least You Need to Know

- Self-hypnosis can help you adopt an abundance mindset.
- Altering your subconscious programming will attract different circumstances and increase financial opportunity.
- The most important belief you need to create financial success is that the change you want is possible.
- Financial struggle doesn't mean you're a bad person, aren't spiritual, or are being punished for doing something wrong. It does mean that your old programming isn't working.
- There are two sides to creating abundance—one side attracts money, while the other gathers it until there is enough to be useful.
- Self-hypnosis can help you attract and save money to build prosperity.

Inspiring Creativity

Creativity is one of the most fascinating frontiers of the mind. Not limited to artistic ventures or works of fiction, creativity is the indefinable ability to link information together in a different way, thus forming a new, unprecedented view of reality. Creativity represents the most significant ability of people who excel in science, problem solving, and invention. Creativity is also the single most significant ability you need to shift your vantage point and create change in your life.

This chapter explores creativity as part of intentional living. Self-hypnosis scripts help you increase creative flow, develop a compelling future for yourself, and overcome your creative blocks.

In This Chapter

- Using creativity for intentional living
- Increasing creative genius
- Designing a compelling future
- Learning from creative blocks

Intentional Living

You know that changing the quality of your life requires changing the quality of your thoughts, attitudes, and beliefs. Making this change is an act of creativity. Creative thinking is the opposite of repetitive thoughts generated from subconscious programming. Creative thinking frees you from the habits that have defined your life and allows you to move to new vantage points that shift your reality. Creative thinking is the prerequisite for changing your life.

Living intentionally is the outward act of creativity where you live a life in which you no longer accept the status quo as representing truth and no longer limit your future to what was true in the past. Living with intention requires you to examine the beliefs behind all of your circumstances and consciously create something different in each action that you take in the present.

 MESMERIZING MORSEL

"If you hear a voice within you say, 'You cannot paint,' then by all means paint, and that voice will be silenced."

—Vincent van Gogh, painter

Having used the scripts in this book, you now have all the tools you need to create a clear vision of your path and consciously attract the circumstances of your life. Your vision must be aligned with your purpose and fueled with the joy you feel when you think of it. As you follow your joy, you'll stay in the flow of life and synchronicity that opens doors that lead you to fulfillment. However, your dreams can't come to you if you're sitting home waiting for them to arrive. You need to be actively pursuing your goals and moving in the flow of life to arrive where you've set your direction.

Every time you use self-hypnosis, you're choosing to change some aspect of your life. This is a conscious decision and, as you look for new vantage points with which to view problems, you're living intentionally. If you've been having a difficulty finding new ways to see your problems, the scripts in this chapter might set your creative juices flowing and allow you to engage other scripts in this book more fully.

Creativity Scripts

No matter what job you have, new ideas and innovative ways of completing tasks benefit you. In fact, the drive to create is one of the most compelling urges humans have. Creativity generates internal energy that motivates action, and creative expression allows you to feel unique, valued, and satisfied. Many feel that the urge for creative expression is the divine spark within.

However, if you're like many people, you might have some doubts about your creative ability. Perhaps as a child you were told by a teacher or parent that you weren't creative and that belief stayed with you. Or maybe you took a creative risk and failed and are now afraid of trying again. No matter what you were told or how many times your creative insights weren't appreciated, you have creative ability. Everyone does. Whether you want to express your creativity in art, music, or writing or desire to solve problems in innovative ways, follow your urge—you wouldn't feel compelled to act if you didn't have the ability.

The first creativity script increases creative flow. You can use it before other scripts in this book, as you're working on a project, or anytime you want to be more open to new ideas. The second script creates your compelling future. You may need to do some homework and decide what you really desire before you start. The more you personalize this script, the more you'll benefit from your session.

 SUBCONSCIOUS SCAFFOLDING

If you haven't already created your vision statement and mission statement with an action plan, it's a good time to do so now. Using the tips in Chapter 6, create your ideal future and insert the specifics into the creating your compelling future script.

The third script removes the blocks getting in the way of a creative project. Everyone experiences creative blocks and it's a most frustrating experience, especially if the lack of forward progress impacts your livelihood. Creative blocks often have an emotional source stemming from pressure, perceived judgment, or a need to recharge. Amazingly, they also can be functional. A block may be letting you know that you have missed something. A block may provide some needed space for fresh ideas to emerge.

No matter the cause, if you're stuck in a project, take yourself to a different location and loosen up. Have fun! Move around, enjoy your body, and invigorate your cells. Enjoy being alive. You can then use this third script and let loose with creative genius! Here are some adjustments you can make to generate creative flow:

- Change your environment; create a conducive place for thinking outside the box.

- Brainstorm with a couple of wild and wacky friends.

- Look for serendipity and synchronicity in your surroundings.

- Free your mind using meditation, yoga, contemplative prayer, or some other mind-freeing practice.

- Move your body—your muscles and your memory are connected, so loosen up with a walk in the woods, dance, or engage in an activity you enjoy.

- Pay attention to dreams, sudden thoughts, and random feelings.

You already possess the personality traits you need to be a creative person. The following scripts help you let loose the sparks of creative genius. As always, use the specifics from your situation to personalize the posthypnotic suggestions and scripts. Don't forget to begin with the induction in Chapter 7. The key to these scripts is approaching them in a relaxed, alpha brainwave state of mind (see Chapter 3).

Increasing Creative Flow

Posthypnotic Suggestions

- I enjoy creative freedom. My mind is free of limiting thoughts as new ideas abound.

- Right here, right now, creative genius flows through me.

- Every problem gives me the opportunity to express greater creativity.

- I am fully open, standing in the flow of creative energy.

- Every day, in every way, my subconscious mind powerfully expresses creativity.

As you step off the last stair and sink into the soft, grassy soil … you notice a wild ocean landscape just beyond the garden's edge. Excitement surges through you. Taking a deep breath … filling your lungs with clear, fresh air … you sprint along the garden path … toward the ocean spray … as waves crash along the cliff face. Hearing the call of gulls … you open and allow your whole being to fill with inspiration and freedom.

As you approach the cliffs, you notice how free your mind is … notice how you're able to think new, creative thoughts. In fact, as the warmth of the sun penetrates your body … the salty air washes over your face … you feel your mind expanding … becoming filled with ideas. You notice your mind is free of limitations … free of old ways of seeing the world. It feels good to be creative …. Energy lifts your body … you feel light and free. You know and say "I enjoy creative freedom. My mind is free of limiting thoughts as new ideas abound."

It feels so good to let your creativity flow. You know you have valuable ideas … and useful solutions to old problems. You remember a time when you didn't believe that you were creative. You remember when people told you that you didn't have creative ability. But now, standing along the cliff edge, feeling free and open … and alive … you know that you accepted and believed limiting beliefs that were not your own. You know that you can choose to let them go. In a symbolic gesture … you shake your body and cast all your old, limiting beliefs away. Dancing in the spray of the ocean … letting the shifting wind move your body … you choose to let your creative genius loose. Suddenly, you feel giddy with excitement, happy that your true self can be expressed. Your heart expands and fills with gratitude as you know and say "Right here, right now, creative genius flows through me."

A huge weight feels lifted from your shoulders as you realize you are creatively alive. You feel full of energy. Just for a moment, you think of a problem you're having … one that seems like it has no solution. At first, you feel discouraged … then you remember that every problem is an opportunity to use your creativity. With every dance step along the cliff … hearing the calling of gulls … moving with the crisp, salty breeze … you notice how much more creative you feel, how much more freedom of thought you have. You know you have the inner resources to solve problems … know that you can tap into more brain power … more creative insight … more freedom of thought. You know and say "Every problem gives me the opportunity to express greater creativity."

 MESMERIZING MORSEL

"When in flow, the creator and the universe become one, outside distractions recede from consciousness and one's mind is fully open and attuned to the act of creating."

—Scott Barry Kaufman, PhD, psychologist and author

Just for a moment, you doubt yourself. You feel afraid that your creative source will dry up. You're afraid you will run out of ideas or lose connection to your creative genius. Then you remember … creativity is energy that flows through the universe. It doesn't run out. Looking ahead, you see a crevice in the rocks … with a huge waterfall that seems to be flowing from the heavens … and you know the water is the juice of creative insight. Feeling excited … anticipating fulfillment … you sprint to the edge of the waterfall. At first, it seems so strong … so vibrant … you're afraid you can't withstand the force. Then you know you have everything you need. Moving forward … stepping into the waterfall … you inhale as your body wakes up … your mind is refreshed … and all old thoughts and beliefs are washed away. Your body opens to the invigorating flow … and your mind is stimulated with new ideas. You see vivid images and solutions, new ways of approaching problems. You hear sounds of inspiration. You feel delight and joy as you know and say "I am fully open, standing in the flow of creative energy."

It feels good to know you have access to this source of creative energy anytime you need a new idea, fresh insight, or inspiration. You know you can make huge changes in your life because you have access to this creative flow. Just for a few moments … stand in the flow and receive creative energy. [Long Pause] When you're ready, you know and say "Every day, in every way, my subconscious mind powerfully expresses creativity."

Now, knowing it's time to go … you turn and head back through the garden. With every step … you have more ideas … you are more alive … and you enjoy knowing how much is ahead of you … how many opportunities to express your creativity await you. You think about your plans and goals … think about the dreams that you want to fulfill … and enliven them with creative energy. Feeling proud, feeling happy … feeling grateful … you walk toward the stairs … knowing you can always return. Reaching the stairs … giving thanks … you start up. On the count of five, you are awake, alert, and happy. It is good to be alive.

One, coming up.

Two, becoming more awake, more alert, more aware.

Three, feeling fine … eyes start to flutter.

Four, feeling great … toes start to wiggle.

Five, feeling awake, aware, and fully restored to normal consciousness.

As you go forward, every time you feel bored, limited, or stuck, you know you are being asked to let go of an old belief. You smile, and then know and say, "I am fully open, standing in the flow of creative energy."

Creating Your Compelling Future

Posthypnotic Suggestions

- I am sincerely grateful for all that I have.

- The future I create is abundant, creative, fulfilling, and purposeful.

- I bring toward me all that I desire: travel, ease, opportunity, beauty, fulfilling relationships, success, and recognition.

- I use all of my abilities and feel satisfied with the results.

- Everything I desire, intend, and work for comes to me now.

- Opportunities to fulfill my dreams present themselves every day, in every way.

- Every day, in every way, my subconscious mind powerfully creates the life of my highest dreams.

As you step off the last stair and sink into the soft, grassy soil … you notice the deep peace and total contentment that sweeps through you. Taking a deep breath … filling your lungs with clear, fresh air … you walk along the garden path, allowing your whole being to fill with peace and freedom. As you walk, you notice all the truly wonderful things that exist in your life … notice and appreciate all that you have. Your heart expands and fills with gratitude. You know and say "I am sincerely grateful for all that I have."

A huge weight feels lifted from your shoulders as you realize that you decide your life. This is exciting to know … because for a while … it seemed your life was out of control … and not going in the direction you wanted. It felt as though you could never achieve your goals … as though life is passing you by.

Now, with every step you take … hearing the calling of birds … feeling the breeze … seeing the beautiful flowers … trees … ferns … you notice how much freedom you have. You know that you create your life. Ahead, you see the entrance to your sacred power spot. Your spirits lift even higher as you walk forward with a spring in your step … feeling light … and anticipating success. Stepping inside … you pause to acknowledge the sacred space … to absorb the ambience.

SUBCONSCIOUS SCAFFOLDING

This is the part of the script where you should add your personal dreams. Be concrete—fill in the details of what you want to achieve, how you want to live, where you want to live, and with whom you want to do this. Engage all parts of it and see yourself working, traveling, or being romantic—feel it, imagine it, and enjoy the emotion of your vision.

Then, moving to the chair that is made just for you … sinking into the comfort … and feeling the surge of energy rise … you fill yourself with creative flow. Closing your eyes … you take a few minutes to imagine the life you want to create. Pause right now and fill your mind with the life you want. Take as long as you need. When you're finished, know and say "The future I create is abundant, creative, fulfilling, and purposeful."

Now, take another minute and fill in any details you may have missed. Pause right now and take all the time you need. When you're finished, know and say "I bring toward me all that I desire: travel, ease, opportunity, beauty, fulfilling relationships, success, and recognition."

As you expand with the enjoyment of living the life of your dreams … reviewing the wonderful aspects that fulfill you, you know and say "I use all of my abilities and feel satisfied with the results."

Now, it is time to leave … and as you head outside … with every step … your back is straighter … you are taller … and you enjoy knowing how much is ahead of you … how many opportunities await. You think about your plans and goals … think about your compelling future … about things you have yet to accomplish …. You know you can do anything you put your mind and heart into. You know and say "Everything I desire, intend, and work for comes to me now."

With every step back through the garden, your compelling future becomes more real. You feel excited with the desire to work hard … to start making plans that will bring your desires into reality. You feel a moment of doubt … can you really do it? And then you smile and know the universe is working with you and you are in creative flow. You know and say "Opportunities to fulfill my dreams present themselves every day, in every way."

Now, letting go of old, limiting beliefs … you know that your subconscious mind powerfully supports you in creating the life of your dreams. You know you can do it … because your subconscious mind is a powerful magnet … and you're willing to work hard to make your dreams reality. Full of the image of your new life, seeing, feeling, and experiencing it … you know and say "Every day, in every way, my subconscious mind powerfully creates the life of my highest dreams."

It feels good to allow yourself to enjoy your life … to be creative … to experience abundance … to feel fulfilled and live with purpose. You gladly release any burden of guilt that held you back … and with relief … relaxing even further … feeling proud, feeling happy … feeling grateful … you head toward the stairs … knowing you can always return. Reaching the stairs … giving thanks … you start up. On the count of five, you are awake, alert, and happy. It is good to be you.

One, coming up.

Two, becoming more awake, more alert, more aware.

Three, feeling fine … eyes start to flutter.

Four, feeling great … toes start to wiggle.

Five, feeling awake, aware, and fully restored to normal consciousness.

As you go forward, every time you doubt your ability to create your compelling future, you know you are being asked to let go of an old belief. You smile, and then know and say "Everything I desire, intend, and work for comes to me now."

Easing Writer's Block and Artistic Stasis

Posthypnotic Suggestions

- Right here, right now, I open to creative inspiration.

- Creative energy flows through me now. Ideas and expression are easy for me now.

- My subconscious mind is overflowing with creative ideas. I have everything I need inside of me to learn from and overcome creative blocks, right here, right now.

- Every day, in every way, I am powerfully supported in creative inspiration and expression.

 HYPNOTIC CONNECTION

The lively compilation of advice from leading creative professionals titled *Breakthrough!: Proven Strategies to Overcome Creative Block and Spark Your Imagination* by Alex Cornell is chock full of fun, unusual methods for overcoming even the most persistent block.

As you step off the last stair and sink into the soft, grassy soil … you notice the deep peace and total contentment that sweeps through you. Taking a deep breath … filling your lungs with clear, fresh air … you walk along the garden path, allowing your whole being to fill with creative energy.

Looking up, you see a tree house high in the branches of a massive oak tree. You immediately feel intense curiosity … an intense desire to explore the view from high above. You sprint to the base of the tree … grasp the rails of a ladder … and begin to climb. As you climb, creative ideas come into your mind. With each step upward … your mind becomes sharper and more focused … filling with new thoughts and images. You notice and appreciate that the higher you go … the more you are surrounded by creative inspiration. Your heart expands and fills with gratitude. You know and say "Right here, right now, I open to creative inspiration." You immediately feel enlivened … and climb faster … as ideas take shape in your mind.

Reaching the top of the ladder … you climb onto the broad platform of the tree house. A huge weight lifts from your shoulders as you realize that you have no shortage of creative energy; it is always flowing …. And this is a relief … because for a while … it seemed that you couldn't access your creative energy …. You felt blocked in expressing creative ideas … and sometimes you felt blocked in having any creative ideas at all. In fact, you remember feeling as though you might never have a creative idea again … as though you weren't a creative person.

Now, looking down … seeing the garden from a new vantage point … everything looks different. The garden is transformed … and birds fly close by … so close you can touch them … and, feeling the sway of the tree house in the breeze … you notice how inspired and creative you feel, how much freedom you have. You know you have what it takes to express your creative inspiration …. You know that, as long as you remain open, you can access creative flow. Smiling happily, you know and say "Creative energy flows through me now. Ideas and expression are easy for me now."

Sitting down in the sun … you see the project you're working on surrounded by a foreboding moat of old fears, doubts, and insecurities. You see that every time you approach your project … you're assaulted by doubts … that rise up as a stuck place within. Now … feeling the strong wind of creative energy … you see that you can build a bridge across the moat. As soon as you realize it … the bridge exists. Walking over it … old fears and doubts rise … and from this vantage point … it is easy to see that most of your fears are simply old, limiting beliefs … trying to protect you from failure. Thanking your block for keeping you safe … you explain that you are willing to take the risk of failure for the joy of creative expression.

Walking proudly over the moat of your fears and self-doubt … you approach a bolted door. It is guarded by a fierce warrior. Standing firm before the warrior, you ask to pass. The warrior points to a chair and you understand that you cannot pass until you receive a message from this block to your creative energy.

You sit … filling with calm and peace … hearing the wind … feeling the sun … relaxing every cell in your body …. You ask "What do I need to know? What have I been overlooking?" You sit quietly and listen. Pause for as long as you need.

SUBCONSCIOUS SCAFFOLDING

Have a large poster-sized paper and colored pens with you as you use this script. Draw images of your project and your blocks. Diagram your ideas, insights, thoughts, and images as they arrive. Approach your work in a new way.

When you're ready … you stand and nod to the warrior … who steps aside and the door opens. Stepping through … you approach your project with renewed insight and a fresh spirit. You smile as you are filled with inspired thoughts and impulses … happy and joyful … standing in creative flow. You know and say "My subconscious mind is overflowing with creative ideas and expression. I have everything I need inside of me to learn from and overcome creative blocks right here, right now."

Experiencing the freedom of pursuing your dreams … you enjoy knowing how much is ahead of you … how many opportunities for expression await you. You think about your projects … about the book you're writing, the painting you're unveiling, the play you're acting in, or the problem you're solving …. You see yourself at your book signing … or gallery opening … or opening night … see all of your dreams fulfilled. You feel satisfied and excited by the creative ventures still ahead.

Knowing that your subconscious mind powerfully supports you in creating inspiration and expression … you know you can do anything … because you are powerfully supported by the creative flow of the universe. You know and say "Every day, in every way, I am powerfully supported in creative inspiration and expression."

Feeling proud, feeling happy … feeling grateful … you say thank you to the inspirational tree house … and climb back down … and walk through the garden … heading toward the stairs … knowing you can always return. Reaching the stairs … giving thanks … you start up. On the count of five, you are awake, alert, and happy. Life is good.

One, coming up.

Two, becoming more awake, more alert, more aware.

Three, feeling fine … eyes start to flutter.

Four, feeling great … toes start to wiggle.

Five, feeling awake, aware, and fully restored to normal consciousness.

As you go forward, anytime you feel a creative block, you shake your body as you release old, limiting beliefs. You smile and know and say "Every day, in every way, I am powerfully supported in creative inspiration and expression."

The Least You Need to Know

- Creative thinking is the opposite of the repetitive thoughts of subconscious programming and a prerequisite for changing your life.
- Living intentionally is an act of creativity.
- Using self-hypnosis is a decision to live intentionally.
- Creativity generates internal energy that motivates action.
- The personality traits you need to be a creative person, you already have, and self-hypnosis can help you access them.

Past-Life Possibilities

Have you ever wondered whether or not you've lived before? Perhaps you traveled to a place you'd never been yet knew the street names and how to find your way through the city. Or perhaps you have a strong attraction to an ancient culture and know aspects of it not written in history books.

The possibility of past lives and reincarnation isn't a New Age invention; it's a persistent belief that exists in many ancient and current cultures. It's compelling to people, not because of the religious doctrines that advocate it, but because of the spontaneous memories many people have of past experiences. If you've ever been curious to know your own past lives, or future ones, you might enjoy investigating the scripts in this chapter.

In This Chapter

- Learning the benefits of knowing a past life
- Discovering how to use the Akashic record
- Traveling to a past life
- Glimpsing into a future situation

Life After Death

It's natural to be curious about what happens after you die; it's a question that's central to most religious beliefs. Even beyond religious doctrines, however, throughout many cultures and across vast spans of time, there is a prevalent belief that some part of you continues after you die. This part is often called the *soul*. Many also believe that the part of you that survives death can be *reincarnated*, or born again in a new body. A Huffington Post poll published in February 2013 revealed that 64 percent of Americans believe in life after death, while a Gallop poll showed even higher results, with an astounding 74 percent of Americans professing belief in life after death.

Because there is no scientific proof, why do so many people maintain this belief? Not surprisingly, personal experience, such as feeling the presence of a loved one who passed, hearing voices, seeing images, or remembering past lives, is the key reason many people believe that some part of us stays around after the body dies. Have you, a friend, or family member had such an experience?

For many people, the most compelling source of information about life after death comes from those who have had *near-death experiences (NDEs)*. An NDE occurs when a person's body has been declared dead, only to come alive later, sometimes several hours or even days later. The experiences of these people while their body is dead is the subject of numerous books, documentaries, and even an hour-long news program broadcast in January 2014 with Anderson Cooper on CNN titled "To Heaven and Back." The incidences of verifiable information they bring upon their return makes the possibility of life after death very convincing.

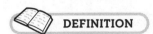

DEFINITION

> **Reincarnation** is the ability for the part of a person that survives death to be reborn in another body. **Near-death experience (NDE)** encompasses the experiences of people who have been declared clinically brain-dead yet come back to life hours or even days later.

The Importance of Past Lives

You may believe in life after death but find reincarnation more difficult to accept. Convincing support comes from the past-life memory of children. A remarkable number of children between the ages of 3 and 5 remember a former life. With no current life experience to explain what they remember, they're able to provide extensive details of a previous existence in different cultures and various time periods. Some even recognize older people in this life and remember knowing them 30 or 40 years earlier, correctly identifying personal stories, relationships, jewelry, and life details.

Are you curious about who you were, where you lived, and what you did in a past life? Past lives certainly hold a certain intrigue, yet there are more reasons to seek past-life information than mere curiosity. Here are some possibilities of what you might uncover and understand:

- The source of your fears and phobias

- The connection between you and people you know

- The dynamics of your relationships

- What you're here to learn

- Why you feel compelled to do certain things

- Your talents and where they came from

- The source of the circumstances in your life

- Where recurring challenges come from

- The wisdom of past cultures

- Spiritual understanding

As you can see, there are vast amounts you can learn and quite a lot of benefit in exploring past lives. You may still wonder how it's possible to regain lost memory. How do you retain details from life to life? Where are they stored?

Accessing Past Lives

The purpose of reincarnation is to learn and grow, and the experiences of your past lives create the conditions of this life in order to complete your growth process. By accessing the memories that exist at the level of your soul, you can learn about your past lives. The self-hypnosis scripts in this chapter helps you shift your awareness and move your perception into your experience of a previous life.

Past-life information is thought to be held in a universal record, sometimes called the *Akashic record*. The Akashic record is where all the information that creates the world and is generated by all that happens here is kept. The idea of an all-encompassing record of life is not a new idea; the Assyrians, Phoenicians, Babylonians, Hebrews, and Greeks held a common belief in the existence of tablets of spiritual wisdom. The repository also has been called the Hall of Records, the Book of Judgment, The Book of Two Truths, and The Book of Life. This record is thought of as a holograph that contains the details of everything that ever has and ever will occur—all the experiences of every person that has and ever will live. Consequently, in addition to whatever else it might contain, it holds a record of the history of humanity.

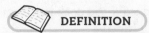 **DEFINITION**

The **Akashic record** is an all-encompassing record of everything that's ever happened, including the life history of every person—past, present, and future.

Most importantly, as a hologram, each of us has access to the information held in the Akashic record. The part of us in connection with the Akashic record is the subconscious mind. Different cultures and present-day intuitives describe inducing altered states of consciousness to access information in the Akashic records. For example, Maya priests smoked special tobacco and went into trances where they "walked among the stars." At the Delphi Oracle in Greece, the priestesses went into trances before answering questions, as do present-day psychics. Most traditions use some type of meditation to shift levels of awareness. Whatever the method, an altered state of awareness is part of accessing the record, which makes self-hypnosis a perfect tool.

Subconscious Travel

Accessing the Akashic record is a wonderful vehicle to explore not only your past lives, but your future in this life or a future life as well. You can think of it as time traveling through your past and future experiences. In addition, why not access information from different locations in this time? If the Akashic record is a hologram, you have entry to all parts of it through your focused attention. The following scripts concentrate on exploring a past life, as well as the future outcome of one of your goals in this life. You can modify the two scripts in this chapter to delve into these other areas.

Remember that the future contains many different possible realities. Which one you end up with is decided by your choices; it's not preordained. So when you use the future script, you're previewing the most likely projection based on where you are right now. If you like where you see yourself, great—continue the way you're going and you'll be supporting that outcome. If you don't like where you see yourself, set a new direction so you can end up in a different place.

As always, use the induction in Chapter 7 before you begin. You might want to spend a few minutes thinking about what you're interested in knowing and personalize the scripts. These two scripts are different from others in this book, as you'll be answering questions in the text as you go. Here are a few tips to get the most from your journey:

- After each set of questions is a pause for reflection and exploration. Take all the time you need to fill in details and, if you can, take the time to write them down.

- When you read a question, close your eyes and allow the answer to come.

- Take the first impression you get; don't analyze it or question whether or not it's real. Just accept it and explore the detail within it.

- If you don't get an answer, move on.

- The scripts are set up to stimulate your subconscious mind, so if you don't get an answer now, pay attention to your dreams.

- You can use paper and pen or a digital device to jot down impressions, feelings, and answers.

- If you're an artist, you may want to draw the images instead of writing, perhaps using symbols to code the information you receive.

- Keep a notebook by your bed for any additional information that comes through your dreams.

- Make sure you have plenty of time and won't be disturbed as you explore.

> **HYPNOTIC CONNECTION**
>
> If you find the information on the Akashic record, NDEs, past lives, and children's memories fascinating, there are great books in the resource appendix on these subjects. For starters, check out my book *The Complete Idiot's Guide to The Akashic Record,* which covers many of these spellbinding topics.

It's a good idea to make a recording of these scripts so that you can focus fully on the process. However, reading in a relaxed state is also dynamic and produces good results. Remember that three dots, a period, or a question mark in the scripts indicate a short pause and should be observed. The scripts are written to give you the most freedom in exploring the areas you are interested in. Enjoy your exploration!

Retrieving Past-Life Memories

 Track 7

Posthypnotic Suggestions

- I'm sincerely grateful for all that I am.

- Past-life information stored in the Akashic record and in my subconscious mind is available to me now.

- I am in control of this experience and at any time can return to the present time by saying "enough."

- I see only information that is for my highest and best good.

- I am ready for any additional information from my subconscious mind and Akashic record about my past lives and easily and safely receive it in my dreams.

Now that you've descended the stairs and entered the garden ... you can use this relaxed, alert state of mind to powerfully support change. As you step off the last stair and sink into the soft, grassy soil ... notice the deep peace and total contentment that sweeps through you. Taking a deep breath ... filling your lungs with clear, fresh air ... you walk along the garden path, allowing your whole being to fill with peace and freedom. As you walk, you notice all the truly wonderful things that exist in your life .... You notice and appreciate all that you are. Your heart expands and fills with gratitude. You know and say "I am sincerely grateful for all that I am."

Suddenly, you see another set of stairs ... stairs going down to a different level, a different vista. You understand these stairs are moving into the Akashic record and if you decide to go down them, you will arrive in a past life. Listening closely, you can hear voices coming from this lower level. You feel pulled toward these voices ... feel like you almost recognize them ... can almost hear what they're saying. You walk toward the stairs ... feeling happy ... safe ... and curious.

You decide you want to descend to this deeper level ... a level where you know all the answers ... to any questions you have. You know that if you go down the stairs, you are in control. You can come back anytime. If you're uncomfortable at any moment ... you can say "enough" and be right back in the garden ... safe ... warm ... comfortable. You feel the sun warm on your face ... your shoulders ... your back ... as you decide you will go down the stairs.

Before you go ... you form an intention of something in this life that you want to understand better ... and now let that intention go ... knowing your subconscious will make the connection when and if it's important.

Now you are ready .... You know and say "I see only information that is for my highest and best good." Starting down the stairs ... you count each step as you descend. When you reach 10, you will emerge in a past life.

  WISE COUNSEL

Past-life information links with current life situations. If you're exploring the source of trauma in your present life, you will benefit further with the support and guidance of a trained hypnotherapist.

One ... going deeper.

Two ... feeling safe and secure.

Three ... letting go of your surroundings ... going deeper.

Four ... feeling safe ... happy ... excited.

Five ... noticing a strong, protective force all around you.

Six ... going deeper ... surrounded in protection.

Seven ... knowing nothing can hurt you ... you are in control.

Eight ... knowing you are in control of the information you receive ... and the experience you have.

Nine ... protected ... safe ... in control ... anticipating enjoyment.

Ten. Eyes closed ... head down ... you move off the last step.

A warm feeling of happiness ... and acceptance flows through you. You know and say "Past-life information stored in the Akashic record and in my subconscious mind is available to me now."

Opening your eyes ... you look at your feet. What are you wearing on your feet? What do your feet look like? Is it day or is it night? Are you inside or outside? Are you male or female?

Take a moment to observe, explore, and record this information. [Long Pause]

Now look at the ground. What is under your feet? Look at your legs ... what is covering your legs? Take a minute and look at your body and your clothes. Hold out your hands and look at them. Are you wearing jewelry? How is your hair styled? Do you have a beard? Notice everything you can about your body, clothes, and accessories. How do they feel to wear, to touch, to smell?

Take a moment to observe, explore, and record this information. [Long Pause]

Now look up ... and notice your surroundings. Take a complete turn and look all around. If you're inside, look at the furnishings, the walls and paintings, the ceilings and floors, windows and doors. Notice the style of the building, the fireplace. What do you smell? How do you feel? If you're outside, look at the landscape; are you near water? What kind of trees, flowers, fences, buildings, and animals are around you? Is the sun out or the moon, or is it a different setting entirely? Is there a breeze? What do you smell? How do you feel?

Take a moment to observe, explore, and record this information. [Long Pause]

Are there people around you? Look at the people and notice what they look like, what they're wearing, and what they're doing. Are they talking to you? Notice how you're interacting. How do you know these people? What culture, what time period are you in? Do you love any of the people present? Is there someone special near you? What are people saying? How are you feeling?

You know, on a very deep level, that you're safe ... and protected ... no matter what is happening. You're in control of staying or leaving and can leave anytime. But now you enjoy participating in the scene around you ... enjoy learning all you can about this past life. You know that if you want ... you can go backward or forward to different times in this life. If you need to know something, you can simply move to another point in the story. In fact, right now, move to a different time ... a different scene that it's important for you to see.

Explore this new scene. Take your time and enjoy being in ... this life. Immerse yourself .... Feel the textures .... Smell the surroundings .... Notice your emotions ... knowing you are in control and can leave anytime.

Take all the time you need to observe, explore, and record this information. [Long Pause]

A huge weight feels lifted from your shoulders as you realize that it doesn't matter if you get all the information from this life right now .... You know your subconscious mind will give you information later ... will send the information in a dream. You know that before you go to sleep, you can say "I am ready for any additional information from my subconscious mind and Akashic record about my past lives and easily and safely receive it in my dreams."

SUBCONSCIOUS SCAFFOLDING

The inducing lucid dreaming script in Chapter 21 can be used with both scripts in this chapter to increase the information you receive through dreams. You may also want to use the meeting your spiritual guide script from that chapter and take your guide with you on this journey.

You've enjoyed the time here in this past life … even the parts that were sad or challenging. It's interesting and important for you to know what you did and who you were. And now you wonder … what were the important lessons of this life? What did your soul learn? What is the gift this life gives to you now?

Take a moment and allow that information to enter into you. [Long Pause]

Now you wonder … is there anything you still need to finish in this life? Anything you didn't say then to the people you loved that you need and want to say now? Any action you were unable to complete before you died? Or is there another piece of information you still need?

Take a moment to complete anything still left unfinished. [Long Pause]

Now … feeling complete … feeling happy … knowing what you need to know … take a moment to fully forgive people in this past life who may have hurt you … and also forgive yourself for any hurt you may have caused. Send love to those you knew before … and know differently now … and when you're ready, simply say "enough." Immediately, you are in the garden … safe, happy, and content.

Hearing the calling of birds … feeling the breeze … seeing the beautiful flowers … trees … ferns … you notice how free and happy you feel. You are excited by all you learned and take a moment to consider how this information changes your current life. Stop to sit on a bench and take the time to consider any additional memories, impressions, ideas, and thoughts.

When you're finished, it's time to leave. [Long Pause]

As you head back toward the stairs … enjoy letting go of old, limiting beliefs …. Know you're in charge of the circumstances in your life … know your choices today create your future. It feels good to allow yourself to enjoy your current life … to be creative … to experience abundance … to feel fulfilled and live with purpose. You gladly release any burden of guilt from your previous life … and with relief … relaxing even further … feeling proud, feeling happy … feeling grateful … you head toward the stairs … knowing you can always return. Reaching the stairs … giving thanks … you start up. On the count of five, you are awake, alert, and happy.

One, coming up.

Two, becoming more awake, more alert, more aware.

Three, feeling fine … eyes start to flutter.

Four, feeling great … toes start to wiggle.

Five, feeling awake, aware, and fully restored to normal consciousness.

Now, every time you want more details to arrive through dreams, as you go to sleep, you know and say "I am ready for any additional information from my subconscious mind and Akashic record about my past lives and easily and safely receive it in my dreams."

Previewing Your Future

Posthypnotic Suggestions

- I am sincerely grateful for all that is in my life.

- I see only information that is for my highest and best good.

- I am ready to see a glimpse of my future in the Akashic record.

- Everything I desire, intend, and work for comes to me now.

- Every day, in every way, my subconscious mind powerfully creates the life of my highest good.

- I am ready to easily and safely receive in my dreams and visions information from my subconscious mind and Akashic record about my future.

As you step off the last stair and sink into the soft, grassy soil … you notice the deep peace and total contentment that sweeps through you. Taking a full breath … filling your lungs with clear, fresh air … you walk along the garden path, allowing your whole being to fill with peace and freedom. As you walk, you notice all the truly wonderful things that exist in your life … notice and appreciate all that you have. Your heart expands and fills with gratitude. You know and say "I am sincerely grateful for all that is in my life."

You are thinking about a goal that you are working to achieve … a desire you have for the future. With every step you take … hearing the calling of birds … feeling the breeze … seeing the beautiful flowers … trees … ferns … you notice how much freedom you have. You know that you create your life. Ahead, you see the entrance to your sacred power spot. Your spirits lift even higher as you walk forward with a spring in your step … feeling light … and anticipating an adventure. Stepping inside … you pause to acknowledge the sacred space … to absorb the ambience … and give thanks.

Then, moving to the chair that is made just for you … sinking into the comfort … and feeling the surge of energy rise … you relax even further. Closing your eyes … you realize that in your power spot … your future exits right alongside your present … in this place, you can relax and allow yourself to travel through the Akashic record to your own future. You don't know what you will find … but you are interested to know how your goals work out. You are relaxed … knowing you don't have to see everything now since your subconscious mind will send you dreams to further your information.

HYPNOTIC CONNECTION

Inventors are often inspired through dreams. Consider Elias Howe, inventor of the sewing machine. The standard sewing needles with point and thread holes at opposite ends didn't work with his machine. One night, Howe dreamed he was captured by natives and ordered to invent a sewing machine by morning. When the sun rose, he had no machine and the natives attacked him, jabbing spears at his body. As they came menacingly closer, Howe noticed that the spears had holes in the spear points. He watched as the spears were thrust at him, moving backward and forward, backward and forward. He immediately saw how to make the correct needle.

Settling into the seat … you see a set of stairs opening into the clouds. You know these stairs lead into the Akashic record … and if you travel along these stairs … you will be part of a scene from your future. You also know that at any time you can say "enough" and be back in you power spot. You know you are safe … protected … and in control.

Excited … happy … you decide to take the stairs … to see five years into your future. Holding your goal in mind … you know and say "I see only information that is for my highest and best good." Then … heading five years into the future … you start along the stairs …counting each step as you go.

One … going deeper.

Two … feeling safe and secure.

Three … letting go of your surroundings … going deeper.

Four … feeling safe … happy … excited.

Five … noticing a strong, protective force all around you.

Six … going deeper … surrounded in protection.

Seven … knowing nothing can hurt you … you are in control.

Eight … knowing you are in control of the information you receive … the experience you have.

Nine … protected … safe … in control … anticipating enjoyment.

Ten. Eyes closed … head down … you step off the last step.

Stepping off the last step, you know and say "I am ready to experience in the Akashic record a glimpse five years into my future."

Opening your eyes … take a look around. Is it day or night? Are you inside or outside? What are you wearing? Do you recognize where you are? What are you doing?

Take a moment to see, feel, and experience the ambience.

Who are you with, and what is the context of the scene? Are there people present whom you don't know yet? Welcome them. Are there people you expected to see who are gone? Send them a blessing.

Observe everything around you. Is there something you need to do now that will impact your future outcome in positive ways?

Ask yourself "What is important for me to know?"

Take a moment to observe, explore, and record this information.

Now, is there something you need to say to the people you're with, or something you need to investigate further before you go? Do you understand what you came here to learn?

Take a moment to explore and record this information.

When you're ready, when you have all the information you need to inspire your actions in the present, give thanks to all the people you've interacted with. Give thanks to the Akashic record and your subconscious mind. Then say "enough" ... and immediately you are back in your sacred spot ... relaxing in the comfort of your special chair.

Take a moment to remember and record the information you received and wrote.

Now, it's time to leave ... and as you head outside ... closing your sacred spot ... giving thanks ... with every step through the garden ... you feel stronger ... happier ... and ready for challenges ahead. You enjoy knowing how much is ahead of you ... how many opportunities await you. You think about your plans and goals ... think about the steps you need to take ... about things you have yet to accomplish .... You know you can do anything you put your mind and heart to. You know and say "Everything I desire, intend, and work for comes to me now."

 SUBCONSCIOUS SCAFFOLDING

This script nicely augments the script in Chapter 19 for creating your compelling future. Using them both may help you fine-tune your direction.

Now, letting go of old limiting beliefs ... you know that your subconscious mind powerfully supports you in creating the best possible outcome in all situations. You know you can do it ... because your subconscious mind is a powerful magnet ... and you're willing to work hard to make your dreams reality. Full of the knowledge of what you need to do to achieve your goal—seeing, feeling, and experiencing it ... you know and say "Every day, in every way, my subconscious mind powerfully creates the life of my highest good."

Relaxing even further ... feeling proud, feeling happy ... feeling grateful ... you head toward the stairs ... knowing you can always return. Reaching the stairs ... giving thanks ... you start up. On the count of five, you are awake, alert, and happy.

One, coming up.

Two, becoming more awake, more alert, more aware.

Three, feeling fine … eyes start to flutter.

Four, feeling great … toes start to wiggle.

Five, feeling awake, aware, and fully restored to normal consciousness.

As you go forward, every time you wonder if the steps you are taking will get you where you want to go, know and say "I am ready to easily and safely receive through my dreams information about my past lives that exist in my subconscious mind and Akashic record."

The Least You Need to Know

- Personal experience, such as feeling the presence of a loved one who's passed, hearing voices, seeing images, or remembering past lives, is the key reason many people believe that some part of us stays around after the body dies.

- People who have been declared dead yet come back to life often have experiences with verifiable information that life exists after death.

- Knowing a past life can help you understand the source of fears, phobias, talents, relationship dynamics, and persistent challenges in your life.

- An altered state of awareness is part of accessing the Akashic record, which makes self-hypnosis a perfect tool.

- Through the Akashic record, you can learn about your past lives, as well as glimpse your future.

Awakening Your Spirit

It's fitting to end this book with a chapter devoted to awakening the spirit. In truth, by working with the subconscious, self-hypnosis interacts with the spirit in profound ways. If the central part of your life is your connection to your spiritual center, this chapter is for you.

All the scripts in this chapter can be used to enhance work you're doing with scripts in other chapters, allowing you to alternate complementary scripts in your self-hypnosis plan.

In This Chapter

- Increasing your self-awareness
- Beginning to lucid dream
- Awakening intuition
- Deepening spiritual practice

Freeing Your Inner Oracle

Increasing awareness is an exciting and important aspect of personal development. Living an authentic life in alignment with your vision and mission is the goal of personal development. The more awareness you have, the better you're able to make decisions that reflect your true self. Awareness begins with paying attention to your emotions, thoughts, attitudes, and beliefs and noticing how they engage the world around you. Simply through self-hypnosis exercises, you've already increased your self-awareness.

You might be eager to expand your awareness and use deeper, more hidden abilities. Intuition and psychic perception are innate abilities that everyone has, but most people never fully develop them. You're probably aware of your gut feelings, hunches, and intuitions and use them to guide your life. The more aware you are of your intuitive process, the more your decisions can reflect your true self.

The first script in this section increases your conscious use of intuition. It supports the awakening of the higher senses within your body and mind and increases your reception of information from your subconscious, making the information conscious. The second script increases your awareness through *lucid dreaming*. Dream states are the perfect medium for the subconscious mind to communicate with you and offer guidance. Lucid dreaming gives you control over what you do and what information you pursue while asleep.

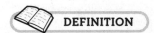 **DEFINITION**

> **Lucid dreaming** is the ability to become aware during a dream that you are dreaming. You can continue the dream while having control over what you do and say.

As always, begin the script after using the induction in Chapter 7 or key 1, instant relaxation. You may also want to keep a notepad nearby to write things down. These scripts can be used in conjunction with earlier scripts for problem solving, past-life retrieval, and easing creative blocks to help increase your reception of the information you need.

Increasing Intuition and Psychic Perception

Posthypnotic Suggestions

- Every day, in every way, I easily pick up intuitive insight and psychic information.

- I am fully alive with psychic ability; my mind, body, and soul are awake.

- My subconscious mind powerfully awakens my intuition and psychic perception.

- My third eye is open and my psychic perceptions are awake. I use my abilities for the highest and best good.

- Everything I know and see, I use for positive benefit and the higher good.

- Every day, in every way, I am more aligned with my spiritual source and better able to receive intuitive messages.

As you step off the last stair and sink into the soft, grassy soil … you notice the deep peace and total contentment that sweeps through you. Taking a deep breath … filling your lungs with clear, fresh air … you walk along the garden path, allowing your whole being to fill with tingling awareness. You know and say "Every day, in every way, I easily pick up intuitive insight and psychic information."

As you walk through the garden … hearing the call of birds … feeling the breeze … you notice how clear your mind is … and how acute your senses are. The smells of the garden … the flower blossoms … leafy soil … fresh breeze … are sharp and clarified. Your hearing is acute … the sounds of the birds calling … the breeze through the tree … all the sounds are sharper and clearer … as though your senses are expanded. Even your eyes see more clearly … see colors more distinctly. In fact … it feels as though your senses are so expanded that you can see … hear … and feel outside of your normal range. Even your body is alive with sensation … feeling the undercurrents of information … that wash over and around you … and are picked up in your energy field. You know intuitive ability is natural and innate … and you are excited by this awakening. You know and say "I am fully alive with psychic ability; my mind, body, and soul are awake."

You know your body and senses are receiving more information than your conscious mind is aware of. And you enjoy knowing that all this information is received and stored in your subconscious mind. It's fun to know that you have the ability to access this information … to be more intuitive and psychic … and you also know … that the more you relax … the clearer your mind is … and the more acute your awareness. In fact, every time you want to know something … you know that all you have to do is relax and tap into your subconscious. You know and say "My subconscious mind powerfully awakens my intuition and psychic perception."

It comes as a surprise to you … to understand that it's okay to know things other people don't know … you understand that the hunches you have are messages from your subconscious … and you trust your hunches and gut feelings … and enjoy following the information you receive. You know that your psychic impressions are increasing … and every day you have more. You can feel your third eye … the spot between your eyebrows … opening. Every day you see and feel more … and trust your intuition more fully. You also know that you use your abilities responsibly. You know and say "My third eye is open and my psychic perceptions are awake. I use my abilities for the highest and best good."

SUBCONSCIOUS SCAFFOLDING

You can use this script along with other scripts to obtain more information on a particular subject. For example, use it with one of the creativity scripts in Chapter 19 for fresh inspiration, with the attracting abundance script in Chapter 18 to see new ways to become wealthy, or with the exercises in Chapter 6 to discover your vision and mission. Tips on how to combine scripts are found in Chapter 7.

Now, letting go of old, limiting beliefs … you know that your subconscious mind powerfully supports you. You know you are increasing your ability … because your subconscious mind is powerfully connected to your spiritual source. Taking a moment, you imagine seeing friends … being at work … solving problems … while following your intuitive insight. You know and say "Everything I know and see, I use for positive benefit and higher good."

You are excited … knowing you have increased insight into problems … and additional information to make decisions. In fact … when you use your abilities, you feel more fully yourself … more completely at one with your path and purpose. Relaxing even further … you smile … knowing you are connected to your spiritual source … that your intuition and psychic perceptions are messages your subconscious is giving you from your spiritual source. You know and say "Every day, in every way, I am more aligned with my spiritual source and better able to receive intuitive messages."

Feeling proud, feeling happy … feeling in control … you give thanks to your subconscious mind as you walk toward the stairs … knowing you can always return. Reaching the stairs … giving thanks … you start up. On the count of five, you are awake, alert, and happy. It is good to be you.

One, coming up.

Two, becoming more awake, more alert, more aware.

Three, feeling fine … eyes start to flutter.

Four, feeling great … toes start to wiggle.

Five, feeling awake, aware, and fully restored to normal consciousness.

Now, every time you feel your body come alive—seeing and hearing more acutely—you know you are receiving psychic information. You know and say "Every day, in every way, I easily pick up intuitive insight and psychic information."

Inducing Lucid Dreaming

Posthypnotic Suggestions

- I easily wake in my dreams and continue dreaming. I have control over my dream actions.

- Lucid dreaming is an excellent canvass for my subconscious mind to give me messages from my spiritual source.

- I am a self-aware observer in my dreams, able to observe myself as I'm dreaming and remember what I see.

- I enter lucid dreams easily and trust my memory to recall everything I need from my lucid dream, exactly when I need it.

- Every day, in every way, my ability to lucid dream improves.

As you step off the last stair and sink into the soft, grassy soil … you notice the deep peace and total contentment that sweeps through you. Taking a deep breath … filling your lungs with clear, fresh air … you walk along the garden path, allowing your whole being to fill with confidence and freedom.

As you walk through the garden … hearing the call of birds … feeling the breeze … you notice how clear your mind is, how sharp your awareness. You realize that you can have this same degree of awareness during your dreams … that you are able to lucid dream at will. In fact, you realize that you often lucid dream … even if you don't always remember. You know that lucid dreaming is very much like self-hypnosis … because you're deeply relaxed, alert, and aware … able to participate in dream images while having total control over your actions. You know and say "I easily wake in my dreams and continue dreaming. I have control over my dream actions."

 HYPNOTIC CONNECTION

Excellent lucid dreaming CDs can be found online at The Monroe Institute (monroeinstitute.org) and Hay House (hayhouse.com).

You know that lucid dreaming is highly desirable …. In a lucid dream, you can learn new skills … meet people … go to spiritual planes … and receive messages from your spiritual source. You enjoy knowing that in your dreams you can explore any part of the universe … can go to any time period … and have total recall. You know and say "Lucid dreaming is an excellent canvas for my subconscious mind to give me messages from my spiritual source."

You also know … that the more you relax … the clearer your mind is … and the better your memory. In fact, every time you need to remember something … you know that all you have to do is relax. You know and say "I am a self-aware observer in my dreams, able to observe myself as I'm dreaming and remember what I see."

You know that a lucid dream is a very creative state of mind and that you can solve many problems … talk to people with whom you need to resolve conflict … and be an ambassador to other planes. You also know that every night as you sleep, you enter lucid dreams. As you go to sleep, you say "I enter lucid dreams easily and trust my memory to recall everything I need from my lucid dream, exactly when I need it."

Now, letting go of old limiting beliefs … you know that your subconscious mind powerfully supports you in enjoying lucid dreaming whenever you desire. As you go to sleep, you need only ask. You know you can do it … because your subconscious mind is a powerful tool. You know and say "Every day, in every way, my ability to lucid dream improves."

Feeling proud, feeling happy … feeling in control … you give thanks to your subconscious mind as you walk toward the stairs … knowing you can always return. Reaching the stairs … giving thanks … you start up. On the count of five, you are awake, alert, and happy, knowing you are a lucid dreaming maestro.

One, coming up.

Two, becoming more awake, more alert, more aware.

Three, feeling fine … eyes start to flutter.

Four, feeling great … toes start to wiggle.

Five, feeling awake, aware, and fully restored to normal consciousness.

Now, every night when you go to sleep, as you enter the hypnagogic state or aware relaxation, you know and say "I easily wake in my dreams and continue dreaming. I have control over my dream actions."

Deepening Your Spiritual Practice

One of the benefits of self-hypnosis is that it enriches your spiritual practice. By teaching you how to induce and use trance states, self-hypnosis helps you find deeper levels of meditation and prayer. In addition, as you saw earlier, self-hypnosis boosts your awareness. Because awareness is the first requisite of spiritual growth, combining self-hypnosis with your spiritual practice is a natural partnership.

As you use the scripts in this book to take charge of your life and overcome addictive behaviors and limiting thoughts, you grow in self-worth and authentic expression. The blocks to spiritual growth melt before your developing self.

In this section, I provide scripts that lead you to insights on your path and purpose. Use the scripts in a self-hypnosis program in combination with lucid dreaming or developing intuition to increase the insights you achieve. You'll need a notebook as you engage these scripts to record the information you receive.

> **SUBCONSCIOUS SCAFFOLDING**
>
> If writing notes is cumbersome, you can use a tape recorder to capture your thoughts and answers to questions. Or, if you are feeling adventurous, try the automatic writing technique provided in Chapter 5.

Finding Your Path and Purpose

Posthypnotic Suggestions

- I easily perceive and know my path and purpose.

- There are no accidents. I am where I'm supposed to be, doing what I'm supposed to be doing.

- My subconscious mind powerfully supports me in knowing my path and purpose. I recognize the signs and receive information through dreams.

- I know who I am and walk my path with purpose. I am in the right place at the right time.

As you step off the last stair and sink into the soft, grassy soil … you notice the deep peace and total contentment that sweeps through you. Taking a deep breath, filling your lungs with clear, fresh air, you walk along the garden path. As you walk past lovely flowers of pink, yellow, purple, blue … your whole being fills with peace and freedom. Moving into the warmth of the sun, feeling the warmth spread over your face … your throat … your chest … warmth moving through your whole body … you smile, recognizing the garden and anticipating enjoyment.

Looking ahead, you feel a surge of excitement as you see the opening to your sacred space. You walk calmly toward this beautiful place … grateful you have somewhere to go to access your higher mind. You move toward the sanctuary of your inner sacred space … with appreciation … excited to ask the questions you have come to find answers to. You stop at the entrance … and pause in acknowledgment of the gift of this sacred place. Stepping inside, you take a minute to absorb the ambience … to acknowledge the space and the objects that are special to you. You know you will find what you are looking for here and say "I easily perceive and know my path and purpose."

Settling into the seat that is made for you … you notice the feeling of acceptance … and notice the upsurge of energy through your system. You are charged and ready to go! Feeling calm … and relaxed … yet charged and ready for action … you allow yourself to move to an even deeper state of relaxed, alert attention. To drop into … on the count of three … an even deeper level of awareness. One … two … three. You are now in a very deep trance … able to see your life … as though watching it from a distance … as though your life is a movie on a screen.

Wanting to understand your path and purpose … the reason you are here on the planet at this time … you allow images of your life to pass before you on the screen of your mind's eye. On the screen … you observe that all the important people who moved through your life … the people … and ideas … that changed the direction of your life … are all together on the screen. You notice them and how each makes you feel. You take a minute … all the time you want … to remember the ways each person came into your life and how you were changed. You realize that none of these people arrived by accident … and you see on the movie screen … the synchronicities that occurred to bring you together. You know and say "There are no accidents. I am where I'm supposed to be, doing what I'm supposed to be doing."

Looking at all these people … remembering the synchronicities … observing the changes you made in your direction … a design begins to emerge …. You begin to see the theme behind all your choices and the people you meet. You begin to see the purpose that holds everything together.

Take a few minutes to fully explore the design … to really see the purpose in your life. Write down the names … and everything you see. Take all the time you want.

 MESMERIZING MORSEL

"Our prime purpose in this life is to help others. And if you can't help them, at least don't hurt them."

—The Fourteenth Dalai Lama

Imagine all you want to accomplish … and know the desire to create these goals comes out of your path and purpose. Your desire is not an accident. Separating your true desire from your ego needs … you also recognize that developing your soul is part of your path. Your growth is not selfish … it is your job. You know that you are growing more fully into your purpose every day. You know and say "Every day, in every way, I walk my path with clarity and live more of my purpose for being here."

Now, when you're ready, ask your spiritual source … and/or your subconscious mind … for direction. Ask to be shown your path and purpose as fully as possible at this time. Take a few minutes to let images, words, and ideas flow through you and onto your paper.

When you're ready … when you have received all that is clear in this moment … you are relieved to know that it's okay if you don't have all the answers now … because your subconscious mind will continue to send you information. You may get sudden insights … have visions … or intuitions. Or you may receive more information in your dreams. You know and say "My subconscious mind powerfully supports me in knowing my path and purpose. I recognize the signs and receive information through dreams."

Feeling proud, feeling happy ... you give thanks to the garden ... your sacred space ... and you. Continue walking back through the garden ... heading toward the stairs ... knowing you can always return. Reaching the stairs ... you give thanks ... saying "I know who I am and walk my path with purpose." Taking a deep breath ... you start up the stairs. On the count of five, you are awake, alert, and happy.

One, coming up.

Two, becoming more awake, more alert, more aware.

Three, feeling fine ... eyes start to flutter.

Four, feeling great ... toes start to wiggle.

Five, feeling awake, aware, and fully restored to normal consciousness.

As you go forward, meeting challenges as you reach for your goals, anytime you wonder if you are in the right place, stand tall and relaxed and say "I know who I am and walk my path with purpose. I am in the right place at the right time."

> **SUBCONSCIOUS SCAFFOLDING**
>
> The idea of purpose and path are very similar to that of vision and mission discussed in Chapter 6. You might use this script and then return to Chapter 6 and combine what you found in this experience with your vision and mission statements.

Meeting Your Spiritual Guide

 Track 8

Posthypnotic Suggestions

- I am a spiritual being engaged in physical reality. I have everything I need inside of me.

- All of the universe is one; every being is interconnected. I have everything I need inside of me to connect with everything outside.

- Through my guide, I have access to spiritual guidance every day, in every way.

As you step off the last stair … and walk out into the garden … you open to the brilliance of light all around. Listening to the birds calling … smelling the blossoming flowers … you feel a surge of excitement … knowing this is going to be a very special day.

You notice that the light seems to be coming from somewhere ahead … and you walk toward it. As you walk … enjoying the beauty all around … you feel the beauty inside your own heart … and your heart expands with light … and joy. You continue to walk toward the light and you begin to see … that the light is alive. You can see individual streams of light … filaments of light … that sway and undulate … and move with awareness. For some reason, this feels very uplifting … and when you see this light … you feel expanded. You are aware that the light in your heart is the same light …. It resonates with the same frequency. You know and say "I am a spiritual being, engaged in physical reality. I have everything I need inside of me."

You now continue to walk toward the light … connecting with the trees … feeling one with the life in this beautiful garden … knowing the essence of the garden is love. Your heart continues to expand as you realize what an incredible gift you enjoy … as a spiritual being … to have a physical experience. Filled with gratitude and love … you round the corner … to the source of the light.

Sitting next to an enormous oak tree … is a being so brilliant … so alive … you need to shield your eyes … even as your heart leaps almost out of your chest … to meet the emanations of this being. Birds, rabbits, deer, wolves, and every type of animal lie at the feet of this being … basking in its radiance.

Turning, the being sees you … and its face lights with pleasure. Inside your head, you hear the words … "I've been waiting so long for this moment … I am so very happy to be here with you." The words blossom in your heart, and you are filled with love, gratitude, and delight.

Suddenly, you realize … this being has always been a part of you … you just didn't see it. Sitting down next to the being in this lovely thicket … surrounded by nature … and standing stones … with the blue sky above … and animals all round … you feel total peace. You know and say "All the universe is one; every being is interconnected. I have everything I need inside of me to connect with everything outside."

The being leans in toward you and asks if there is anything you want to know. And you do. Take as long as you like to ask questions and talk with your spiritual guide. If he or she has a name, ask it. Write everything down. Take as long as you want. [Long Pause]

When you're finished … when you have everything you need … you stand to leave. You're momentarily sad to be leaving the warmth of this light … yet you know you must. You know that it is your job to keep this light in your heart … and that you can connect with your spiritual guide anytime … anywhere … through the light in your heart. You know you can ask questions … and receive answers. The answers may come through intuition … through a vision … or sudden insight …. The answers may come in a dream. Or you can meet your guide in your sacred space and speak directly. You know and say "Through my guide, I have access to spiritual guidance every day, in every way."

MESMERIZING MORSEL

"There is no need for temples, no need for complicated philosophies. My brain and my heart are my temples; my philosophy is kindness."

—The Fourteenth Dalai Lama

Feeling uplifted … you give thanks to your guide … to the special place you are in … to the garden … and to the light within yourself. Walking back through the garden … heading toward the stairs … you know the light is inside. Reaching the stairs … you give thanks … saying "I know who I am and walk my path with purpose." Taking a deep breath … you start up the stairs. On the count of five, you are awake, alert, and happy.

One, coming up.

Two, becoming more awake, more alert, more aware.

Three, feeling fine … eyes start to flutter.

Four, feeling great … toes start to wiggle.

Five, feeling awake, aware, and fully restored to normal consciousness.

As you go forward to meet challenges, keep the light within alive. Anytime you feel lost or alone, stop, know, and say "I am a spiritual being engaged in physical reality. I have everything I need inside of me right now."

The Least You Need to Know

- Awareness of emotions, thoughts, attitudes, and beliefs and how they engage the world around you is enhanced through self-hypnosis.
- Intuition and psychic perception are natural and innate.
- Dream states are the perfect medium for the subconscious mind to communicate with you and offer guidance. Lucid dreaming gives you control over what you do and what information you pursue while asleep.
- Self-hypnosis enriches your spiritual practice by inducing a trance that enables you to attain a deeper level of meditation or prayer.

Glossary

addiction   A strong and harmful need to regularly have something (such as a drug) or do something (such as gamble). An unusually great interest in something or a need to do or have something.

Akashic record   An all-encompassing record of everything that's ever happened, including the life history of every person—past, present, and future.

altered state   A state of mind different from your everyday level of awareness.

auto-suggestion   A posthypnotic suggestion that you give to yourself during a self-hypnosis session.

centenarian   A person who has lived for 100 or more years.

conscious mind   The part of your mental process you are aware of. That part that is objective and handles daily awareness, observations, logic, and rational thinking.

critical positivity ratio   The ideal ratio of positive to negative thoughts that determine whether or not a person is able to attain their goals and flourish in life.

hypnagogic state   The state between waking and sleeping characterized by alpha brainwave states and often occurring with odd sensations, visions, sounds, body movements (such as sudden jerking and eye rolling), and deep insights and perceptions.

hypnosis   A purposefully induced altered state of awareness in which positive suggestions can be integrated into your belief system, characterized by deep relaxation with an alert, clear mind.

hypnotherapy   Hypnosis used in psychotherapy by trained psychologists, psychotherapists, and psychiatrists.

hypnotic induction   The process of establishing a trance state. *See also* altered state.

hypnotic regression   The process of using hypnosis to lead a subject back in time to re-experience past events and process the varied emotions buried in the subconscious.

ideomotor effect   Unconscious motions that reflect psychological states that can be used to communicate with the subconscious mind.

limbic system   The part of the brain that manages emotional memory.

lucid dreaming   The ability to become aware during a dream that you are dreaming. Allows you to continue the dream while having control over what you do and say.

mind-body medicine   A wholistic approach that takes into consideration the impact of the mind and emotions on physiological processes.

mission statement   A declaration of how you intend to enact your values through life that defines the path you will take to fulfill your purpose.

muscle memory   A form of procedural memory stored in the neural patterning of your brain that relates to body experiences and associated emotions.

near-death experience (NDE)   The experience of being declared clinically dead and then coming back to life hours or even days later.

negative hypnosis   Hypnotizing yourself to not see something that is in plain sight.

posthypnotic suggestion   A suggestion made to a hypnotized person that specifies an action to be performed after awakening in response to a specific cue.

procedural memory   Memory that increases through repetition of an activity until it becomes a subconsciously performed action.

psychoneuroimmunology   The field of medicine focused on the influence of emotional stress on the nervous and immune systems, especially in relation to disease.

reincarnation   The ability for the part of a person that survives death to be reborn in another body.

self-hypnosis   Hypnosis induced by the person being hypnotized.

subconscious   Mental process that's not consciously known or felt but has tremendous impact over the quality of your life.

subconscious programming   The unexamined attitudes and beliefs that drive behaviors.

trance   A deeply relaxed and alert state of mind with altered brainwave patterns, usually in the alpha brainwave range.

vision statement   A declaration of your core values and where you see yourself fitting in the world that's usually enacted through the mission statement.

visualization   Constructing images in the mind's eye that enact desired outcomes.

Resources

You can learn more about self-hypnosis and other topics discussed in this book with the following books, CDs, and websites.

Hypnosis Training and Certification

If you're interested in becoming a certified hypnotist, there are several good organizations to check out. Although there are no licensing requirements or regulated certification standards, these organizations maintain the standards of the field. The first two offer hypnotherapy training for health-care professionals, while the third offers training in clinical hypnosis for non-health-care providers.

American Hypnosis Training Academy
ahtainc.com

The AHTA focuses on the clinical use of hypnosis as an adjunct for health-care professionals. It is an approved continuing education provider for mental health and allied health professionals, including psychologists, social workers, and mental health counselors.

American Society of Clinical Hypnosis
asch.net

This is the largest U.S. organization for medical hypnosis used by many mental health practitioners. It was founded by Milton H. Erickson, MD, in 1957. The ASCH has been a large promoter of the clinical use of hypnosis and offers professional training and certification.

National Guild of Hypnotists
ngh.net

The National Guild of Hypnotists, Inc., is one of the first organizations to create standards for the field of hypnosis and provide quality training. It is a not-for-profit, educational corporation that provides certification to non-health-care providers and encourages dialogue and development of self-hypnosis techniques.

Finding a Hypnotist

If you're looking for a hypnotist or hypnotherapist, there are several good directories. Most training facilities offer directory services as well. The following are websites of training facilities that are members of the three main associations.

- American Association of Professional Hypnotherapists: aaph.org/directory_search

- National Board for Certified Clinical Hypnotherapists: natboard.com/index_files/ Page548.htm

- National Guild of Hypnotists Referral Request Form: ngh.net/referral/request-form

You can also look for training facilities in your area and ask for direct referrals.

Books on Self-Hypnosis

If you want to read more about self-hypnosis, these books are by leading authors and offer a large assortment of additional scripts.

Blair, Forbes Robbins. *Instant Self-Hypnosis: How to Hypnotize Yourself with Your Eyes Open.* Sourcebooks, Inc., 2004.

———. *More Instant Self Hypnosis: Hypnotize Yourself As You Read.* CreateSpace Independent Publishing Platform, 2011.

———. *Self Hypnosis As You Read: 42 Life Changing Scripts.* CreateSpace Independent Publishing Platform, 2013.

Hadfield, Michael. *Change Your Life with Self Hypnosis—Unlock Your Healing Power and Discover the Magic of Your Mind.* CreateSpace Independent Publishing Platform, 2013.

Knight, Bryan M. *Self-Hypnosis: Safe, Simple and Superb* [Kindle edition]. Amazon.com, 2012.

O'Brian, Cathal. *Powerful Mind Through Self-Hypnosis: A Practical Guide to Complete Self-Mastery.* O-Books, 2010.

Starr, Jo Ana, PhD. *Quantum Self Hypnosis: Awaken the Genius Within.* CreateSpace Independent Publishing Platform, 2011.

Self-Hypnosis CDs

If you're looking for self-hypnosis audio CDs, the following are good additional sources.

- Glenn Harrold: glennharrold.com
- The Milton H. Erickson Institute of the Bay Area: miltonherickson.com
- The Monroe Institute: monroeinstitute.org
- Weil: drweilproducts.com

Books and Resources on Additional Subjects

There are many topics in *Idiots Guides: Self-Hypnosis* that you may want to delve into more fully. The following is a sampling to get you started. Take note of the old and truly great books that have stood the test of time.

Developing Intuition:

Schulz, Mona Lisa, MD, PhD. *Awakening Intuition: Using Your Mind-Body Network for Insight and Healing.* Harmony Books, 1998.

Journaling:

Grason, Sandy. *Journalution: Journaling to Awaken Your Inner Voice, Heal Your Life and Manifest Your Dreams.* New World Library, 2005.

McDonald, Quinn, and Tonia Davenport. *Raw Art Journaling.* North Light Books, 2011.

Pendulum Dowsing and Muscle Testing:

Diamond, John. *Your Body Doesn't Lie: Unlock the Power of Your Natural Energy!* Grand Central Publishing, 1989.

Olson, Dale W. *The Pendulum Charts: Knowing Your Intuitive Mind.* Crystalline Publications, 2003.

———. *The PENDULUM Bridge to Infinite Knowing: Beginning Through Advanced Instruction Complete with Pendulum Charts.* Crystalline Publications, 2011.

Visualization:

Gawain, Shakti. *Creative Visualization: Use the Power of Your Imagination to Create What You Want in Your Life* (25th anniversary edition). New World Library, 2002.

Wyatt, William. *Visualization: Creative Visualization Techniques to Change Your Life Forever (Visualization, Visualization Skills, Creative Visualization)* [Kindle edition]. Amazon.com, 2013.

Mind-Body Medicine:

Chopra, Deepak. *Quantum Healing: Exploring the Frontiers of Mind/Body Medicine.* Bantam New Age Books, 1990.

Hay, Louise. *You Can Heal Your Life.* 2nd edition. Hay House, 1984.

Pert, Candace B. *Molecules of Emotion: The Science Behind Mind-Body Medicine.* Simon & Schuster, 1999.

Sarno, John E., MD. *The Mindbody Prescription: Healing the Body, Healing the Pain.* Warner Books, Inc., 1999.

Past Lives:

Andrews, Synthia, and Colin Andrews. *The Complete Idiot's Guide to The Akashic Record.* Alpha Books, 2011.

Newton, Michael. *Journey of Souls: Case Studies of Life Between Lives.* Llewellyn Publications, 2002.

———. *Destiny of Souls: New Case Studies of Life Between Lives.* Llewellyn Publications, 2000.

Stevenson, Ian. *Twenty Cases Suggestive of Reincarnation.* University of Virginia Press, 1980.

———. *Children Who Remember Previous Lives: A Question of Reincarnation.* McFarland & Company, 2000.

Weiss, Brian L. *Many Lives, Many Masters: The True Story of a Prominent Psychiatrist, His Young Patient, and the Past-Life Therapy That Changed Both Their Lives.* Simon & Schuster, 1988.

———. *Only Love Is Real: A Story of Soulmates Reunited.* Grand Central Publishing, 1997.

Positive Thinking:

Achor, Shawn. *Before Happiness: The 5 Hidden Keys to Achieving Success, Spreading Happiness, and Sustaining Positive Change.* Crown Publishing, 2013.

Allen, James. *As a Man Thinketh.* Tribeca Books, 2011.

Hill, Napoleon. *Think and Grow Rich*. Wilder Publications, 2008.

Peale, Norman Vincent. *The Power of Positive Thinking*. Touchstone, 2003.

Shinn, Florence Scovel. *The Game of Life and How to Play It*. DeVorss Publications, 1978.

Self-Development and Spirituality:

Andrews, Synthia. *The Path of Energy: Awaken Your Personal Power and Expand Your Consciousness*. New Page Books, 2013.

———. *The Path of Emotions: Transform Emotions into Energy to Achieve Your Greatest Potential*. New Page Books, 2013.

Andrews, Synthia, and Sherry Rogers. The Emotional Translator App. thepathofenergy.com.

Chopra, Deepak. *The Seven Spiritual Laws of Success: A Practical Guide to the Fulfillment of Your Dreams*. Amber-Allen Publishing, 1994.

Cornell, Alex. *Breakthrough!: Proven Strategies to Overcome Creative Block and Spark Your Imagination*. Princeton Architectural Press, 2012.

Dyer, Wayne W. *Excuses Begone!: How to Change Lifelong, Self-Defeating Thinking Habits*. Hay House, 2009.

Keyes, Ken. *Handbook to Higher Consciousness*. Eden Grove Editions, 1997.

Myss, Caroline. *Sacred Contracts: Awakening Your Divine Potential*. Three Rivers Press, 2003.

Tipping, Colin. *Radical Forgiveness: Making Room for the Miracle*. Quest Publishing & Distribution, 2002.

Tolle, Eckhart. *A New Earth: Awakening to Your Life's Purpose*. Plume Books, 2005.

Williams, Paul. *Das Energi*. Entwhistle Books, 1982.

———. *Remember Your Essence*. Entwhistle Books, 1999.

Young-Sowers, Meredith L. *Spirit Heals: Awakening a Woman's Inner Knowing for Self-Healing*. New World Library, 2007.

———. *Wisdom Bowls: Overcoming Fear and Coming Home to Your Authentic Self*. New World Library, 2006.

Index

B

C

Q-R

T

U-V

W-X-Y-Z

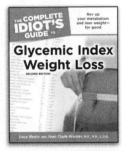
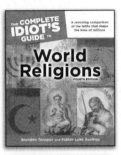

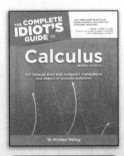

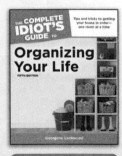

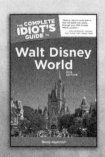